WRESTLIANA
Toby Litt

GALLEY BEGGAR PRESS

First published in 2018
By Galley Beggar Press Limited
37 Dover Street
Norwich NR2 3LG

Text design and typesetting by Tetragon, London
Printed in the UK by Clays, St Ives, and TJ International, Padstow

A CIP record for this book is available from the British Library

ISBN paperback: 978-1-910296-89-9
ISBN limited edition: 978-1-910296-90-5

For my father and his grandsons.

You wrestle with your family your entire life.

JUNOT DÍAZ

CONTENTS

PART ONE

TAKING HOLD

I

WILLIAM LITT

My father likes to tell a joke, a story. Not on the page, in person. He does this better than I do. He's friendlier and less self-conscious. He laughs, gives details when you need them, skips the boring bits, draws you in. One of the best true stories he knows is that of his great-great grandfather, William Litt. It has everything – a strong, handsome, tragic lead man. It involves crime, disloyalty, poetry and love. It's a mystery story. It even has some epic fight scenes.

Since I was a boy, my father has told me this story – his version of it, anyway – perhaps a dozen times. He describes William's triumphs, as champion Cumberland & Westmorland wrestler and as writer of the first history of wrestling, and his failures in just about everything else. He speaks of William's secret life as a smuggler, and his loss of a small fortune. He says that William was a sporting hero throughout the north of England, but that even today people are bitter about the debts he left behind. (When my father told the barman in the pub William used to run that he was his great-great grandson, he was told, 'I wouldn't mention that name in *here*.') The story always ends the same way. William hops on a boat out of Whitehaven and flees to Canada – to 'escape the local lord'.

This was the story my father told me when I told him and my mother that I wanted to be a writer. I was 16-years-old. We were sitting around the dining table – oval, pine.

I remember a pause.

I was relieved to have got it out, the announcement. I had been building up to telling them for years.

My father lounged in a Windsor chair that creaked at every shift. My mother sat upright on a chair like mine, wooden and antique but plain.

From primary school on, I had been desperately trying to work out what I should do, what I should be. Dinosaur hunter. Vet. Soldier. Astronaut. The idea of having a vocation, something to give my life meaning, appealed to me long before I knew what a vocation was. I was drawn, I still don't know why, to the idea of apprenticeship to a difficult craft.

'Writing can be a very lonely business,' said my father. He knew because his sister Shirley's second husband had written and written, novel after novel, none of them published – and had left Shirley very much alone while doing so. 'But if that's what you want to do, that's what you should do.'

I can't remember what my mother said, probably just that they both just wanted me to be happy.

We got up from the table.

'Ee, son,' my father finished by saying, in the Lancashire accent he puts on when he wants to disguise wisdom as wit, 'p'raps it's in your blood.'

He meant William.

About ten years later, when I had published a book, my father began to add a coda whenever he told me some newly discovered fact about William's life: 'It's a great story – *you should write it.*'

But I had never taken this up – God, no!

Wasn't I exactly the wrong person to tell William's story? I was a puny Southern desk-worker who played video games – what did I have to do with this rugged Northern sportsman?

Figure 1. At the oval, pine dining table, signing copies of my first book for family and friends. Photo taken at my father's insistence; smug expression, entirely down to me.

I knew nothing about Cumberland and Westmorland wrestling, the kind of wrestling William loved – at which he was good enough to win two hundred belts.

Although I'd grown up in Ampthill, a Georgian market town, in a Georgian house surrounded by Georgian furniture (bought and sold by my father, who dealt in antiques) most of what I knew about that period had come from Jane Austen.

The one physical connection I had with William was the family copy of his densely worded novel, *Henry & Mary*. This was kept on a bookshelf in the hall. I had been curious about it when I was a boy, because when you opened it, you didn't just see print. It had some old-fashioned handwriting in the back. Someone had copied out a poem called 'The Enthusiast' and written under it 'by William Litt "Author of Wrestliana"'. I had added some scribble, in pencil.

It was true that William and I had writing in common. But he was known as the author of the first ever history of wrestling – an early and important piece of sports journalism. My first book was called *Adventures in Capitalism*. In it, I wrote about made-up characters living in a very shallow, extremely technological now. I wrote about quick lives going violent and perverse and weird and sometimes haunted. That's the kind of writer I was, not a historian or a historical novelist. I told the stories I wanted to tell, and they were about the world *I* lived in and the time *I* knew. My father was the antique dealer. The past belonged to him.

What I was really worried about, and had always been worried about, was that my father didn't just own the past; he owned the present and future as well. He owned the whole world.

My writing had always been part of a struggle to prove my own existence, my own complete independence, from my family, but most of all from my father.

If I did owe anything to William Litt, if there really was something in the blood, then that blood had come to me through my father – and that was something I wasn't ready to admit.

Yet.

Without me knowing it, my father had begun to do some of his own research. In 2005, he wrote to the Secretary of the Cumbria Family History Society. An article about William Litt had appeared in issue 109 of their magazine. He had heard it was very interesting. Could he have a copy?

Unfortunately, the Secretary replied, all copies were gone, even her own – but she could put my father in touch with the authors, Mr and Mrs William Hartley of Egremont, Cumbria.

My father wrote to the Hartleys, Bill and Margaret, who were delighted to hear from him. They knew exactly who Yours Sincerely

David Litt was, because William Litt was also an ancestor* of theirs. He was there in the family trees they had constructed, over the course of thirty years of research.

From local newspapers, they'd excavated William's patriotic poems, his sports reports and his combative letters. In parish records, they'd discovered the fates of his children and grandchildren.

I got to read some of these in 2009. A visit had been arranged. My father and I took most of a long rainy day to drive up from Ampthill to Cumberland, to the Hartley's comfortable bungalow.

They were very welcoming, quietly enthusiastic. Bill is a spruce, gentle voiced man. He had made much of the Georgian-style furniture in the house, chests of drawers and side tables. Margaret, equally soft-spoken, immediately made us feel comfortable – by serving us a proper roast dinner.

During the next couple of days, Bill took us to the sites of William Litt's life. They were all very close together – his birthplace, the farm on which he grew up, the pub he mismanaged.

I was curious but not fascinated. Already, my father and the Hartleys had come to believe I was taking notes for a book I'd write, probably a historical novel with William as hero.

Finally, Bill took us to a cosy new-build cul-de-sac in Cleator Moor. Our family place.

Not my place.

For a start, I didn't speak the language.

I knew that in order to write *The Life and Adventures of William Litt*, a novel convincingly set in eighteenth and nineteenth century Cumberland, I would have to spend at least a year mastering the dialect.

---

* Bill Hartley is a blood relation of ours through his great-grandfather, who married Nanny Litt, one of William's daughters. This makes Bill my father's third cousin, and my third cousin once removed.

Figure 2. Father and son.

The last evening of our visit, Bill took down his leather-bound dictionaries from the shelf beside the fireplace. They were full of wonderful words, words I would have loved to use, Oomer, Sneck-Posset, Yabble,* but these dictionaries were not small.

And what would the story be? The paper trail – as the Hartleys shared it – was fascinating, but limiting. I didn't want to make things up about William, and not enough was known to make a biography.

But these were excuses. The real reason was still my father.

As we drove back south the day after Bill took our photographs in Litt Place, I felt guilty. I didn't think I would write this book, but I didn't

---

* Oomer means shade, Sneck-Posset is when a man has the door shut in his face, figuratively or literally, Yabble means wealthy (literally, able) as in 'A varra *yabble* man'. Other Cumbrian words that have entered general use include Boggle, Eldritch, Gumption, Hugger-mugger and Swap. But how much better is Lowpy-back than leapfrog? And Black-kites for blackberries?

want to tell my father. We stopped in a pub and had a pub lunch. I could have said then that it wasn't going to happen, but I was scared to disappoint. Or make him angry.

'Do you think you've got enough?'

'Yes,' I lied.

I wasn't uninterested, I was just unable. So I went home and continued work on a novel. It had a subplot involving the poet John Keats, a contemporary of William, but was a long way away from Georgian Cumbria.

I didn't tell my father, and Bill and Margaret, that I wasn't writing about William, I just let other books, and life, get in the way.

I was father to two young sons, Henry and George. I had a job, teaching creative writing.

I think everyone understood.

And then, on February 13th 2012, my father's birthday, my mother died.

Afterwards, for several weeks, I stayed with my father. I cooked his favourite meals – macaroni cheese, liver and bacon – foods my mother used to make. I watched *Bargain Hunt* and *Pointless* and the six and nine o'clock news with him. I did what I could, but it wasn't enough.

My parents had been together for forty-six years. Theirs was the best marriage I've ever seen, though they were an odd couple, physically. My father was 6'5"; my mother, 5'1".

Even when I was very young, I knew that although I'd definitely be bigger than my mum, I'd never be taller than my dad. The first memories I have of him aren't so much of a human being as of a landscape. When I was a toddler, I used to climb him. He would be sitting on the sofa. It seemed to take me ages to get from his knees to his chest. He went on for miles.

Figure 3. If the family portrait (by a German painter called Hannelore Köhler) is to be believed, I and my two sisters are the offspring of a giant and a witch.

I remember summer holidays in Cornwall – after swimming together in the sea, I would sit shivering between his legs, his vast towel wrapped around us. This was like being inside a sea cave. If I shouted, there came an imaginary echo. I felt very safe. I knew my father would protect me, would defend my two sisters.

One year, there was a huge guard dog that used to patrol the front garden of the bungalow next to ours. I remember it was a German Shepherd. When we children tried to sneak past, the hairy-muscly-teethy thing would rush at us, snarling, barking.

As we ate dinner, after a particularly terrifying walk back from the beach, I asked my father what he would do if the dog got out. He said, 'I would put it over my knee and break it, like that.' My mother tutted, but I believed him. All three of his children believed him. It took no imagination to see our father performing impossible feats of strength.

We knew that, at school, he'd been 'shot-put champion of Shropshire'. In the sea at Cornwall, he would swim out so far that he was beyond our sight. He disposed of troublesome wasps by crushing them between forefinger and thumb.

As a boy, I was never afraid of getting lost in a big crowd, because I knew my father would be the tallest person there, and I'd always be able to find him.

But old age isn't kind to men who have been big. My father now had type 2 Diabetes and continued to buy cakes and biscuits from the nice lady at the local farmer's market. He walked with a stick. Getting out of a chair took a paragraph rather than a line.

Those weeks after my mother's death were tough. My father missed her like a limb, and saw and heard her around the house. He suffered. He seemed completely defeated.

If I wanted to write the book he wanted to read, I had to write it soon.

It's something lots of us have in common. We want to be different, to be original. We start out thinking that we come from nowhere and owe nothing to no one. And that this is all good and necessary. Idiosyncrasy, self-reliance – yes.

Then, as years pass, we realize just how dependent on others we've always been, and how similar to them we now are. And rather than resenting this (although sometimes it's still oppressive and daunting), we come to welcome it. We're not alone.

Finally, we arrive at a point where we realize, we have to go back and take a good hard look at what *really* made us who we are. We have to acknowledge our debts. We have to measure ourselves against our forebears.

For me, with my mother's death and with my father's grief, this time had come. It had come from looking up and looking down – looking up at my father, who was becoming frail and forgetful and had never asked me to write anything *except* the story of William; looking down at my sons, who were desperately looking up at me for clues on how to grow up, how to be a man.

There are things I'd wanted to write about, ever since I began writing, but had never found a way to approach: being badly bullied at boarding school, and deciding the best I could do was never pass any violence on; going from being sporty (Public Schools Relays and First Fifteen) to being anti-sport; spending most of my life – like so many of us do – sitting looking at words on a computer screen.

In the Autumn of 2014, I sat down and read William's book *Wrestliana* for the first time – and I suddenly saw a way in.

Through William.

Even during his lifetime, a friend referred to him as 'a kind of anomaly in nature'* – an unprecedented combination of athletic superiority and literary talent.

William was like an ideal combination of my father and I. Here was a man who was *both* a wrestler and a writer – who was *both* physical and intellectual.

This '*both*' is absolutely not me, and it's not lots of other men in the West, either – men who mainly work at desks, on computers. Achieving any kind of balance between body and mind is something we find almost impossible. Perhaps this is because, nowadays, in order to compete at any skill, there's no choice but to hyperspecialize.

If you're an athlete, you train so many hours of the day that you never have time to read a book; if you're a programmer or a manager or a writer, you spend so many years at the desk that your muscles go slack, your belly grows and your spine gets crocked. And if you're well-balanced, then you must be a well-balanced no-hoper.

---

* *Cumberland Pacquet*, 12 January 1824. This was probably written by Robert Gibson, the editor.

I had been thinking a lot about modern masculinity. Not only because, as the father of sons, that was where my limited experience lay, and where my day-to-day dilemmas took place. (Should we let them play this macho video game? Do we need to have another talk about nature/nurture?) But because the push to the extremes of body and mind seems at its worst amongst Western men. The two outlying male tribes, Jocks and Nerds, have become completely culturally separate. Their rituals and sacrifices are completely different. Each defines itself by hating the other. You couldn't possibly be both, could you?

And yet back in the 1810s, my great-great-great grandfather *had* been able to exist successfully in the wrestling ring and also in literary society.* And because of this, he seemed to me an ideal figure: someone from whom I could learn things I needed to learn.

I decided to write a book about William, and to pay tribute to him by calling it *Wrestliana*.† By doing this, I would explicitly take William on, on his home ground. Because all of this 'being a man' stuff was something I needed to wrestle with.

To be a better son and to be a better father. To be a better man.

---

* Coincidentally, that was round about the time that the two tribes of masculinity began to define themselves and separate. The sportsmen began to professionalize, the poets began to disdain sport.
† 'Wrestliana' meaning a grab-bag of things to do with wrestling, just as Victoriana is stuff to do with Queen Victoria. (Although half the people who I've mentioned the book to insist on referring to it afterwards as '*Wrestlemania*'.)

PART TWO

WRESTLING

2

BEGINNING

William Litt was born the 8th of November 1785, a Tuesday. He was christened six days later at St Mary's, Cleator.

I'd seen the church, very near Litt Place, a squat stone building on a rugged plain between high hills and grey sea.

The Hartleys had provided me with a chronology, and I began to work out what the dates meant.

His father, John Litt, was born 1744, and so was 41-years-old when William was born. His mother, Isabella Litt, born 1751, was 34-years-old.

Isabella was Scottish, from Dumfriesshire, and it seems likely that her father was one William Rome* and that her mother was Henrietta Holiday. (What a wonderfully happy name.)

The chronology gave me very few details about the women in the family. Their lives were not recorded as the men's were.

John Litt's father – the son of a Scotsman – was also called John Litt. His mother was Eleanor Beeby.

By the time William came along, John and Isabella already had four children: Eleanor (1778), who was to have nine children of her own; John (1780), who became a farmer and corn inspector; Joseph (1781), later a surgeon; and Thomas (1783), who was to die at Montego Bay, Jamaica, having become a mariner.

---

* Whether Isabella Rome's maiden name suggests an Italian or Roma origin is unclear. The Litt men subsequently have tended to be olive skinned with dark hair.

After William, two more children joined the family: Isabella (1788) who died in the eighteenth year of her age, and Nanny (1792), who also did not live to see nineteen.

Having decided I would write about violent physical engagement, body against body, I immediately fled to my comfort zone: books.

Wrestling – seeing it and doing it – I would leave for later, as late as possible. Maybe avoid it completely.

My first task was to read everything by and about William. I had a heap of photocopies done by the Hartleys, but I needed to see where all this stuff came from. For a newspaper article, say, I wanted to know what had been printed around it. What was the news? What was being advertised?

Normally, I work at home, in my study. My usual research method for novels is to assemble a large number of important books on whatever subject I'm writing about, and then ignore them completely.

I buy authoritative works of reference, with very good intentions, and for the security of having them to hand. But over the years I've realized that, for me to say something alive about a subject, I need to be energetically ignorant and still enthusiastic rather than exhaustedly well-informed and bored to death. I always felt it was better to write confidently with errors of fact, then correct them later, than to write a tentative note here and a doubtful sentence there, and then try but fail to make it come to life.

This would have to change. I was now dealing with facts, real lives.

I would have to go to the British Library.

Although some of the fiction writing I'd done did involve 'research', nothing before had taken me into the Newsroom.

This long, L-shaped balcony within the British Library is quietly filled with the whirrings and occasional screechings of microfilm reading machines. The people sitting at them look like they never wrestle with anything tougher than a hard *sudoku*. As I walked in, I immediately felt at home.

Outside was a dank, clammy November morning. I'd stuffed my coat in a locker and found my way to a corner of the building I hadn't known existed.

From the librarians waiting behind their high counter, I collected a few small cardboard boxes. Then I went confidently over to one of the microfilm machines, sat down, unboxed the long filmstrip and began to fumble with spools and knobs.

Other, more experienced researchers, sitting nearby, winced at the thought of damaged celluloid.

One of the librarians, having spotted me for a newbie, hurried over and showed me how to feed the microfilm over and under the metal reels.

She pressed a key on the keyboard, and upon the large flatscreen weeks of pages began to whiz past. There's no other way of describing it than as a March of Time shot from a movie. Whirling black and white text, whirling-whirling, and then, when it stops, a masthead. *The Cumberland Pacquet.*

I thanked the librarian, then began to look for the pages I needed.

'Wow,' I thought, 'this is *proper* research.'

Luckily for me, William Litt was famous. His doings, as well as his wrestling bouts, were reported in all the newspapers of the north-west. He also contributed to *The Cumberland Pacquet*. The writings of his contained within its pages included letters defending his reputation as a wrestling umpire, a beautiful account of the 1824 Regatta on Lake Windermere and, between 1812 and 1840, eighteen songs and poems.

Surrounding these were reports of the Napoleonic wars and of Lord Byron's escapades, accounts of mining tragedies and ships lost at sea, advertisements for skilled farm labourers.

I found William's poetry, always on the top-left hand part of the page – Poetry Corner. It appeared as by 'W. Litt' or just 'W.L.' Those initials alone were enough to identify him locally.

But most of what we know about William, from his own pen, appears in his two books – *Wrestliana*, a history of wrestling from its origins, and *Henry & Mary*, a novel expansively subtitled:

A LOCAL TALE;
ILLUSTRATIVE OF THE PECULIAR HABITS, CUSTOMS,
AND DIVERSIONS
OF THE
INHABITANTS
OF
THE WEST OF CUMBERLAND,
DURING THE GREATER PART OF THE EIGHTEENTH
AND PRECEDING CENTURY

Wrestliana – published in 1823 – contains some very small snippets of autobiography, particularly to do with William's life in the ring. He's not modest about his achievements, but then – he says – wrestlers have no need to be:

> ... supposing two individuals, one a celebrated wrestler, and the other a distinguished football-player, [are] present at any place of amusement where there is a large collection of people; the wrestler will be noticed and gazed at by almost every person present; while the other will be regarded with comparative indifference.

I could easily imagine a scene from this: William, at a county fair, the centre of admiring attention. And the voice that spoke in *Wrestliana* was one that was used to being listened to, taken seriously.

Henry & Mary, much more suggestive of William's early life, appeared in two editions. The first, published in 1824 – a year after *Wrestliana* – kicks off with a couple of pages of 'Preliminary Observations'. In these, William confessed that there was 'more *truth* than *fiction*' to his Tale. He had observed '*real* dates and facts'.

If you were to categorize it now, you would say that *Henry & Mary* was a romantic paranormal adventure story. It isn't just influenced by the internationally bestselling Waverley novels of Sir Walter Scott, first published about ten years earlier, it's a wholehearted attempt to re-do them within a Cumbrian setting. Elements of the plot are very similar to Scott's *Guy Mannering* – both have a witch-like figure who pops up and makes predictions, both have a beefy hero who suffers many reversals. This is very much within the genre Scott was inventing and developing.

But Henry's physical achievements, his great love Mary, his falling among smugglers and his repentance – all of these come out of William's own youthful experience.

It's very hard to talk about *Henry & Mary* without using clichés. So, I may as well give in and describe it in nothing but.

Henry & Mary is the tragic story of a pair of doomed lovers, Henry Clementson and Mary Armstrong. Henry, a strong, handsome young man, meets and falls head over heels in love with beautiful, kind Mary. Their first encounter takes place at a lively County Fair in Arlecdon, where Henry wrestles against Mary's weak-willed brother Tommy. Henry defeats him with ease. Tommy and all his family are heavily involved in the contraband trade. Among their associates, present at the Fair is one Kadgie Brown, a great brute of a man now entering his dotage. Henry is befriended by the whole lot of them. He has fallen in with a bad bunch.

On the night of their first meeting, Henry and Mary take a romantic moonlit stroll with another couple. Their wandering takes them past a spooky graveyard. Suddenly, they are addressed by a witch-like figure. It is the tragic Eleanor Anderson. Years before, Eleanor's fiancé mysteriously disappeared, and she haunts the spot where she believes he was murdered and secretly buried. Mad-looking Eleanor mournfully prophesies that Henry and Mary have met under a bad planet; they may avoid its evil influence but...

Eleanor becomes terrified at what she sees in their future, breaks off, and flees.

During the weeks that follow, Henry wins Mary's affections, and she promises to be his bride.

Encountering Eleanor Anderson again, one dark night, Henry hears her prophesy her own death – in seven days' time.

Come the seventh night, Henry is stationed outside Eleanor's desolate house when the ageing giant Kadgie Brown arrives. Kadgie confesses that it was *he* who murdered Eleanor's fiancé, and says he intends to ensure she leaves behind her no evidence of his guilt. If necessary, he says, he will kill her, too.

At the very last moment, having overheard the whole scene, Henry leaps forth and dashes Kadgie to the ground, foiling his evil plan. Her reputation vindicated and her prophecy of her own doom fulfilled, Eleanor dies. It remains to be seen whether her prophecy for Henry and Mary will also come true...

Weary months pass, and Henry becomes increasingly impatient to marry Mary, but does not have the wherewithal to do so. However, Tommy Armstrong persuades Henry to make a sound investment... in contraband goods. The Armstrong clan are always looking out for muscle and money.

The first night's smuggling goes well, a large profit is made. But the second time Henry goes along to unload the boats, the Customs Men attack and Tommy is shot.

Henry manages to get the rapidly fading Tommy home to his father and mother. After witnessing the senseless violence, Henry has resolved to quit smuggling. He confides this in Mary, who is pleased but inwardly heartbroken over her mortally wounded brother.

Disgusted with all he has become, Henry sails for Virginia on the Balfour with his good friend Captain Harrison.

One night during the return voyage, Henry dreams a terrible dream of Mary, waxing thinner, her skin lustrous as pearls. At the climax of the dream, Mary dies.

Almost immediately, the Balfour comes under attack from pirates. In bravely fighting them off, Henry sustains a deep cut to the head and a bullet wound above the heart.

Soon after they dock in Liverpool, a friend arrives with terrible news for Henry. Henry already knows what it will be. 'Tell me when Mary Armstrong died,' he says. Mary expired, it turns out, at the very moment he was dreaming of her.

A broken man, Henry returns to Cumbria to make his final farewells. He then enlists and voyages to Cuba, where he dies heroically in the attempt to retake Havannah for the British.

With his death, Eleanor Anderson's prophecy is fulfilled. Henry and Mary, who met under an evil planet, were destined never to be together.

A second edition of *Henry & Mary* was printed in 1869, twenty years after William's death. Along with William's own 'Preliminary Remarks', this contained an anonymous 'Memoir of the Author'. It's clear that the Memoirist (as I soon began to think of him) was one of William's literary circle in Whitehaven. The most likely candidate is Robert

Gibson, the town's main publisher. Robert Gibson was editor of both of William's books; he also ran *The Cumberland Pacquet*. Whoever the Memoirist was, he knew and admired William.

> In person, Mr. Litt possessed a rare combination of physical strength, with the most perfect symmetry of form. His height was about six feet, and his countenance and manner were manifestly thoughtful and pleasing. His conversational powers were also remarkable. His voice was singularly fine and powerful; and one accomplishment he possessed above all men we have ever known – he was, without exception, the very best *reader* we ever listened to.

A far more aggressively critical account of William's life appeared in a book whose full title was *Wrestlers and Wrestling: Biographical Sketches of Celebrated Athletes of the Northern Ring; to which is Added Notes on Bull and Badger Baiting*. The authors were Jacob Robinson and Sidney Gilpin. 'Sidney Gilpin' was the pseudonym of a Carlisle printer, George Coward. Coward seems to have been a dodgy character, accused of plagiarism. *Wrestlers and Wrestling* didn't come out until 1893. However, it does contain some gossipy details about William's life that aren't elsewhere.

Their conclusion is brutal.

> ... from the time he left the paternal roof, his course through a check-ered life to the bitter end, was marked by a series of disastrous failures.

For a man born over two hundred years ago, William's is a very full record. But not the whole way along. Until he begins to speak – that is, to *write* – for himself, William is a figure against a background; and the background is far more detailed than the figure.

For instance, in my library research, I discovered there was a severe drought during the months William's mother, Isabella, was pregnant.

I found this because John Bragg, a Quaker shoemaker living in Whitehaven, kept a diary. He wrote, 'a general complaint of want of water prevails all over England'.[*]

I also learned that three months before William was born, a pony belonging to his father was stolen – probably from the commons of Cleator Moor. This, from *The Cumberland Pacquet*, may be the only surviving piece of writing by John Litt. It is gruffly vivid, grumpily humorous:

Aug. 9. 1785. A bay mare, 13 hands 3 inches high, star in forehead. Flock mane. Seemingly nicked but not nicked. Small lump on the back the size of a plum. Information to John Litt, of Bowthorne.[†]

No anecdotes of William as an infant have survived. Nothing has come down through family rumour about feats of strength or early scraps with his brothers. I knew from the Hartley materials that his family called him 'Will' or 'Willie'. On his first birthday, as John Bragg the shoemaker noted, an earthquake was felt across the whole northwest – 'preceded with a rumbling noise – very calm & quiet air, very alarming to most of people'.[‡] But I could find out nothing more, not for certain.

Yet easily available – from books and maps – are all the old names of the fields of Bowthorn Farm near Cleator Moor, William's birthplace.[§]

---

[*] *The Diary of John Bragg from Whitehaven*, Cumbria Family History Society, 1999, p. 121.

[†] Caesar Caine, *Cleator and Cleator Moor: Past and Present*, Michael Moon, 1973, p. 160. A bay mare is chestnut with black 'points' – meaning lower legs, ears, mane and tail. The 'nicked but not nicked' suggests the pony's tail has not been cut, to make it carry high, but naturally looks that way. The plum-sized lump seems large rather than small, but perhaps plums were smaller then.

[‡] *The Diary of John Bragg from Whitehaven*, Cumbria Family History Society, 1999, p. 122.

[§] Caesar Caine, *Cleator and Cleator Moor: Past and Present*, Michael Moon, 1973, p. 54.

They come from a language still half Danish: Crugarth; Fir-garth; Land Heads; Well Dale. I found these names, in their hard matter-of-factness, extremely evocative. Stone Field; New Moss; How Guards; Hingrihow Croft. William later referred to himself as a 'broken plough-boy'.* So from an early age he would have been out on the land, helping with the harvest. Ley Field (Far); Ley Field (Near); Gill-Gap. He would have walked to and fro, down Water Lane to the Watering Place, along Ley Field Lane. My imagination began to range. Perhaps Willie had taken Hingrihow Island for his summer castle, and imagined it rivalled the ruined medieval castle at nearby Egremont. He may, cold, wet and bored, have brought in the sheep from Croft.

The names of the farms surrounding William's father's farm suggest a windswept wilderness: Netherend, Low House, Galemire.

But the most suggestive of all was Bowthorn.

As I sat in the library, looking at the maps, I remembered visiting the territory itself.

In 2009, Bill Hartley had driven my father and I the short distance from his bungalow to Bowthorn.

Bill had showed us that above the door were carved the date '1685' and the initials 'E.M.S.'

And I had felt, for a moment, as if I were standing outside Wuthering Heights – over the principal door of which, as readers of the opening of Emily Brontë's novel will know, are carved the date '1500' and the name 'Hareton Earnshaw'.

In the whole of that first trip up to Cumberland, this was my deepest moment of connection with William. I imagined him, as I had often

---

* This is a line from 'Freedom – An Apologue', published in the *Cumberland Pacquet*, 18 November 1812.

Figure 4. Distant hills, so we are facing east from William's birthplace, Bowthorn Farm.

Figure 5. Bill Hartley, left, looks on as my father, right, walks up the hill towards the front door of his great-great grandfather's birthplace.

imagined myself, sitting eating his supper near the fireplace in the kitchen of the Heights.

Remembering this, five years later, from a desk in the British Library, I felt slightly hopeful. If the boy Will had had a childhood like that of Heathcliff and Cathy, in a rural wild, then perhaps I had a way of understanding him, writing about him. Wuthering Heights was a place with which I'd once been obsessed.

The set books for my A level in English – the books that, along with Keats's poems, made me want to be a writer – were about as bleak and perverse an assembly as English Literature houses: *Hamlet*, Thomas Hardy's 'Emma' poems, Webster's *The Duchess of Malfi*. Death, death and a smidgeon more death. But it was Emily Brontë with whom I became infatuated, and *Wuthering Heights* that I really loved. I was, I thought, a bit like Heathcliff.

The English teacher who led me through *Wuthering Heights* was keen – for reasons of his own – to douse this self-love. Like a sandy-haired Abraham Lincoln, stiff in body and accent, Earnest Carwithen stood at the front of class. 'I don't know about you,' he said, 'but for myself I have the humility to know that I'm more Edgar Linton than Heathcliff.'

Edgar Linton is wild Cathy's fake husband – a disgusting, sickly milksop who likes reading poetry. Heathcliff, you probably don't need me to tell you, is a dark, virile destroyer who likes causing pain.

In the mid-1840s, Emily Brontë was dividing men into two types: mental and physical. For her, the physically weak are worthless.

I still secretly thought I was more like Heathcliff than Edgar Linton.

★

Later that day in 2009, after we came back from Bowthorn, Bill put a book in my hands. It was Caesar Caine's *Cleator and Cleator Moor: Past and Present*. This is, he said, the best history of the area.

When I had finished with the newspapers at the British Library, and had moved on to the books, Caesar Caine's history was one of the first I ordered. I soon found that Bill had been right.

The Reverend Caesar Caine was Cleator's vicar from 1910 to 1922, but where he truly lived was in the past. He confessed – as Margaret Hartley might also confess – that: 'I have occasionally moved about in a daydream, more conscious of the Steeles, the Benns, the Towersons, the Litts, the Robertsons and Parson Barnes' family than of the living people of the present time.'*

In particular, he was a great enthusiast for the farmhouse at Bowthorn – the situation of which, he said, could hardly be finer. As I read, I imagined how lucky William was to grow up there. 'To the westward and southward from the farm buildings, situated close to the common, the rolling moorland, rich in heather and gorse, stretched as far as Keekle Bridge in one direction, and as far as Crossfield and Jacktrees in the other. Eastward, there was a splendid view of undulating country with numerous farms, terminating in the splendid assemblage of hills around and beyond Ennerdale Lake.'†

But Caesar Caine continued on after this, and with his every word my *Wuthering Heights*-inspired imaginings began to collapse.

'This ancient homestead must have been indeed "lovely for situation,"' Caine lamented, 'before the iron industry destroyed the fair prospect by monstrous black furnaces, mountainous slag heaps, and huge chimneys belching forth dense smoke.'‡

Oh dear.

---

* Caesar Caine, *Cleator and Cleator Moor: Past and Present*, Michael Moon, 1973, p. v.
† Ibid., p. 45.
‡ Ibid.

★

My imaginings of Bowthorn as akin to Wuthering Heights, and the surrounding landscape as like the pre-industrial world of Emily Brontë's Yorkshire moors had been, literally, undermined. Cleator Moor sounded far more akin to William Blake's 'dark satanic mills'.

Cut off from the rest of the country by the hills of the Lake District, the county of Cumberland has never been affluent.

Whitehaven, within walking distance of Bowthorn, was a busy port, and there were opportunities for young men to go to sea, and perhaps die there, but not really to become rich. Some young men would have joined the army, fought at Austerlitz or Waterloo.

Most young men worked the land. Farms were widely spread out; families connected by blood or trade. Many farmers in the borders were self-sufficient, meaning not only they fed themselves but also dressed in homespun cloth of blue. They wore wooden clogs.

This was the rustic world into which William was born, a world he memorialized in *Henry & Mary*, but it was not to last.

William's figure emerges not only from a local but also from a global background. The dates of his life were to be 1785–1850. These very neatly bracket the dates of the Industrial Revolution, which Eric Hobsbawm in his great book, *The Age of Revolution*, puts between 1789 and 1848. This was, Hobsbawm excitedly wrote, 'the greatest transformation in human history since the remote times when men invented agriculture and metallurgy, writing, the city and the state'.[*]

---

[*] Eric Hobsbawm, *The Age of Revolution: 1789–1848*, Vintage, 1996, p. 13.

And Will Litt did not witness the Industrial Revolution distantly. All he had to do was stand on the doorstep of his father's house and look out at the smelting works and slag heaps. Nor did he witness the Industrial Revolution innocently. It helped pay for his upkeep as surely as antique dealing paid for mine.

Shortly after William's seventh birthday, on December 4th 1792, his father John went into partnership with a Jonas Lindow – taking over the Langhorn pits. It was not until 1803 that their labours, or more likely the labour of their workers, started to show a profit. From that year, between one October and the next, 5,374 tons of iron ore were brought out – at a royalty of one shilling per ton.* The mine came to be known as 'Litt's pit'.

There has been mining in Cleator Moor for over five hundred years. To this day, the ground is prone to sudden subsidence – and to the discovery of forgotten chasms beneath fields and streets. Maps of the area are thick with 'Mine (Dis)' and 'Shafts (Dis)'. But the history of iron ore mining in Egremont has been one of 'disconnected spurts of activity separated by long periods of stagnation'.† And this was true for Litt's pit. If John Litt hoped to become rich through industry, he was to be disappointed. 1803 was the mine's only truly productive year. When Jonas Lindow went bankrupt in 1815, the mine had to be re-let.

The Litts – Caesar Caine tells us – took a lease on Bowthorn in 1798, after the death of Edward Steele, the last of the male line of the Steeles. But the Litts were living there before then, because it is listed as the birthplace of their children.

Bowthorn is not a big house. It would have been crowded and noisy; two or three to a bedroom.

I tried to imagine William's early life.

---

* Very unusually, coal as well as iron ore was also produced by Litt's Pit; it stands on a geological border above haematite and coal.
† *The Egremont Heritage*, Egremont Town Council, 1982, p. 17.

Pulling together all the sources available, this was what I found:

Will was a healthy boy, strong, energetic, yet also given to indolence. He lay upon the village green, watching the wrestling matches of the field workers and craftsmen. As soon as he was able, he joined in. His later writings are always a rough and tumble. If his character has a keynote, it is combativeness.

But Will was a listener, too – and in particular he liked listening to the old folk. His knowledge of wrestling went as far back as his grandparents' generation. I imagine him, a young fan, pestering anyone who might have details of legendary bouts from thirty or forty years before he was born.

Will was a happy boy who loved his mother and respected his father. In a poem of 1839, 'The Bells That Hang in the Old Church Tower', he called his childhood 'a golden time / When the heart was gladsome, it knew not why'.[*] He referred to himself (ignoring the Industrial Revolution for a moment) as one 'rear'd 'mid the mountains wild / Where the grey thrush sang, and the heath flower smil'd…'

One scene from *Henry & Mary,* vivid and tender, seems to give us a picture of Bowthorn as William remembered it. On the clean white-washed walls of the comfortable sitting room hang prints of The Ark and the Tower of Babel. There is a brass tea-kettle, candlesticks, &c. The father's books for reading, or noting down the transactions of the day, are lying open on the green cover of his desk. And is this a glimpse of mother Isabella? If so, she seems central, occupied, inscrutable. 'While her rosy children of different ages, are innocently amusing themselves by… endeavouring to attract… attention from their parents'. 'She, whether listening, or bearing a part in the conversation between her husband and brother, is busy with her needle'.[†]

---

[*]   *Cumberland Pacquet,* 12 February 1839.
[†]   *Henry & Mary,* 1st ed., pp. 342–343; 2nd ed., p. 194.

In the same poem of 1839, mothers are a byword for the most loved thing: 'And he loves, like a mother, his village bells'.

Even after reading everything William wrote, I cannot find a similar statement about fathers or about his father; nothing that would suggest love separate from respect.

In fact, almost everything John Litt did in his life came under public attack, at one point or another, by his son. The assaults seem systematic.

John Litt was a farmer. Here is what William had one character in *Henry & Mary* say about the farming life:

> If you commence farmer, you may toil yourself from morning to night; perform the labour, and subject yourself to the drudgery of a brute beast, to procure a scanty subsistence – that is, if you are fortunate...*

John Litt's main income came from his position as 'Commissioner for the Inclosure of Waste Lands'. This was a lucrative job, but one that risked making Will extremely unpopular with some locals – like being the son of the man charged with closing down the village playground, or paving over the allotments.

In both his books, William digressed – with no apparent need – into long condemnations of the removal of land from common ownership. Looked at in one way, William's entire life was centred around these spaces, for it was on common lands that his beloved wrestling took place; including William's own most famous bout, that against the cobbler Harry Graham.

What could be more direct than this, from *Wrestliana?*:

> In the vicinity of Whitehaven, the best wrestling was at Arlecdon Moor; but the inclosure of that common has now put a stop to it.

---

* *Henry & Mary*, 1st ed., p. 258; 2nd ed., p. 148.

In *Henry & Mary*, the lament is overt – perhaps the most gushingly heartfelt and bitterly comic thing William was ever to write:

> Hail! scene of exalted triumphs, immemorialized in the pages of Wrestliana, long shalt thou live in my remembrance! What though the green tops of the best of vegetables now wave over the place where the mighty have fallen! … Yet what is all this to those sensitive thrills of delight, which, emanated from thy listed ring, have made hundreds forget for a time there was such a thing as eating, or even drinking, in existence?

The implication, to me, is clear: William's father – because he helped enclose of the Moors of Arlecdon and Cleator, annexing them for the aristocracy, for the Lowther family – killed the people's pleasures. Put a stop to them.

Fathers, like farmers, are boring drudges. Fathers put a stop to fun. They fence in playing fields, and make them profitable. They end waste.

When I reached this conclusion, I began to doubt myself. How could I be certain these digressions referred to William's father?

But I knew that if I were to publish something about antique dealers, to say – for example – they were all crooks, that couldn't be about anything but my father.

I began to suspect a boyhood crisis for William – a crisis against his father.

It involves the death of a hare.

3

HARE

Hare coursing was the great pastime of Cumberland in the late 1700s. Back then, sport meant bloodsport. All classes were devotees – the yeoman and the labourer, the gentleman and the beggar. Because of the roughness of the terrain, foxhunting on horseback was too dangerous – or too likely to result in a half-dozen lamed animals rather than a single dead one.

The hunt gathered early in the day, and looked for the hare's tracks. When they had followed these to where she was hiding, the hunt began. (The hare was always referred to as 'she'.) There was no formal pack, as for foxhunting. Instead, farmers brought their greyhounds and terriers, mongrels and whelps. The tradition was for a swarm of onlookers to pursue the pursuing hounds.[*] Caesar Caine writes, 'The interest and excitement which could be aroused by a hare hunt seems incredible. I have an account of a Whitehaven Hunt in December 1787. Two thousand people, horse and foot, followed...'[†]

We know from an advertisement[‡] that William's father was one of the organizers:

---

[*] Details from J.S. Gibbons, *The Hare*, Longmans, Green, and Co., 1896; and Walter Scott, *Guy Mannering*, Penguin, 2003, pp. 134–135.
[†] Caesar Caine, *Cleator and Cleator Moor: Past and Present*, Michael Moon, 1973, p. 392.
[‡] Ibid., p. 393.

Oct 13, 1790. Cleator Hunt. The annual hunt at Cleator will be on Monday, the 25th day of October inst., the hounds to be cast off at the usual time [8 o'clock in the morning], and dinner upon the table at Wilson's, precisely at 2 o'clock.

Mr. Thomas Curwen/Mr. John Litt } Stewards

I can't prove that 4-year-old Will was present at this hunt. But, from the account of hare coursing he gave in *Wrestliana*, I am sure he was taken along on many similar mornings. He knows every fleck of ritual, and writes with an intimacy almost matching his disgust.

From the first time I read it, I've thought that this passage contained William's best and most passionate prose[*] – and so it's only fair to let him run beyond bounds.

When he stretched his legs, William could be a fine, muscular writer: personal as well as polemical; always ready with an image to back up his argument.

And as I hurry along with him here, breathlessly following the tonguing hounds, I feel I am approaching a kill – a kill witnessed in early boyhood. Here is horror.

In some countries they hunt for subsistence, – in some for safety, – and in others for pleasure only. In the United Kingdom, the last is the only motive; and generally speaking, the objects are three – the stag, the fox, and the hare. Of these, the hare is the most general... Hunting is equally esteemed as an exercise as well as an amusement, combining two of the greatest earthly blessings, – health and pleasure; and we will not detract from the pleasure it affords, by stingily urging the consequences which may result from the pursuit of it; such as overheating, catching cold, breaking a *limb*, or possibly a *neck*, &c.

---

[*] *Wrestliana*, 1st ed., pp. 60–63; 2nd ed., pp. 41–43.

Caesar Caine notes that *Wrestliana*, here, '"runs down" hunting in order to "run up" wrestling' – because wrestlers, as William always stresses, very rarely get injured.

What spectacle can be more animated and alluring than a well-attended chase? The sight and music of the dogs, eagerly followed, directed, and encouraged by horse and footmen, form such an overpowering combination of incidents as supersedes by its irresistible impulse almost every other consideration! The traveller and the labourer, the gentleman and the beggar, will all equally gaze on the enchanting scene, and often tempted by its magic influence, deviate from their immediate avocation for the pleasure of witnessing it a few minutes longer. But does the sight instil into the breast of any generous and reflecting man one praise-worthy sentiment, or furnish him with any example of noble or manly emulation? Alas! no. We fear when duly considered, it is a striking proof of the frailty of man, and his deplorable proneness to be led away by sensual propensities. The *fear* of one animal, and the *ferocity* of others, are the sole cause of the pleasure he experiences. The hare, the most timid of quadrupeds, aided by speed and very circumscribed natural sagacity, endeavours to elude its pursuers, and preserve itself from a death the most terrific and horrible even a reasonable mind can possibly suggest. The dogs, guided by instinct and natural ferocity, and capable of enduring much greater fatigue, preserve the same tract, and mutually guide and encourage each other in the work of destruction. The little animal, instructed by self-preservation, retraces, or traces over again, nearly the same ground, and would often baffle its ferocious pursuers; – and what hinders it? Man, endowed with reason and reflection! Man! the boasted lord of the earth interposes! For what motive? To preserve the weak from the strong? No! Quite the contrary! To guide and impel the latter to the work of blood and murder! Thus not only encouraging, but joining on terms of equality with *dogs* and *horses* in the deed. But surely it is some powerful motive which thus induces him to derogate from his natural dignity? Some means of acquiring honour, profit, – or benefitting the community at large? No! We are again reluctantly obliged to answer in the negative. No honour can be acquired either in the pursuit or the death of so weak and timid an animal, except that false notion of the term which arises from the circumstances of tempting Providence more than his companions, by some dangerous leap, or other similar cause; which even then he must share with his horse: and between profit, – the desire of benefitting others, – and hunting, we need scarcely observe there is an insuperable bar. – Aided by man, the final result is generally as follows: – The poor helpless animal, quite exhausted with terror and fatigue, is no longer capable of active effort. It lays itself down in the vague expectation of concealment, and there awaits its fate; or rises only to meet a death replete with terrors. A few terrific squeals nearly drowned by the exulting cries of its pursuers, announce the termination of its cruel fate. The note of triumph is sounded by its *generous* and *pitying* enemies, who congratulate each other on the sports of the day, and point out the respective merits of the *meek* and *gentle* assistance, which are often distinguished by the names of Charmer, Lovely, Comely, &c.; and sometimes enlighten and edify each other, by seriously asserting that the hare hearkens with pleasure to the pursuit! and that the moment she is caught the terrors greatly subside! We will subscribe that they are not long in doing so, as they will vanish with life; – but we cannot say we ever heard any of those instructive and *very knowing* gentlemen contend, that the dying shrieks of the wretched animal, were notes of satisfaction and pleasure!

Am I wrong to place John Litt, the steward, among those '*very knowing* gentlemen' guilty of 'the work of blood and murder'? Probably not, when the owner of the 'Cleator Greyhounds' was one Jonas Lindow, John Litt's business partner. Is it pushing things too far to see, through this incident, Will's brutal detachment from his father? Even more, his disgust and dismay? The boy who grew up to be the man who wrote these words was looking to be furnished with noble examples of honourable deeds worthy of manly emulation. He found none of this in hare coursing – he found only wretchedness and terror.

Nowhere else in *Wrestliana* does the grown-up William seem less of his place and of his time. He separates himself from the bloodlusting Cumbrian crowd, for whom hunting would have been the epitome of sport. His argument is rational but his reaction was visceral. He could not control it. William's language is that of horror at men and empathy with the hare.

The first time I read this passage in *Wrestliana*, I thought I understood William's attitude – that he was, in a twenty-first century way, against cruelty to animals. How could he write about the suffering of a hare and not feel the same way about the suffering of other creatures? If he was against one kind of bloodsport, why not all of them? But as I read on, I saw that it was not so simple. Later in *Wrestliana*, he makes his opinions clear.

William opposed hare coursing not because of its dependence on agonized death, but because it just wasn't *sporting*. He also disparaged angling (using, as he wrote, 'artificial means to destroy or deceive... a fish'*). However, because two cocks, put into the ring, faced only one other of their species, and it was a fair fight between them, he supported it.

---

* *Wrestliana*, 1st ed., p. 66; 2nd ed., p. 46.

Surely no man in his senses, unless totally blinded by prejudice, can pretend to argue, that an equal combat between two birds which need no incitement but their mutual and natural animosity, can possibly be either cruel or barbarous, compared with league-ing, and combining with twenty, thirty, or forty ferocious animals to worry a defenceless one!*

When I realized this, I found William's values regarding animals confused and confusing. His logic was bracing. But what he said of the hare's death went beyond the intellectual. I could see him, at a tender age, running up to the screaming creature. I could see him, white-faced, disillusioned, appalled. Hares are notorious for the anguish of their death-cries, and for the amount they bleed. I could see his father, mortified, pulling him away.

Years later, when he wrote the first of his two books, William would show that he had forgotten nothing of what young Will saw, or what he thought and felt.†

---

* *Wrestliana*, 1st ed., p. 66; 2nd ed., p. 46.
† Both William's eldest son, William Litt, my great-great grandfather, and his son's eldest son, also William, and his son's third son, John, my great grandfather, were to have a lifelong concern with the welfare of animals. They were veterinary surgeons.

4

DADS VS. LADS

In Brockwell Park, London, just inside the Rosendale Road gate, there is a patch of ground between two diverging paths shaped like an upside-down triangle. Tall trees stand at each corner. Every time I walked past it, during the year I spent researching William, I felt guilty and proud. Elsewhere in the park, the grass was thick and green and healthy. But at the centre of the triangle was a fuzzily oblong area of flattened mud. This is where, every Sunday afternoon, the Dads vs. Lads match took place. One or two of us fathers were there in January, when the boys lifted the ice off a nearby puddle and smashed it on the path. Many more, perhaps fifteen fathers, were around for the later, sunnier days.

Henry, who was 10-years-old, and George, 8, never wanted to miss a Sunday. If we had to go to a family gathering, or they were invited to a birthday party, they would get extremely upset.

With an intense year of tackles, passes, and running, running, up and down the triangle, we wore away the grass so completely I was worried it wouldn't ever grow back.

I became a father at the age of thirty-six. When we had the scan for my first child, and I was told it was a boy, I saw two clear images of his future. One was of him learning to ride a bicycle – me letting go, in slow motion; the other was of us kicking a football back and forth. If he lived, if I lived, I knew these things would happen.

And they did. The bike riding was a big moment of potential father–son connection. From my own boyhood, I remembered learning how to keep going without stabilizers. This had become one of my mother's stories about me. At 99 Dunstable Street, there was an apple tree in the garden, with a lawn around it, and I tried and failed, for a week or more, to ride around it once without putting my foot down. My mother, standing at the sink, watched me through the kitchen window. She had obviously said something to annoy me, and perhaps to provoke me, because, when I finally succeeded in keeping going, I ran back inside and defiantly said to her, 'I *have* got a sense of balance!'

Henry loved the way his bike looked – red and yellow like a fire engine – but he hated riding it. We'd made the mistake of buying a bicycle with inertia braking. Unfortunately, this meant that to get the bloody thing going from a standstill required an infant Hercules. Henry never got moving without a push. The stabilizers, too, slowed him down. He became dispirited. He hated the bike, and me for putting him on it.

The big day, stabilizers removed, I tried to persuade Henry to the park. Inside, I was preparing myself for the slow-motion moment as he joyously and independently cycled away from me. He cried all the way down the street. As we approached the gates, he wailed, 'No!' In the end, it became obvious that I was being cruel, and we turned back home.

Kicking the football back and forth went better. I didn't force it, it just happened. I wasn't trying to train a professional. If Henry wanted a kickabout, that was fine. I would have been just as happy throwing a Frisbee. In fact, I would have been overjoyed.

★

My memories of playing Frisbee with my father all take place in 1970s California light – light as soft as a Fender Rhodes piano recorded on analogue tape: Paul Simon's "Still Crazy After All These Years". We would play on Cornish and French beaches. And I was never closer to my father than when twenty or thirty metres away, zinging our Frisbee up into an onshore breeze, slinging it off on an arc so lopsided that it seemed the Frisbee would splash down way out to sea – then watching (with my father watching, too) as the beautifully weighted plastic saucer zoomed back in towards him; so accurately that he didn't even have to move his feet to catch it. Then he would do the same, even more outlandishly, back to me – and it was a wonder the few people left on the sundown beach didn't all stand up to applaud.

We were as good at Frisbee as The Carpenters were at harmonizing.

Surely, I believed, we would win the Father–Son Frisbee gold medal, if the Olympics were sensible enough to start holding that event.

And if the Frisbee wasn't thrown with perfect aim, because the wind lifted and took it further off, I would try to impress my dad by making desperate diving catches that had me sprawling in the sand. Then I would stand up and put an extra load of spin on the next throw, so the Frisbee would seem to stop for a minute, directly above Dad's head, just out of reach, until it fell like an apple out of a tree, straight into his hand.

Yes, for a couple of summers, we were the champions.

Together.

I knew I couldn't compete with my father. I had never beaten him at any sport he took seriously.

The closest I ever came was at squash. We were not in one of the recently built glass boxes but in one of the older, white-walled courts at the Flitwick club. It was a Sunday morning. (I know this because if it had been any other morning, I would have been at school.) For some reason, I had gone out to an eight–one lead. I was serving really well, and needed only one more point for victory.

My father had promised me £10 if I beat him.

Just as I was about to serve, my mother appeared in the wide-screen-shaped gap in the brickwork, high up at the back of the court.

She asked my father when we'd be finished, and he told her the score.

'Oh,' she said, and stayed to watch.

We resumed the game.

I served, lost the point.

Perhaps beating my father whilst my mother watched was a much harder thing. Or perhaps, with my mother watching, my father decided to start trying his best. Probably a combination of both, but my father won every remaining point in the game.

I lost eight–nine.

I became angry. To cover this, I jokingly blamed my mother for interrupting my flow. 'If you hadn't come along, I'd've won.' Secretly, though, I was glad that my father remained undefeated. Beating him was something I would achieve one day, when I was worthy – but I never did.

We never played squash again seriously.

I don't know why not.

When I ask my father, he can't remember.

Both William's father, John, and my father's father, John Percy, were in their mid-forties when their sons would have been of an age to want to muck around, to play physical games.

I doubt that John Litt ever wrestled seriously with William, and he seems too staid a character for horseplay.

John Percy was worn out from the war. He liked a round of golf, far from children.

I am glad, however unserious it is, that I've been able to join in with Henry and George at Dads vs. Lads. They've seen me score some goals. They don't associate me entirely with a desk and a computer. And George will still, now and again, ask me if I could score five out of five penalties against the England goalkeeper, or if Usain Bolt would really beat me from here to that tree over there?

Figure 6. George's drawing of 'Daddy at the Desk'.
(Daddy doesn't look very happy.)

I enjoy being a hero to them. I am delighted by their ludicrous belief that I'd stand a chance against a professional sportsman of any sort. I know this will end very soon, and they'll think I'm 'dead'. (As Everton's star midfielder in a football magazine on their bedroom floor is 'dead'.) Maybe, when they're older, they'll realize that where I'm at my best is at the desk, on the computer.

I remember believing my own father was invincible. But, with him being as big as he was, I had more reason. I didn't imagine him winning sporting events. Instead, I had a repeated fantasy that took place at a particular location.

Behind the Spar minimarket, directly opposite my bedroom window at 99 Dunstable Street, was a car park. This is where we'd always park the Peugeot 504 – and then, to get home, we'd walk up a side alley, over a little paving-stoned hillock, and through an arcade of concrete pillars.

Here, in my imagination, was where a gang of four local dossers would stop Dad and me. And here, an event I seriously yearned for, my father would send all of them flying over brick walls and through glass windows. Just once, and with me there to witness it, he would be able to unleash his full, fearsome, dog-snapping strength.

Sadly, we were never mugged – and part of me still mourns this scene that never took place.

I wonder if my sons have similar fantasies about me, kicking arse.

Fights with winners and losers, someone being beaten, someone doing the beating – there are far more nuanced ways of looking at male identity, masculinity.

My partner, Leigh, is an academic. She teaches English literature at the University of Westminster. Her specialist areas are early twentieth century writing and contemporary fiction. Recently, she has been writing about novelists who (like me with this book) have temporarily or permanently abandoned writing novels and turned instead to non-fiction – because made up stuff has started to make them feel nauseous, self-disgusted.

Leigh is tall, strong, and can jog further and faster than I can. School games lessons, however, were some of the worst hours of her life. She loves watching Wimbledon, but if all other sport disappeared from our house for the rest of the year I know she'd be delighted. (With Henry and George around, that's not going to happen.)

When I showed Leigh an early draft of this book, she said, 'I know what you should call it – *Bein' a Man.*'

It was a family joke. When he was 2-years-old, still bumbling around in nappies, Henry came up with a little thing he'd do – tensing his arms so that the tiny muscles bulged and his head wobbled from side to side with the strain. He was like a small bodybuilder, displaying his pecs to the judges. (The pose exists and is called the 'Most Muscular'.) This performance, he said, was *bein' a man* – and, because it was so funny, we filmed it, making the usual joke about eighteenth birthday montages.

In our house, bein' a man was something innately ridiculous, and to be laughed at. But as the boys have grown up, I've become aware that they will be encountering people, especially men, for whom bein' a man is the most serious business of all. How should I advise the boys to cope with them? Men's men. Should they just try to avoid them? That's not really an option. The world is dominated by men frantically, and often violently, demonstrating just how manly their manliness is.

Men tend to endure what they are, rather than examine or explore it. (And they make others endure it, too – especially women.) They are often oblique. Don't just tell your best mate you love him. Go out together, get drunk, get more drunk, start a fight, get beaten up, get chucked out of the bar, then tell your best mate you love him. That's the furthest extreme. Lots of men would just do the getting more drunk bit.

Men are not simple creatures. But many men like to make a very simple impression. They like it to be known that the argument about them personally is over – and they won.

It's hard to resist this. I realize, I'm making a lot of very general generalizations. But I find it hard to say anything specific about manhood because the subject resists that. It wants to be described in action. Words are for liars. The truth is a well taken penalty kick.

In the west – and probably to a degree, the rest of the world – manhood is partly a rage for simplification – not just a simplification of itself as a subject, but the repeated assertion that there isn't a subject, because that's just how things are, because it's all obvious, alright?

(As I wrote these words, the woman sitting next to me on the train said into her phone, 'Philip's at home, watching TV in his pants.')

Perhaps my picture of all of this is stereotypical, but a lot of men live and die by these stereotypes.

Some of the more nuanced ways of examining manhood and masculinity look at how it is performed. These are the ways Leigh would respect. They don't take machismo's surface explanations for it's deep reasons.

I once had a creative writing student, a lesbian air-stewardess, who had done a fascinating piece of research for her PhD. She had become a drag queen, and had developed quite a successful act in gay men's clubs. But the thing was, she had done this *as a man*. Before she dragged up as a drag queen, in the dressing room, she had secretly to drag up as the man who was about to drag up as a woman.

She told me how she'd applied make-up to her neck, to fake an Adam's apple. She would put on her male voice, and then her male-mimicking-female voice. She was very funny about how she'd managed to pass not just once but twice. To pass as what she was but wasn't.

I asked her what she'd learned. What was the conclusion of her PhD?

She gave a grimace. It was too sexually head-spinning to explain. But then her face lightened, and she found the best way of putting it.

'Darling,' she said, 'it's *all* drag.'

A punch in the face is not drag.

★

I am aware that this is a very male book, and that it seems to take masculinity very much on its own terms. It's about wrestling, for God's sake.

There is a big subject here, but it presents itself flickeringly. If you are a man, you are faced – moment by moment – with thousands of micro-conflicts. Unless you stay indoors, in bed, under the covers, you can't avoid them.

Who will win the Battle of the Zebra Crossing? Who will triumph in the Getting Off the Train First Sweepstake? Who will win the Eternal Factoid Smackdown down the pub?

There's a simpler, less nuanced explanation, too – simpler than sport. The entire world is about penis size, or compensation for lack thereof.

The more nuanced approaches to masculinity may be more accurate, but they aren't much help in Brockwell Park on a Sunday afternoon when a 10-year-old is attempting to nutmeg you for the third time.

The match is called Dads vs. Lads because Mums hardly ever take part, and Lasses (with one exception) never.

When I'm playing, I have to make a split second choice: Do I let the Lad nutmeg me? Do I let the Lads win?

My father, clearly, believed that it did a boy no good to think he could beat a grown man at squash, at anything, until he himself was a man, and won fair and square.

I belong to a less macho school of fatherhood. Perhaps it's generational. New man; househusband – keywords of the 1980s, when my view of the world was being formed.

If I become tempted to let loose, on the football field, I remember the Competitive Dad sketches on the Fast Show. In these, a similar knockabout in the park always degenerates as the embarrassed children witness the unleashing of their father's rampant will to triumph.

What did boys learn from that kind of behaviour? It's Dad dancing to the power of a thousand.

Once a year, there's a proper, formal Dads vs. Lads match, with plastic goalposts and medals given out to the winners. The result isn't definite until the final, last second goal. (We always let the Lads win.) But there are lots of little moments where an individual Dad has to make a decision. How fast do I run here? How much muscle shall I put into this tackle? Do I let that cheeky little git nutmeg me *again*?

I usually allow myself one goal per match.

When it comes to Dad vs. Dad, on the wing, things can suddenly become full-on.

The best example of this escalation is the Father's Race, on school Sports Day. At Rosendale School, the state primary where Henry and George go, Sports Day is about as All Shall Have Prizes as you can get. The worst a child will come away with is four 4th place stickers. Each year, the Dads are called on to line up for a 50-metre sprint.

Henry and George used to beg me to take part, so I did; now they beg me not to, so I don't.

Everything is immensely unserious, on the start line – completely about showing willing, taking part – until about five seconds before the *on your marks*. At that point, a dozen more Dads, younger, more muscled, arrive out of nowhere and start to bring their elbows into play. By *get set*, the atmosphere on the track is one of mock-focus. Jokes are made, men laugh. But on *go*, some of the Dads take off as if they would rather die than come anywhere but first.

I tried my best not to come last.

I usually finished about fourth from last, but at least I was ahead of the games master.

After the finish, the top three disappear – and I never see them again, in playground or at school gates, until the following year's Dad's race. I end up believing some young men only become fathers in order to win the Dad's race at Sports Day.

There can only be one winning team in Dads vs. Lads, whether we let them nutmeg us or not.

We are slowing while they are speeding up. We are beginning to flail just as they are starting to fly.

It is our job to be vanquished.

To be a father is to be a loser.

Usually willingly.

5

BOARDER

In 1947, aged eight, my father found his father dead, slumped over the lawnmower on the long, sea-facing back lawn of 20 Clifton Drive, Lytham Saint Annes.

John Percy had been very much a distant, Victorian father – observing his newly-bathed youngest son each evening, round the side of the *Times*. Head and all four limbs still intact. 'Very good, very good.' Now off to bed.

My father insists it was the war killed his father. During the D-Day landings, John Percy had been in charge of sanitation for the whole South of England. Not a conventionally heroic role, but vital: if half the Allied troops had been shitting themselves with diarrhoea rather than fear, the 6th June 1944 might have gone very differently.

Once John Percy was dead, my father was left with his older sister Shirley (teenage, but before the invention of teenagers) and his mother, Muriel. They had chickens in the garden, because of rationing. This female-dominated interlude didn't last long.

'He died, and I was whipped off fairly rapidly,' my father remembers. 'I wasn't allowed to the funeral. I went to the Mattersons.'

The Mattersons were friends of the family who had a house in the Lake District. 'It was very *Swallows and Amazons*, that bit.' And then my father went to boarding school.

First, he went to a Preparatory School, Charney Hall, Grange-over-Sands, near Lancaster. 'My mother wanted me out of the house.' Then, aged thirteen, he went to Shrewsbury School.

He thrived there.

He was always a big lad.

One legend has him going on a hiking holiday and taking his dumbbells in his rucksack, so that he could do some weightlifting in between climbing peaks.

By the time he left, he'd broken the school record for putting the shot. It's a good tongue-twister: 'Shrewsbury School's Shropshire Shot-put champion.' His photograph hung for many years in the Games Pavilion.

Another photograph was found recently – my father throwing the discus.

Figure 7. Nice shorts, Dad.

It looks to me as if the discus were heading off into orbit. I can't imagine it ever dropping.

Imagine a punch thrown with that force.

My father *loved* boarding school.

We have no certain evidence that William Litt hated his boarding school, but it's hard to see what he would have found to like.

The school he almost certainly attended was St Bees, founded in 1583. St Bees is a chilly, windswept, isolated place – jutting out into the Irish Sea, the westernmost point of the North of England. Close by is Fleswick Bay, where smugglers used to bring in contraband on moonless nights.

'Enter so that you may make progress' is the inscription above the long-bricked-up door of the school.

The headmaster at the time William would have been there was The Reverend John Barnes.

The defining anecdote about Reverend Barnes is that, when unwilling or unable to give the Sunday sermon, he occasionally sent boys from St Bees to preach in his stead. (This, I have to say, makes me rather like him.)

Reverend Barnes' pedagogic approach was that of all unwilling teachers: force the children's noses further and further into books, make them learn hard stuff by heart.

On Friday the 27th May 1796, when William would have been 10-and-a-half years old, the patrons of St Bees dined in the schoolroom, to celebrate the flourishing state of that Seminary and to commemorate founder's day.

'At this meeting,' according to a report in *The Cumberland Pacquet*, 'some remarkable instances were given of the retentive powers of the mind, in the recital of Latin and English poetry. The students afforded the highest satisfaction.'

'The silver medals were awarded to Mr. ROBERT BENN of Hensingham and Mr. BENSON of Cockermouth, for reciting Gray's "Elegy," and to Mr. WATSON of Whitehaven for reciting Thomson's Poem "Spring," which contained 1,174 lines, to Mr. PONSONBY of Hail and Mr. BOWERBANK of Croft, near Darlington, for reciting the Second Book of Virgil's Aeneid which contains 804 lines...' (Gray's "Elegy" is a mere 128 lines.)*

I imagine the adults, proudly smug; the boys, semi-fossilized with boredom.

Although we have no idea whether William enjoyed school or not, we do know that, when given his liberty, he headed somewhere completely different. He went to the village green. He hung around with the sons of craftsmen and labourers.

He chose to fight.

My father, also, chose to fight.

Within my family, it's the best-known story of his time at Shrewsbury School.

I asked him about it recently. He chuckled. 'It was Tim that put me up to it.'

Dad was talking about his best friend, Tim Bevan, later to become a Brigadier in the King's Shropshire Light Infantry.

Tim was House Captain of Boxing, Oldham's Hall.

'Annual inter-house boxing came around. Tim needed a bruiser. Although he was nearly as tall as me, he was the weight below me. Light heavyweight. Tim was a quite a good boxer. But he was short of a heavyweight boxer. So, like a chump, I stuck my hand up, said, "I'll do it."'

---

* William's published books, history and novel, contain quotations from Thomson's *The Seasons* and Virgil's *Aeneid*. But, at this time, it would have been unusual for a schoolboy not to have studied them – and to miss Gray's 'Elegy' would have been unthinkable.

This was not the very first time my Dad had been in the ring, but he wasn't very experienced.

I asked my Dad, did Tim Bevan give you any tips, before he sent you in? 'Yes,' said Dad, '"*Hit* him."'

'Him' was the house master's son, David Matthews. As such, it might have been a good idea for my Dad to make the bout resemble a contest but...

Dad comes out at the bell. Thumbs the sides of his nose with his big juicy boxing gloves. Two steps forwards. And in a few seconds, it's all over. His fists go blam, left and right, like torpedoes fired from a submarine. They don't need to be brought back. Doof! Doof!

'I did knock the poor chap to the floor,' said Dad. 'He was hospitalized. I broke his nose, I think.'

'Were there repercussions?' I asked.

'No, no. Bill Matthews, who was the house master, took it all very much in his stride. He was a very phlegmatic man.'

My father fought and won.

I didn't.

I suppose there must have been a *first* fight, one I lost to The Other Boy and that set *him* up as the winner and me as everything else. I wish I could remember it, but I can't; it's not available – forgotten or, more likely, repressed. Instead, I remember a small incident from my first evening at Culver House (my boarding house) – before the nasty stuff began.

After eating, a few of us boys were given permission to go and play football on the school playing fields. (Note: This access never happened again.) These wide acres of grass were behind a high wire fence and tall hedge a couple of streets away from Culver.

At this point in proceedings, I was getting on well with The Other Boy, whom I'd only just met. He was a bit silly, a bit cool. He had a very brown face topped off by a floppy quiff. I thought he looked liked a cross between Elvis Presley and a St Bernard. Perhaps he had just come back from summer holiday abroad. He was a bit of a rebel. We were going to be good friends, I could tell.

After we crossed Clapham Road, The Other Boy immediately began to climb over the tall iron gates to the playing fields. He was high up in the air, one leg on either side of the spikes, when I decided to see if the gates were unlocked – they were, and The Other Boy swung round in a big ridiculous arc as I and the other boys with us strolled effortlessly through.

Everyone laughed, and The Other Boy laughed along – I remember this. I remember because later on, when The Other Boy became my worst bully, I would wonder if this was when he began to hate me. Quite without meaning to, I had defeated him, humiliated him. His easy way into the playing fields had been comically undermined by my easier one.

I can't remember the first fight between us, but perhaps, for The Other Boy, this was it. If so, without trying, I won it; I wasn't to win many more.

No, I can't remember the first fight, because all the fights soon became one, and it wasn't so much a fight as a situation, a steady state of being hurt.

(Why, I thought at first – Why doesn't my father come and rescue me? Why doesn't he break the bullies, like he'd have broken that dog? Why? Because I never told him anything was wrong. That would have been weak.)

Of the three years I spent as a weekly boarder at Culver House, this is how they appear to me:

The Other Boy has me down, defenceless, my hands trapped by his knees, my body beneath his body.

This is the worst place to be. At least, it's the worst that I've been in this far in my life.

I'm hot. I know my face is pink and bulging. Everything else in the world has disappeared. There is only this bed with the green cover and two bodies, one on top, one beneath. Sometimes The Other Boy's hand smells of toothpaste and sometimes of cock, but usually of both. His hand covers my mouth to make sure I'm quiet. I feel my mouth, full of spit.

It started just after lights out. He waited until the house master was gone then jumped on me, began the fight. I wasn't quick enough or strong enough. I lost.

When someone has you down, you can't do anything, can you? You are the purest kind of loser. They are in total charge. You are nothing but their victim. You can't *do* anything to them, and they can do anything they want to you. They can punch you or force you to open your mouth and then spit in it. You can try spitting up at them, but it will fall back in your face.

Completely defeated, the only thing you can do is think – think about what you will do once you're free again, once this pain ends. Because it *will* end. It has to. The Other Boy will get bored. He has to sleep. Eventually. Someone might come in. Hopefully not the house master, because then The Other Boy will be punished really badly, and he'll make you suffer even more, later. This won't go on forever, though it will definitely happen again.

I have to decide what to do, when he releases me. There are boys who will start the fight again, and maybe they'll win and be the one on top. Anger can make you stronger – anger of a first defeat, a defeat because the opponent cheated or ambushed you.

If someone grabs your arm from behind, pushes it up, you can't *do* anything, you're powerless, but you haven't *lost*.

But this getting-back-into-it always seemed ridiculous to me – the reversal of power just made clear how limited that power was.

There are boys who will get up and start the fight again, and lose again. They are likely to be treated worse, the second or third time they are pinned down, as the bully will be getting bored.

The bully is already looking for the best way out of the scene. Once they've spat in your mouth, what next? Well, what? 'Give me your...' 'Promise me that you'll...' 'If you ever X, then I'll Y...'

In order to get out of the pin, the loser will promise anything. The bully is already looking out for his own dignity, looking out for a gain. What can they get from the loser? 'Give me your... Yes?' Punch. 'Yes? You promised – you *promised*. Everyone heard you. You *have* to.'

No, when you are a pure loser, you can't *do* anything, when you're pinned down, but you can *decide* something. You can decide to change your life.

At some point, at Culver, I decided that I was never going to fight. I was never going to use my strength on younger or smaller boys. I was going to be as unphysical as possible – because the physical was where you got hurt. Hurt was caused by physical force. Physical force was bad.

I lived with The Other Boy in my dorm for three years before I resorted to magic. A short while before this next and final incident, I believed that, through the force of my psychic powers alone, I'd broken a friend's arm – in order to give him and the rest of my Ampthill gang a demonstration of my powers. John Fortescue fell off a log or off his bike, and broke his arm or wrist.

I had made this happen, I knew, by silently and intensely willing it. My thought-magic had worked, against unsuspecting John Fortescue. I was so powerless, I'd been reduced to Bedfordshire voodoo.

Back at Culver, I decided – after this successful trial – to use all my magic force to get rid of The Other Boy. I expect some small rituals were performed. Mainly, it was visualization. I thought of him gone.

And then, in a scenario I could not have made more perfect if I'd written it in a short story, he fucked up entirely and was expelled.

The perfect scenario my powers brought about was this: during morning break, The Other Boy sneaked away Someone Else Who Bullied Me's briefcase, his leather schoolbag, took it into one of the toilet cubicles, and ripely shat in it. Then he replaced it on Someone Else Who Bullied Me's peg.

I expect The Other Boy expected to get away with this. How could shit be tracked down?

I don't know how or why he was caught. It happened almost immediately.

Looking back, I can see that he was an extremely unhappy little boy, perhaps quite disturbed, and that he wanted to force some form of crisis.

One evening that previous year he had tried to run away from the boarding house, in bare feet. Sometimes he cried with homesickness. I didn't know much about his home. Except that it had orange carpet on the stairs.

I remember how scared I was on The Other Boy's last night at Culver. There were no longer any consequences to his actions. He could do anything to me, what did it matter? Perhaps he'd kill me – psycho that he was. Of course, the house master didn't think to separate him from the rest of us. The Other Boy slept in his usual bed – to the right of the door, separated from it by an ugly chest of drawers. I expected a last hurrah of agony, but The Other Boy – in disgrace, probably fearing his parents, his father, maybe already having spoken to him on the phone – slept meekly.

This was the last time I used magic.

★

'What do you want to be when you grow up?'

If you had asked me, around the age of eight or so, I would probably have said, 'A soldier.' By the age of thirteen, after Culver, I was a pacifist – and if you had asked what I wanted to be, I wouldn't have answered. I didn't have an answer. I no longer had any idea what I wanted to be. But I knew it definitely wasn't a doer of violence.

It all went together, a big jumble of thought and hate and not wanting to have to fight. In there were John Lennon singing 'Imagine' and 'Working Class Hero' and 'Give Peace a Chance', a few things I'd heard about Mahatma Gandhi, the Campaign for Nuclear Disarmament. I was a Cold War Kid. For me, all escalations of violence terminated in the atomic bomb. Cartoons showed cavemen with clubs turning into politicians with Inter-Continental Ballistic Missiles. The logic of force was the logic of Mutually Assured Destruction.

After The Other Boy was finished with me, I wanted to be unphysical. If it had been possible, I'd have chosen not to have a body at all. But that choice wasn't available. (Not until I began dematerializing

Figure 8. The photo I show people to prove to them that I did once have hair. Lots of hair.

into words.) Instead, in order to make life easier for myself, I needed to pass as physical. Whilst at school, I would have to play up and play the game.

Before I went to BMS, I would have defined myself as sporty. Sportier, really, than I was allowed to be. Alameda School in Ampthill didn't take itself too seriously, in terms of competition. During games lessons, we played football. (I remember coming off the pitch, one frosty afternoon, my pink fingers so cold that they couldn't undo my shoelaces.) We climbed ropes in the sports hall. We had a sports day. That was about it.

At BMS, a public school, things were far more competitive, far more serious. Partly because I was in the boarding house, and therefore easily bring-inable for events, but also because I was quite well-coordinated and fit, I represented the school at lots of sports. I thought I was a fast swimmer, especially breaststroke, but never was asked to show my paces. Instead, year after year, I was consistently in the second team for rugby. Early on, they had made me play hooker – dogged punch-bag in the middle of the scrum, glory boy of throw-ins. I couldn't escape that position; I wasn't fast enough to be a wing or aggressive enough to be a flanker or fat enough to be a prop. We played against Stowe and Haberdashers' Aske's. I couldn't escape until the season changed.

About halfway through my school career, I had my most glorious sporting moment. After doing lots of circuit training for a rugby tour of the Netherlands, I became very fit. The school steeplechase that year saw me finish seventh. I was recruited for the cross-country team, and joined the athletics team – I was assigned to the 800 metres, a wonderful, killing distance, neither sprint nor slog. But 800 metres was the event of my sporting hero, Sebastian Coe, and another English victor, Steve Ovett.

Seb Coe running, one of the greatest sights I've ever seen on a television. Birdcage ribs above very British legs, superbly pale toward the upper thigh. Floating, as if a hundred birds inside his lungs were winging him forwards. By the time Steve Cram came to the fore, I was losing interest; Cram's appalling flipper-footed style made me pray someone else would beat him — it didn't matter what country they came from. I wanted that flailing embarrassment out of my sight. Earlier, though, I'd read *Running Free*, Sebastian Coe's co-written autobiography. I'd also read about Sir Roger Bannister's four-minute mile and, one year, took part in the four by 800 metres at the Public School's Relays. This was held on a proper all-weather running track, on the Iffley Road, Oxford. The very place the four-minute mile had been broken.

BMS were in the lead when I took the baton and still in the lead when I handed it over. Our anchor leg runner was our weakest, and we finished outside the top three. But I'd worn the vest and the spikes. I ran a time of two minutes nine seconds — as close as I'd ever come to the pace of a four-minute mile.

I was sporty, or sporty enough to pass.

But it wasn't what I felt I was best at.

6

MY BEST DAYS

The men I feel saddest for are those whose schooldays really *were* the best days of their lives.

The washed-up high school sports star has become an American archetype. Rabbit Angstrom, hero of John Updike's Rabbit novels, was once almost-great at basketball. Jack Kerouac turned to writing after a knee injury ended his American football career. In 'Glory Days', Bruce Springsteen sings of having a few drinks with a guy who used to be a great baseball pitcher – and they can't talk about anything else, because there's nothing else to talk about. Sport takes everything, leaves nothing – nothing except aches and jokes. *Match of the Day* banter.

For my own sons, I hope they peak around the age of sixty-four and a half. Obviously, that means they're going to be doing something mental rather than physical. But I don't want them to spend their lives reminiscing about goals they once scored or saves they once made.

William said of himself, in *Wrestliana*, 'my best day was in 1806, 1807 and 1808' – which makes it quite a long day. He meant his best wrestling day. He would have been 21-years-old when he began to peak. School would have been over for a while – and the two main sources on William's life mostly agree about what he was up to, during that time, which wasn't a great deal.

The Memoirist says that he was leading 'what may be called rather a loose, gentlemanly kind of life'. This involved living with his parents at Netherend and 'taking just what portion of the duties of the farm he pleased, and at such times as best suited his inclination and convenience'.

Wrestling and Wrestlers is more specific, and more critical. William's parents, they say, saw that 'young Litt had rendered himself in some measure unfit for the Church'. To try and give him an alternative they 'placed him with a neighbouring farmer to get an insight into practical, as well as theoretical, agricultural pursuits'.* Elsewhere the authors give their gloss on the word 'unfit' by writing: 'Attending wrestling and racing meetings unfits many persons for a steady and attentive devotion to business'.

Their word 'devotion' was carefully chosen. William, around 18-years-old, had shown himself to be unfit for the business of devotion and incapable of devotion to business. This lack of application might have something to do with alcohol, and the easy money of gambling, and low company. If *Henry & Mary* is as autobiographical as I believe it is, and if its straying hero Henry is a stand-in for William, then these early years of manhood led him into temptation.

Why did William not take to farming? It may be, simply, because – as my father would say – it was 'a bit too much like hard work'.†

To get an idea of the yearly round of farming in Cumberland, I searched the British Library for contemporary documents. I lucked out, and found a diary kept between 1811 and 1859 by William Fisher of Barrow. His notes are extremely laconic, perhaps simply those of an exhausted man, but record how much sheer grind was involved in growing crops and tending sheep and cows. One sentence for January 20th reads, 'Begun to plow' and then adds 'March 23 had done plowing'.

---

* *Wrestling and Wrestlers: Biographical Sketches of Celebrated Athletes of the Northern Ring*, Wordsworth Press, 1893, p. 65.
† Years later, in one of his *Letters on Canada*, No. 3, William refers to 'such a laborious life as tilling the ground'.

(Two months trudging behind the blade! – enough to break any plough boy.) Sewing the corn takes from the 2nd to the 20th of April, after which the barley takes another ten days. The milch-cows are laid out in early June. July is mowing hay in the meadows. August 10th to September 12th is sheep-shearing. In late October, the milch-cows are laid in. The diary has nothing to say about winter.

William did not become a farmer. This, for him, is the moment of great regret – both main sources agree.

'On arriving at manhood, with a vacillation much regretted in after life, farming was neglected and abandoned',* says *Wrestling and Wrestlers*.

'Memoir of the Author' gives a more elaborate explanation:

> In after years he looked back on this period of his career with feelings of great pain, and attributed his subsequent misfortunes and want of success in life to the fact that the golden time of youth had been allowed to pass over so unprofitably, and to the circumstance that he had not been brought up to look forward to any particular occupation as a means of living.

From our point of view, two hundred years later, William seems to have been a definite success in two areas – as a wrestler and as a writer. And as, for us, these are both acceptable ways of making a living, and of defining oneself as a man, he seems hardly to have been a failure at all. But William was a gentleman, and the son of a gentleman. It was only in the years after he retired from the ring that professional sportsmen began to gain recognition.

Paul Johnson says in his book *Birth of the Modern*, 'In no respect did the modern age proclaim its arrival more significantly than in the rise

---

* *Wrestling and Wrestlers: Biographical Sketches of Celebrated Athletes of the Northern Ring*, Wordsworth Press, 1893 p. 65.

of competitive, organized, regulated and mass-directed sports. In the past, sports usually had been regarded as the resort of the idle, frivolous, dissolute and even the disaffected – "sporting meetings" were often a pretext for treasonable gatherings of the discontented gentry and their followers. Suddenly, at the beginning of the [nineteenth] century, it became identified with healthy outdoor exercise and, equally important, with moral cleanliness: *mens sana in corpore sano*'.

Later in life, William regretted his youth as feckless, undirected. He hadn't laid the foundations of prosperity, or learned a useful trade. But it's clear he did devote himself to something, wrestling. I take this brief paragraph from *Wrestliana** as disguised autobiography:

> To arrive at the top of the tree in either wrestling or boxing, a complete knowledge of the science, and varied and effective action are indispensably necessary; and neither of these requisites can possibly be acquired without practice of every description. What we mean by practice of every description is, practice with superiors, equals, and inferiors, both in respect of science and weight; and to form a complete master, such practice is absolutely necessary.

Despite being the son of the Commissioner for the Enclosure of Waste Lands, William must have been liked by other wrestlers. If he had not been, he would not have gained the opportunity to train. There is no way he could have forced or bought his way in. Natural talent wasn't enough. He had to be one of the lads. In *Wrestliana*, it's clear that whilst none of the wrestlers were full-time professionals, many of them had occupations that gave them a kind of daily preparation for the hard lifting and muscular strain of the ring. Millers, for example, such as the famed William Richardson, of Caldbeck.

---

* *Wrestliana*, 1st ed., p. 48; 2nd ed., p. 32.

From frequent practice in lifting and removing loads with his arms, in which the knee and foot are sometimes used as auxiliaries, he might have acquired more strength in the leg when striking out, and felt less incommoded when balancing and turning his man, than if he had been brought up to almost any other trade.

To compete with, and sometimes to defeat, men whose daily business was hard physical labour, William must have been anything but idle in his youth.

This was the time when, in the words of the poem 'The Enthusiast' – handwritten in the back of the family copy of *Henry & Mary* – William 'had been / In very youth, the Champion of the green...'

He must have put in the hours.

Malcolm Gladwell's book *Outliers* popularized the idea of the 10,000 hours rule – that in order to become an expert in any given discipline (playing the violin, writing short stories, bricklaying) a person needs to have spent 10,000 hours doing that thing.[*] Former table-tennis champion Matthew Syed, in *Bounce*, refines Gladwell's definition. Achieving excellence doesn't just demand putting in the hours, it requires ten years of directed practise.[†]

I found this an incredibly persuasive idea, when I first read it. And when I applied it to myself, it seemed to fit. I began writing fiction seriously in about 1986; my first book was published in 1996. But I also had my doubts. It's not that I believed in innate gifts that took a sportsperson all the way or in inevitably triumphant artistic genius; more that I thought – before the hours – the basic physiology

[*]   Malcolm Gladwell, *Outliers: The Story of Success*, Little, Brown, 2008.
[†]   Matthew Syed, *Bounce: The Myth of Talent and the Power of Practice*, 4th Estate, 2010.

or neurology also needed to be in place. I was relieved to find this argument put far better than I could put it in David Epstein's *The Sports Gene*. This is a point-by-point takedown of Malcolm Gladwell's argument, for which Gladwell was gracious enough, or self-publicizing enough, to give a cover quote saying that it's 'A wonderful book'. David Epstein finds a way to explain what makes champions. For example, some of them may have a talent not for a particular sport but for being trainable.

What all of these accounts of sporting achievement leave out is what I see as central: a certain degree of fuckedupness. No one starts wanting and needing to be the world's greatest X without some kind of very sad prompt. Occasionally, but not always, this is abuse they've suffered. Often, what gets a person to put in 10,000 hours is a simple desire for revenge.

Out of my own past, I came raging against bullies – I wanted to make sure my voice was the one that was listened to, not theirs.

If it takes ten years of dedicated practise to achieve the highest level, that would place William's serious dedication of himself to wrestling in 1795, when he was 10-years-old. Seems about right. And, if so, this would have required a lot of hanging about on the green, throwing and – more often – being thrown.

Perhaps the village green really was as idyllic as the place Susanna Blamire, the self-styled 'Muse of Cumberland', lays out in 'Stoklewath; or, the Cumbrian Village'.*

Now on the green the youth their gambols keep,
Stretching their sinews in the bounding leap;
Others the wrestler's glory would maintain,

---

* Susanna Blamire, *The Muse of Cumberland*, 'Stoklewath; or, the Cumbrian Village,' from *The Poetical Works of Miss Susanna Blamire*, collected by Henry Lonsdale, M.D., 1842, pp. 11–12.

Twist the strong nerve and fill the swelling vein;
One youth his pip blows from the rocky hill,
Seated like Pan above the clacking mill;
Another strikes the violin's cheerful string,
Light to the dance the bounding virgins spring;
'Tis most part nature, yet some art is found
When one—two—three lies heavy on the ground...

This vision is like something off the side of a Greek vase, or the painting by Edgar Degas, 'Young Spartans Exercising' (without the nudity, I guess).

The idyllic greens were later to be enclosed, by William's father.

How good was William, as a wrestler?

Well, when a copy of *Wrestliana* came into his hands, he would add beneath his name the words 'Winner of 200 belts'. That means he won two hundred competitions, small and large. Each competition would have had a number of rounds, sometimes three and sometimes as many as six or seven. This suggests William won well over 1,000 competitive wrestling bouts.

His most impressive statistic is that for ten consecutive years, on Arlecdon Moor, William went undefeated. The place was his fortress. He was perfect there.

Elsewhere, he didn't do so well. His record at the Carlisle races wasn't good. The further from home he went, the less well he did.

In this, William was like Antaeus – the wrestler from Greek myth who couldn't be defeated on his home turf. It took wily Hercules to figure out Antaeus' weakness. To beat Antaeus you needed to lift him off the ground. By holding him in the air, breaking the link between man and land, Hercules took away Antaeus' strength. After figuring this out, Hercules was easily able to bear-hug the previously unbeatable wrestler into submission.

William was good enough at wrestling to seem mythic.

And what was I doing, when I was twenty-one, twenty-two and twenty-three?

I was reading – reading and writing. When I finished reading a book, I noted it down in my diary. In 1990, I read 101 books; the next year, 109; and 1992, it was 104.

I read Graham Greene and Jane Austen, Harold Pinter and Samuel Beckett, Elizabeth Bishop and more Graham Greene. I read on the metro and in trams. I read for whole anxious, blissful afternoons.

I also wrote and rewrote three novels (never published), and either wrote or co-translated 265 poems.* I kept a daily diary. I wrote a weekly letter to my parents. For my employers, a private English school, I created dialogues for English courses.

This was me, taking a large chunk out of the necessary 10,000 hours of directed practise. Much of what I wrote was an attempt to drag myself away from the sludge of adolescent self-pity and self-hatred.

Forgive me, but I sometimes used to ask myself if I would prefer to be happy or that vague thing I thought of as 'great' – as in 'a great poet', 'a great writer'. It wasn't a real question, this, because I knew the answer already. I was just pushing myself onwards. Of course, I would do anything, write any number of words, trash any number of years, to become 'great'.

If I looked up from my book, from my desk, which I must have done sometimes, outside the window was post-revolutionary Prague.

---

* Most of the translations will be published in *Impossible Green Country*, Jantar Press, 2018.

I arrived there on Easter Sunday 1990 and stayed for exactly one hundred and twenty weeks.

In retrospect, I am partly amazed how much work I got done, but mostly I am sorry how little I allowed myself to enjoy myself – and I am even more sorry how negligently I treated Magdalena and Virginia, my first and second girlfriends.

Magdalena had fled Prague in 1968, as a little girl, with her mother. She grew up in Sweden, and spoke English and Swedish better than she did Czech. Magdalena was dark haired, pale skinned. She worked in the National Theatre. I loved her. I couldn't believe she was going out with me, and I treated her so badly she soon wasn't.

Virginia was English. She had come to Prague to learn Czech, Early New High German and to start a PhD about a Protestant from the start of the fifteenth century known as Peter the Englishman. Gini was auburn haired, freckled. She ended up working for an educational foundation funded by the billionaire George Soros. I loved her. I couldn't believe she was going out with me, but she stuck with me for several obsessive years.

I was so boring.

I never wanted to do anything except read and write. The most exercise I took was a walk up to Prague Castle.

Whenever I missed a day at the desk, I became convinced I was worthless. If I wasn't writing, I might as well be dead.

1990, 1991 and 1992 were a high point for Europe.

I could have seen much more of them than I did.

If 1806, 1807 and 1808 were William's best day, then these years were a high point for Great Britain, too – or, at least, the beginning of the glory days. Political historians love the pungency of this era – very posh men in stinky wigs trying to top one another's eloquence, or undermine one another's parliamentary oomph.

Walk in through the side door of Westminster Abbey, and you find yourself dwarfed by pale marble versions of these democratic giants. They stand, refreshingly noble, secular but god-fearing, voluble even in their silence – Charles Fox, George Canning, William Pitt the Younger. 1805 had brought victory at Trafalgar, the sea-battle against the French and Spanish Navies that set up a hundred years of 'Britannia Rules the Waves!' But this is more to do with the Winston Churchill school of history, those who believe that Britain's finest hour always comes when the nation is on the back foot. Thus, 1940, after the evacuation of Dunkirk, when Hitler could go sightseeing in Paris, and on through the heroics of the Battle of Britain; thus, 1805 – after Napoleon had defeated both the Austrian and French armies, at the battle of Austerlitz, and had Europe at his mercy.

What was my father – young David H.B. Litt – doing, at the age when William was having his best days?

The answer is simple: National Service. Stationed in West Germany, he dated German blondes and translated love letters to German blondes for his fellow Tommies. He polished his boots to a bright shine, and hated it. If he misbehaved, the Sergeant Major had him peeling potatoes all day long. Mainly, he drove a tiny armoured Daimler Dingo Scout Car with five gears forwards and five in reverse. He was in the cavalry, the Royal 17th/21st Lancers. Their cap badge was a skull and crossbones that wouldn't have been out of place on a Jolly Roger. Their motto was 'Death or Glory'.

All this machismo fed in to my pre-Culver House fantasies of becoming a soldier.

'My father,' I used to tell my friends, 'was in the army.'

He enjoyed it, but left as soon as he could – these were not his best days. Those came quite a bit later.

My father was only ever 'Dave' to Australians, and down Flitwick Squash Club, where 'Davids' were completely unknown.

I was 'Tobes', my sisters 'George' and 'Charl', and my mother (as she winced) 'Hell'.

This isn't to say my father isn't good at informality. He can talk to and get on with anyone – that's his best gift. I think he shares this character trait with William. They both liked to get on with everyone they met. With William, I think it was almost a mania – and one that eventually undermined him.* With my father, it seemed something natural and relaxed. On family holidays in France, he would embarrass my sisters and I by chatting (in French) to the *patissier* and the *boulanger*, and anyone else who happened to be in the shop. He would make them smile and laugh and nod, we – hanging around over towards the door – didn't quite know how or why.

'Da-*ad*, come *on*.'

Within the antiques trade, which can be extremely bitchy and factional, he had fallings-out but – as far as I know – he did forty years business without making an enemy. Perhaps this was because he was never quite as successful as he might have been.

The great *What If?* in my father's career was what if he had taken or gone shares on a shop in London – some eponymous emporium, halfway along the Fulham Road. This would have meant moving up from brown furniture and, instead, buying and selling the gilded, the inlaid and the lacquered.

---

* There is evidence that William's brewing business failed because he was too generous in his terms. The Memoirist says, 'he refused nobody who thought proper to favour him with an order' and that 'his book debts soon became very heavy'. I think William was afraid to ask men to pay him back what they owed him, because then they would like him less.

There were offers and opportunities (dealers love to talk about trading up), but Dad never really wanted to risk making the leap. He'd kept the Dunstable Street shop in Ampthill, and also capitalized on the pine craze by opening another shop, *Yesterday's Pine*. Later on, he switched from selling English to French furniture. It was easier to get hold of. For years, he had a stand at Battersea Decorative Antiques & Textiles Fair. This chi-chi event takes place in spring, autumn and summer in a permanent plastic tent near the Peace Pagoda, beside the muddy Thames.

And it's in Battersea, I believe, that my father had his best days – on the stand, just chatting away. He would charm rich Americans, and rich English. They were, he says, 'very nice people'.

Within a couple of minutes, they had ceased to be customers and he – like the very best salesmen – had ceased to be a salesman. I often watched this, proud and slightly awed at my father's likeability.

The little group of them would stand, close together, surrounded by stock, mirrored in the lichen-like mottle of Louis XVI glass, talking about schools or holidays or dentistry and – oh, yes, we'll take it – somehow, without it being difficult or even a decision, the deal would be done. Almost without having been spoken, the price was agreed. Everyone was happy, laughing, nodding.

A few days afterward, my father would deliver the chandelier or candlesticks to some very large residence – to an American wife or, sometimes, to Lady this or Viscount that. And he'd have a cup of tea, and continue to chat. His customer would close the door on him feeling better – they'd feel like his friend, because that's what they were. And in this way, he paid for my food, clothes, and the second half of my education.

'I had some wonderful customers,' Dad says, with emotion. 'We had some in the South of France – we more or less furnished their house.'

What it comes down to, this gift, is simple: my father likes people, and so people like him back.

But not so much they start to call him Dave; they're not generally that sort. His customers were relaxed, polite and keen to get on with everyone.

Unlike some people I could mention.

7

ONE OF THEM LOSES

'When two men say *Hello* in the street, one of them loses.'

I say this once, slowly and clearly, and then – the only statement I ever repeat immediately – I say it again, with exactly the same intonation.

'When two men say *Hello* in the street, one of them loses.'

I want it to sound a little intimidating, but also mock-macho. My teaching style needs to fit what I'm teaching, and this sentence is one I use when I am teaching dialogue.

In the creative writing class, I identify three kinds of dialogue: Winning, Hiding and Ignoring. Two Men Say Hello is my best example of Winning. What it demonstrates is how little is needed for a decisive shift in power relations to take place. This is the kind of dialogue you often hear between armed, up against it men, in Hollywood movies.*

'I'm top dog.' 'No, I'm top dog.'

In *How to Write a Blockbuster Screenplay* manuals of the less thoughtful variety, the student is advised to rack up the conflict in each scene – particularly if the scene feels pointless or flat. If you can get the characters screaming at one another, the theory goes, the truth of

---

* Sometimes, even speech isn't needed, just presence, silence. A baddie greets Clint Eastwood, sarcastically; Eastwood says nothing. The baddie has no follow-up line. Eastwood still says nothing. The baddie becomes embarrassed and then, to cover this, becomes angry. Eastwood has won.

who they are and *what is at stake between them* will come out more clearly and entertainingly.

In a restaurant, all the other customers will pretend to ignore a couple bitching at one another at conversational level, but if the couple start screaming everyone is granted permission to turn and gawp.

After a few months in the British Library, I had moved on from historical research to research into wrestling – specifically Cumberland and Westmorland wrestling. It was taking me over. I was starting to think of everything in terms of wrestling.

Speech was wrestling. Pursuing any kind of a career was wrestling. Getting a sentence into proper shape – wasn't that wrestling, too?

As I tried to get to know William better, I thought about what we had in common.

William had been a writer. With his novel, *Henry & Mary*, William had entered into competition with the great novelist Walter Scott, and he'd lost.

With *Wrestliana*, William had written a book that people still wanted to read two hundred years after it was published. Would I manage that, or would he beat me?

For several years, I attributed the Two Men quote to Norman Mailer. I remembered reading it, or something like it, and I remembered it being something to do with the hyper-machismo of Norm. It didn't appear in, but was very much in keeping with, the rest of Martin Amis's wonderful profile of the great American novelist and plonker, republished in *The Moronic Inferno*.* Here Amis tells how Mailer got

---

* Martin Amis, 'Norman Mailer: The Avenger and the Bitch', *The Moronic Inferno*, Penguin, 1987, pp. 57–73.

into a fight with two sailors whilst walking his poodle in New York. The sailors called Mailer's poodle queer, and *nobody* called Mailer's dog queer. Mailer returned home, having taken a hell of a beating, his left eye practically hanging out, but ecstatic, on cloud nine. The implication is: Mailer only took his poodle for a walk – that Mailer only *had* a poodle, in order to get into fights.

After a while, I became uneasy about using a quote I couldn't locate – particularly because some students took offence to what it implied about men, about human beings, about a general lack of human niceness. It made them feel awkward, particularly in the coffee break that usually followed this part of the session. A humanity that is seen as speaking this way is all about the Will to Power. Winning dialogue can seem to turn everyone into Hitler.

I once got into an argument with the writer John Boyne. 'All that "one of them loses" stuff,' he said, 'It's crap – it's just crap.' We were in a bar in Norwich. This was years after we both attended Malcolm Bradbury's creative writing MA. In John Boyne's novels – such as *The Boy In The Striped Pyjamas* and *Crippen* – straightforward self-sacrificing goodness exists, and characters often speak to one another without attempting (in the words of chess Grandmaster Nigel Short*) to 'trap, dominate, fuck'.

But when I'm teaching dialogue, I am trying to stop students writing second gear novels – and I am trying to help them avoid the worst kind of dialogue, that in which it is obvious that the characters are speaking not to one another but out of the page, directly at the reader, on behalf of the writer. (I want to get this piece of information across, the writer thinks, but I don't want it to be some heavy chunk of exposition, so I'll have X and Y take a drive through some symbolically meaningful scenery and talk it all through, even though they're both saying stuff they know the other already knows.)

---

* As reported by Julian Barnes in the article 'Trap. Dominate. Fuck', *Granta 47 'Losers'*, edited by Bill Buford, 1994.

On my website, I used to have a page called A S K I N G S, where I went fishing for answers to questions such as:

> If a human body were dumped from a spaceship, what would happen to it in terms of decomposition? Would it freeze, desiccate and then shatter?

> Where does that fluffy, scummy stuff come from, that seems to end up in the bottom of a glass of water in which home-made ice cubes have melted?

> Why is nothing that we eat in England made out of pigs' milk?

> Did dinosaurs get cancer?

> What is the shortest English word containing all the vowels, a e i o u, in that order and also in any order?

I put up the Mailer quote in 2004, with a plea to help me identify it. Three years later, after Mailer died, web-friend Iain Campbell pointed out that 'in his recent obituary in The *Guardian*, they mentioned that quote though the exact phrasing is different. They give it as: "When two men pass another in the street and say 'Good morning,' he once said, 'there's a winner and a loser'."'

In 2012, another email, this time from James Scudamore, came telling me that 'I've just read this in *Advertisements for Myself*:

> If anyone can pin Tolstoy, it is Ernest H. Somewhere in Hemingway is the hard mind of a small-town boy, the kind of boy who knows you have a real cigar only when you are the biggest man in town, because to be just one of the big men in town is tiring, much too tiring. You inspire hatred, and what is worse than hatred, a wave of cross-talk in everyone around you. You are considered important

by some and put down by others, and every time you meet a new man, the battle is on.

Mailer's sentences are diffuse and un-hard-hitting. (I prefer my version.) But the thought, and the sentiment, are pure American machismo. (I'll come back to this, and to the dire consequences it has for pencils.) The moral, though, could be derived from any episode of any great English TV sitcom – 'I'm Alan Partridge' or 'The Office' or 'The Thick of It'. Each utterance however small is, in the mind of its speaker, for the win. Every single word is intended to be the last word.

Even when they're not wrestling, men are always wrestling.

When the dialogue class resumes, I get the students to write a dialogue in which two men (I make it men to keep it simple) are talking about a subject that is *not* the real issue between them. Their subject might be how they wash their cars or the latest X-Men movie, doesn't matter. What the student needs to ensure is that, with every new thing that is said, by one man or the other, there is *escalation* – the conflict must increase, the stakes must get higher. The both of them want to end up as Top Dog.

And then, when all the students have had time to write a page, usually in a room that has suddenly energized, I get some of them (the ones who sniggered as they scribbled, or looked particularly appalled at what they were allowing themselves to put on paper) to read their dialogue aloud.

Before they start, I ask the others in the class to listen out for any hint of conciliation or backing down. Are there any lines where one of the men says 'Maybe' or 'You might be right about that?' If so, cut 'em. Within this model of dialogue, these lines need to be crossed out in heavy black marker. They're not getting us where we need to be going – which is not just conflict but violence.

Hopefully, someone within the group will have been forced – due to the level of conflict their dialogue has reached early on – to have A or B make a physical threat, or throw a punch, or – best of all (for teaching purposes) – produce a gun. This will allow me to go smoothly into a digression on Quentin Tarantino's addiction to Mexican Standoffs.

It's no accident, I'll say, that in the first four scripts of QT's that made it to the screen – *Reservoir Dogs, True Romance, Pulp Fiction, Natural Born Killers* – there is a Mexican Standoff. Meaning, that everyone in the scene – five, six or seven characters – has a gun, draws it, and points it at the person who is pissing them off the most. (This is a trick Tarantino, at least in part, took from Hong Kong cinema of the 1980s. It's still there in his more recent films, too – the ones I haven't bothered seeing.)

When someone pulls a gun, I tell the class, they take off from speech – the argument is over. Speech has been outdone. The gun-pointer may not have won the argument, but they are winning the exchange. They are Top Dog. The defeated man is likely to speak a line to the effect of, 'Hey, anything you say, buddy.'

With a gun at my temple, if the bearer requires, I will admit that 2+2=5, that I know the combination to the safety deposit box, that my mother was a whore and that I like nothing better than sucking dick, etcetera. Anything to make it alive into the next moment.

Who is Top Dog? It's the guy with the biggest gun.

The problem for the screenwriter (Bonjour, Quentin) is that, once that first gun is out of the holster and pointing at the first head, you've reached a definite highpoint, so how do you get out of the scene? Do you allow an anti-climax, or do you try to find an even higher high?

Answer, more guns. Two, three, four, five, six, seven.

Answer, Mexican Standoff.

A rapid succession of better and better tooled up Top Dogs can be thrilling—

click, 'I win'

click, 'No, I win'

clunk, 'No, I win'

ker-CHUNK, 'I think you gentlemen will find that *I* win.'

As Sean Connery's character in *The Untouchables* puts it, definitively: 'He pulls a knife, you pull a gun; he shends one of yoursh to the hoshpital, you shend one of hish to the morgue.'

All together now: 'Thatsh the Schicago whey.'

Brilliantly macho dialogue from master of brilliantly macho dialogue, David Mamet.

And so, the logical outcome of employing the Winning model of dialogue is the Mexican Standoff. If you keep escalating conflict, you'll pretty soon get to guns. Or you'll get to the arch-villain with his finger on the red button of his Doomsday Device.

Not all Winning dialogue gets here, outside Hollywood. Mostly, dialogue stays on the level of truth-telling. What's beneath it is the question, 'Who is right, you or me?'

In a simplistic way, within these limits, Knowledge is Power. What tactics does X use to defeat Y? He tells Y something Y didn't know. 'You think you know everything? You are such a sap.' Or, in philosophical language, 'My world-picture is fundamentally more accurate than yours.' For example, 'It's not just that I drive a better car than you. All this time you think you've had a happy marriage, your wife's been sleeping with Z.'

Serious, John Boyne-type disgust can occur, within students, at this point. 'But people *just aren't like that.*' This often means *Men may be like that but women aren't like that.*

Often, to teach is to provoke. I don't expect students to accept this model of dialogue as accurately describing all human interactions.

But after reading this chapter, I invite you to watch any Hollywood movie. Could Winning dialogue explain why the characters seem to be so unnecessarily pissed at each other? Why are they always trying to teach one another lessons?

Dismiss my conjecture – then, when you're feeling smug, listen to the next conversation behind you on the bus, or between two children in a shop. Tell me no one was trying to win.

I once heard a horrible news story, about a fatal shooting in America. Two young men had gotten into an argument about whether Paris was in France or France was in Paris. This doesn't seem worth dying over, though there's clearly a right and wrong answer. But that wasn't the issue – it was whether X or Y had the truest picture of the world. And everything depends on that.

The loser of any exchange can still depart the scene, believing they are right – unless they are dead.

Being in the wrong is right next to being wrong and being wrong is just another way of saying *Loser*.

Facetious is the shortest word in the English language including all the vowels in alphabetical order.

Writers look askance at winners, at winning. What we win – or far more often don't – are Literary Prizes, and these are not contests we can do much to try to win. Yes, we can write the very best book we are capable of, and hope prize judges like it when they come to read it – one or two years later. Or we can even try to write the type of novel – reassuringly chunky, emotionally wrenching – that judging committees seem to favour. But we can't actively *take part*. It's not sport. We aren't present to clip away Ian McEwan's heels, to throw Hilary Mantel to the ground.

Most writers are likely to feel oppressed by gaining rather than losing a prize, because it will be for something accomplished by an earlier version of themselves. Prizes are given to writers for who they once were. The winner of the Olympic 100 metres final was the fastest man on *that* day; the Booker Prize winner was the person who completed that novel six months or a year earlier, and perhaps even more so they are the person who had the idea for that novel six or seven years before that. The writer may feel that they are struggling to get back to that previous self's level. Almost certainly, they will feel they have gone beyond that stage, in insight if not in quality of prose.

Writers look at winners as if they were not exactly *cheats* but annoying favourite children of an openly unjust father. The pet child, outside the family, is usually everybody's pet hate. Writers, tribally, view Winners as our oppressors. We are the goers-away, the mullers-over, the grumblers, the questioners of the whole society that creates few winners and many losers. For most writers, to win is to become a traitor to the tribe. It is through our losses that we became writers. The instantly and repeatedly rewarded individuals become something else: monsters. We, we console ourselves, are ugly, but we have the prose style. I have always lulled myself with those words from Leonard Cohen's song 'Chelsea Hotel #2' – ugly, but...

There are no wins within language. A novelist can't *beat* the English tongue. Nor is it possible for her to *defeat* the Novel or the Short Story. Perhaps, in gamer slang, you could say about them – if they wrote innovatively enough – that they 'pwned' a form. Maybe it would be accurate to say, 'Hey, in 1921, James Joyce was really pwning The Novel – that *Ulysses* smacked down everything else.' The most that any writer can hope to do is invent a popular genre – as Walter Scott did the historical novel or Edgar Allan Poe the detective story – although what comes after you will almost certainly be superior.

Wrestling with language, that isn't how I think of what I do with words. The wrong kind of struggle, on the page, will leave traces of damage in the finished rhythms, word choices.

I am frustrated by the poverty of words in English describing smell or scent. But it's not something with which I wrestle. The words I need are not difficult to use, they are just absent – not being able to get a grip on them *is* the issue.

I love writing ghost stories, but I wouldn't say I had wrestled with the ghost story genre. I entered into it and it, like a spirit, entered into me. The only haunted house an artist can enter is her own psyche. Unless I am the right person to write that genre, right at that moment, the writing won't come out right. Grace is our daily bread.

Booker, Pulitzer, Nobel – the future renders every literary prize null. All writers, in regard to posterity, are in the position of drug cheats – their glory can be taken away, found to have depended upon falsity. That people in the past thought something great is of historical interest, nothing else. It's what people in the present think that counts, perpetually.

Most of what most of us writers produce is, in this context, failed. And I sometimes feel that, within my lifetime, I have seen *The Canterbury Tales* and *Paradise Lost*, fading, failing. The present finds them too antiquated, too demanding, too ambitious, too Christian.

In which case, what hope of surviving do this afternoon's anxious typings have?

About macho writers, American ones, as promised. And pencils. This used to amuse me so much that I began collecting examples. The problem, for many male American writers, is that they imagine they have to justify what they do as not-cissy, or they have to show that although, okay, they do *write*, and writing is a bit of a cissy activity, they themselves are demonstrably not-cissy. In order to achieve this slight of hand, they have to realign writing with manual labour.

Hence, pencil abuse. Hemingway said that he sharpened twenty pencils before starting work on a story. Ben Hecht wore down an estimated seventy-five to a hundred pencils a week. But the winner is John Steinbeck. He sharpened twenty-four pencils each morning and wrote with them until each one was blunt. After many years of doing this, he had to use his left hand to slide the pencil between the fingers of his hugely calloused writing hand, because that hand could no longer pick a pencil up. Every few months, he sandpapered down the calluses so he could keep writing.*

Why? Because he was a man, a real man, dammit, and writing (to avoid being cissy) has to appear more like carpentry than mental arithmetic. A good writer shapes, hones, polishes. It's not just about desk work. A writer does not merely risk back-strain reaching out for their copy of *Roget's Thesaurus*. A writer does not spend hours debating with himself whether to employ Oxford Commas. A writer doesn't merely keep typing whatever comes into his drifty head. (Even if, really, that's what most of us do.) No, they sharpen pencils and more pencils.

European male writers don't tend to bother with posturing. They accept that writing is cissy. Most of them are not bothered being thought cissy or gay or effeminate. I mean, imagine Kazuo Ishiguro looking at himself in the mirror in the morning, wondering if he was 'Man Enough.'

★

---

* I can't find the website or book in which I read about Steinbeck's macho mania. If you do, please let me know.

I once felt like I was a winner. It wasn't a prize, but it came close.

Being chosen as one of the *Granta* Best of Young British Novelists seemed the literary fictional equivalent to being selected for the England Under-18 Football Squad.

Squad, not team – only eleven were in the team. Some might be substituted on or off, during the match, depending upon injuries, tiredness or lack of performance.

Of the twenty of us, brought together in 2003, some have gone on to carve out successful international careers, scoring lots of big match goals: Sarah Waters, David Mitchell. Others are still there or there-abouts in the Premier League: A.L. Kennedy, David Peace. Others, like me, trog along in the Championship. One or two seem to have given up the game entirely.

This is all what you would have expected. But, at the time I was chosen, my inclusion felt as if it proved something: I hadn't wasted my life.

There was a launch party. Everyone glammed up, in the way writers only tend to for the Booker or Baileys' Prizes. I wore a pale suit and the most beautiful tie I'll ever own – a silk neither green nor grey nor gold, but something amazingly in-between. Six or seven photographers surrounded me and went click click click, using flashes. This was more lens-attention than I've received at any time, before or since. But, curiously, I have never seen a single photograph taken at that party. Which makes me wonder whether they were really photographers or actors paid to say, 'Over here' and do catastrophic things to all of our egos.

'This,' I thought, 'is what Elizabeth Hurley' – flash! flash! – 'must feel.' You remember Elizabeth Hurley, don't you? No? Well, no matter. 'This is how Salman Rushdie must feel.'

I heard that Salman appeared at a Chelsea Football Club home match and, being spotted, the fans – having no other chant prepared – sang, 'One Salman Rushdie, there's only one Salman Rushdie'. He's really the only truly famous writer of our time.

This is lucky. Fame is bad for writers. A writer needs to be able to sit on the top deck of a bus, and hear how people talk when they don't think anyone is listening. Invisibility is a necessity. Bob Dylan can never enter a room that doesn't contain Bob Dylan – and those rooms have too much in common for him to be interested in them. He's no longer going to overhear good material. Why go out? (He doesn't go out.)

Successful writers have lots of readers, and enough income not to have to do anything but write. Some of the *Granta* bunch became very successful.

Let's not be falsely okay with this – I wanted what they seemed to have, and I still want it. But I know I have already had more attention than is usual for a writer. (Over here, Toby.) I may already have had more attention than is *good* for a writer. (Click, I still hear it.) My ego craves another chance to do its giddy little dance. Look at me, oh, look at me. Also, a couple of prize wins would allow me to have bits of my house that are falling apart put back together.

Most of all, I would like to be able to do the being-successful thing with the greatest reluctance. After months of persuasion, to grant an interview – like a king. Writers who are in this position can get the maximum publicity without seeming to pursue any publicity.

But then, of course, give me any success and I'd want to mess with it. I'd follow a genuine bestseller up with anything but a sequel. I'd do it again – but upside down and back to front and under a pseudonym.

Because if you do it the way other people do it, you haven't proved – to your self – that you're better than other people. This is how I think. And if you're not better than your contemporaries, no one in the future is going to need to read you.

You must always be, drumroll, a smartarse – and we all know what people like to see happen to a smartarses.

★

The Totleigh Barton centre in Devon is a medium-sized white farm-house that once belonged to the poet Ted Hughes.

I was there in the summer of 2005 with the novelist Ali Smith, teaching a residential creative writing course for the Arvon Foundation.

Many writers 'do an Arvon' once a year, as a welcome way to earn £1,000 and perhaps sell a dozen of their books.

Both Ali and I had novels that had been entered for that year's Booker Prize. Hers was called *Hotel World*, mine was called *Ghost Story*. We also shared the same publisher and the same editor.

I had tried to prevent myself going too often to the computer in the centre's office, and checking the Booker website, to see if the longlist had been announced. I had wanted to avoid knowing when the announcement would be made – I knew it was imminent.

One morning, halfway through the week, Ali (who hadn't been going to the centre's office at all) got a phone call, then another phone call, then another. I knew this because, at Totleigh Barton, there is only one small patch of grass within which you could get a phone signal – and that patch was right outside the converted goose shed in which I dormed. Ali was on the phone all morning. My phone did not ring.

When I checked the website, *Hotel World* was longlisted, *Ghost Story* wasn't.

In the first moment, losing is like bad heartburn – at least, that's how it feels to me. I blush and sweat but the worst thing is the losing hitting me right in the chest; somewhere in the middle, between the lungs. I feel like a great alien ball of burning iron has appeared there, sizzling away just to the right of my heart.

When they lose, sportspeople often say they feel 'gutted'. But that feeling comes a little later, because the iron ball of defeat has only just started to sink down through my body. I feel it dragging my face along with it, forcing a frown as my face melts from the inside.

Oh God, I hope no one speaks to me now. What could I say?

After the first moment is over, I feel diminished, older. What I want most of all is for time to reverse – can't everyone just back up to the moment before this happened? Then we can run it again the way I wanted it to go. But still the loss is there, I can feel it descending within me. Around it, I feel the whole of me getting heavier and smaller and less worth being.

As soon as the ball scorches my stomach, I feel nauseous, and when it evaporates my intestines, I feel completely undermined: I know I will never be able to speak to anyone and make eye contact again.

Hitting my pelvis, the ball of loss sends agony down my femur bones but is diverted forwards.

Out it falls, to lie briefly on the floor in front of me – invisibly – as I stare down, before it burns off toward its rightful home, the boiling core of the world.

Despite the damage it's done, it remains unchanged. The failure I started with was the failure I ended up with. All I can do is change my attitude towards it. And I feel – because I can't put it any better than an athlete – I do feel completely gutted.

For the rest of the week, Ali was extraordinary. She didn't tell the Arvon students of her listing. She commiserated with me in a way I found genuinely consoling.

On the morning she spoke on the phone to everyone congratulating her, I was fiercely jealous. I was burning with resentment.

So, I went for a walk.

I'd been to Totleigh Barton before, and I knew there was a longish hike down high-hedged country lanes that took you round in a big circuit.

It was what I needed. I set off.

The day was blue sky gorgeous. I tried to let it cheer me up, but I just became angrier and angrier. I was a failure. My efforts to write the novel had been a waste. If I couldn't even get longlisted – and it was a long longlist – what was the point? *Ghost Story* was just as good as *Hotel World*, wasn't it? Perhaps it wasn't. Perhaps I was rubbish, and no one had told me. Perhaps I should give up writing. But *Ghost Story* wasn't a bad book. Round and round, the same thoughts.

I knew that this was an important moment. I wasn't sure I'd ever write a better book than *Ghost Story* (I'm still not sure if I have) – so this might have been my last chance to win a big literary prize and become one of those writers who seem, for a while, to be everywhere, to be the writer everyone should read. And who, for the rest of their writing lives, can be reasonably certain of being published and making a living and having a house that doesn't need a lot of fixing.

I felt shit.

I kept walking.

And then, fairly desperately, I remembered what are known as the Buddha's Four Noble Truths.

I had always been interested in Buddhism, ever since my best friend Luke introduced me – when I was a mystical 11-years-old – to Jack Kerouac's *The Dharma Bums* and to the works of Lobsang T. Rampa. Rampa's books detailed his youth in Lhasa, watching flags fly above the Potala Palace, and his initiation into the mystical secrets of Tibetan Buddhism. After his third eye was opened, Lobsang astral travelled, experienced powerful cosmic visions, was exiled from his homeland and had long conversations with his cats. Lobsang T. Rampa was, it later turned out, the pseudonym of Cyril Henry Hoskin. Cyril Henry Hoskin wasn't a Tibetan lama, writing his spiritual autobiography, but an English plumber.

Since then, I'd read some more reliable books on Buddhism; enough to be able to remember the basics of the Four Noble Truths.

I knew about the first Truth, which said that suffering was inevitable, and the second Truth, that explained how suffering arose – that suffering comes from not getting what you want.

I was so jealous of Ali, one of the people I like best in the world, and so angry that my own book – that *I* – hadn't been recognized, that I was suffering an extraordinary amount of pain.

Unnecessary pain.

I looked at the green hedgerows and kept walking. Everything around me looked wonderful. It was a fantastic day. I was healthy. My family was safe.

Not a word of my book or Ali's book was different than it had been before.

Why was I angry? What exactly did I want? Wasn't I, right then, the clearest possible example of suffering through wanting something intangible?

I had allowed myself to become attached to something non-existent, and now I was suffering not because of anything I'd lost but because of not having gained this non-existent thing.

Being longlisted would have been good for my writing career, but I doubted it would have boosted me as much as *not* being longlisted was killing me.

I decided to accept I wasn't going to be a winner. Not just in this case, with this prize, but possibly, probably, with every prize from now on.

It would be too much to say that I came back from that walk a Buddhist. But I had wrestled with myself. And the only thing that had given me any purchase was an idea of the Buddha's.

I thought his Truths might have some truth in them.

If I was going to be a loser, I was going to have to find some way of living with that.

8

C & W W   V S .   W W E

28 March 2015

All winter long I'd been a library rat. I had read books on farming and folklore, the Industrial Revolution and wrestling. I had read and reread *Henry & Mary* and *Wrestliana*.

For as long as I could get away with, I'd avoided the non-verbal world. But this was becoming silly.

I'd been looking at illustrations of wrestling throws demonstrated by gentlemen in Victorian dress—

Figure 9. An illustration from William Armstrong's *Wrestling*. Two men toppling like a very genteel tree. Leigh says, 'Get a room, chaps'.

—By now, I knew this was a well-executed back-heel by a wrestler who had gained a tight, high grip on his opponent. But I still hadn't got myself along to a real match. Typical writerly behaviour, typical me.

So, I couldn't put it off any longer. With every page I turned, I felt further away from my subject. I needed to see some Cumberland and Westmorland Wrestling close up. It was time to get physical.

Or, at least, to watch someone else getting physical.

I needed to make contact.

Years before I began seriously researching William, I had done the easy thing and Googled him. Apart from scanned in copies of *Wrestliana*, there wasn't a great deal to be found online. One man was responsible for most of what appeared there: Roger Robson.

An article by him on the *Whitehaven News* website under the headline 'William Litt was the very first' was the thing that snagged me. It began by saying, 'Anyone interested in the history of Cumberland and Westmorland Wrestling knows the name of William Litt.'

Roger Robson had been in touch with Bill and Margaret Hartley, and was able to sketch out most of the details of William's life. He'd also come to his own conclusions on William's character: 'egocentric' was the word. William, he said, boasted about his wrestling career, expressed opinions on all subjects and flaunted his education.

Roger Robson's interest in William went deep enough to read *Henry & Mary*. It was, he wrote dryly, 'not the most entertaining novel', but the parts of it about wrestling were 'fascinating'.

Anyone interested in what's happening today in Cumberland and Westmorland Wrestling knows the name of Roger Robson.

Figure 10. Roger, just after winning at Grasmere. I would cast him as James Bond over Roger Moore, wouldn't you?

He took over from 'Clicker' as the *Cumberland News'* C&WW correspondent, and continued for thirty-seven years.

He writes from experience. In 1970, Roger was 12 Stone Champion at Grasmere Sports.

I started to come across Roger's name almost daily when I seriously began researching William. He ran the website of the Cumberland and Westmorland Wrestling Association – reporting on what seemed like every single match that took place. There were often photos credited to a Jill Robson.

If William was the author of *Wrestliana, the* book on C&WW, then Roger – it turned out – was the author of *the other* book. His book was called *Cumberland and Westmorland Wrestling: A Documentary History.**

It was clear that Roger Robson was the man to ask, if I wanted to see some wrestling first hand – or even to do some.

On the website of the Cumberland and Westmorland Wrestling Association,† I found Roger's email address, and put together a message introducing myself.

---

*   Roger Robson, *Cumberland and Westmorland Wrestling*, Bookcase, 1999.
†   You can find it at www.cumberland-westmorland-wrestling-association.com – the best source on C&WW there is.

I hoped Roger Robson would at least be curious to hear from William's great-great-great grandson.

All I needed to do was work up enough courage to press send. After a day or two, I did.

I began by introducing myself, and describing the book I was trying to write, and then I asked if Roger could put me in touch with a wrestler or a coach. 'Is there anyone in London I can speak to about it?'

Roger replied, promptly and definitively, 'I know of no-one in London with any knowledge of C&W wrestling'.

This made me think: from alpaca farming in Albania to the Zoroastrian zodiac, you can find someone who knows about *most things* in London. C&WW was amazingly local if that were true. (Turns out it was.)

Roger continued, 'Another problem is that the indoor training at the academies tends to finish at the end of March, when the hour changes and all the farm lads who wrestle are working overtime on tractors'.

He said that, if I wanted to see anything, I better get up to Cumberland by the end of the month. On Saturday the 28th was the Academy Shield – the biggest club event of the year.

Roger sent me some details – a poster that had obviously been put together in Microsoft Word. The event was to start prompt at 7.30 in Bootle Station Village Hall. That was Bootle – Bootle the village, not the used-as-a-comedy-name suburb of Liverpool. (When I mentioned this to a friend from the North West, he said 'Bootle! That's *proper* West Cumbria.') There were to be five teams competing, from Waberthwaite, Kendal, Milnthorpe, Carlisle and Rothbury (in Northumberland). For the younger wrestlers, competition would be by age – Under 9, 12 and 16 years. For the grown-ups, by weight – Under 8, 10 and 12 stones, then All Weights.

There would be a raffle. There would be a Pie & Pea Supper for £4, but Wrestlers ate for free.

After wrestling, I hoped.

I checked with Bill and Margaret Hartley that it was okay for me to stay with them, then wrote back to tell Roger I was coming. I booked my train ticket.

When I arrived at Carlisle, Bill Hartley was there at the station to greet me. He looked unchanged since I'd seen him on the trip with my father in 2009. Spruce, dressed in tweed. 'How was your journey?' he asked.

'Very good,' I said.

It wasn't exactly true. I had made lots of notes about what I saw about the window, as the train made its way along the grey coast.

I'd seen a sports store and gym, beside a large car park. Wind shaped woods. Chickens under the trampoline in a garden with green sheds. Joggers crossing a heath. The sea. Rocky beaches and distant Scottish hills. Hard headlands. Unfussy waves.

Making notes is what I do when I'm really nervous.

I was worrying about the evening. Ever since I'd booked to travel, my anxiety had been increasing. Would I be welcome? Would they make me hand out a prize or make a speech? Would they force me to wrestle?

Bill might be amused at seeing me in the ring. Although as a younger man he never wrestled, he did become a black belt in judo, and he enjoys – in his gentle Cumbrian accent – pointing out the similarities between an inside hope and an *uchi mata*.

Figure 11. Bill in his judo kit.
Cast him as a Bond villain,
don't you think? Great shadow.

Over another of Margaret's generous dinners, I found out more about the Hartleys.

For much of his working life, Bill was a building surveyor, sometimes discovering five hundred foot mineshafts beneath living rooms. But his vocation came from his grandfather – a joiner – who had once said of his own sons, 'I've got three lads and isn't yan of them could knock a nail in a turnip.'

His grandson, though, was early on apprenticed to John Gill, cabinetmaker and undertaker. ('I quite like making coffins,' says Bill, 'it were alright.')

Alongside the surveying, Bill made dozens of Georgian-style chests of drawers and tables. As I'd already seen, he'd furnished their bungalow, and was still making exquisite walking sticks with handles shaped like the heads of hares. He gave me one of these, a gift for my father.

Of William and himself, Bill says, 'I were born in the wrong time – I shoulda been alongside him; I'dah been alright.'

With a fine mixture of affection and exasperation, Bill and Margaret's daughter, Jane, later told me a story to sum up her father:

The family television had broken – it wouldn't work unless the ON button was constantly pressed in. Rather than call an electrician, Bill went into this workshop and came out half an hour later with something a lot like a wooden backscratcher, only with an extended finger rather than a curved set of nails at the end. This he set up at an angle, so that it pressed the ON switch in, and thus the TV was fixed.

If Bill would feel more at home in 1810, Margaret is quite happy to live in the present – because the internet is where she can make discoveries and connections. She is a comfortable, comforting presence, slow moving and slow speaking. But mention the past, and everything turns quicksilver. However much I have found out about William, I know that Margaret can zip around the past as rapidly as Google Earth around the present. 'Ah,' she says, 'well, you know, of course, they were related – only they didn't know it.' And then she will give a little hum of inconclusiveness – there is always more for her to find out, too, and she's glad of that.

That evening, Bill Hartley drove me down to Bootle. We passed the Sellafield Nuclear Power station, brightly lit up against the sea.

We arrived in the dark. We'd only made one wrong turn.

Bootle Village Hall reminded me of Ampthill Scout Hut, where I used to do Cubs, and where – on the warm asphalt roof – I shared my first cigarette with Andrew Money, a stolen from his mum's handbag Embassy Mild.

The Hall was grey, low, with a floor space about the size of a tennis court. There was a disabled access ramp from the car park, a row of rectangular double-glazed windows then a row of square windows above them. It was surrounded by fields but had a playground out back with swings and a slide.

Bootle Village Hall was the opposite of glamorous.

I wanted what happened there not to be an embarrassment.

I didn't want to wrestle.

Just inside the door was a small foldout table with ice-cream tubs on it containing notes and change – I'd anticipated this, or something like it. I'd done a lot of anticipating.

I'd anticipated the smell of fried, unhealthy food, the smell you often get in British sports venues.

I could smell boiling potatoes.

I'd anticipated being disappointed more people weren't there, and that the sport wasn't more successful.

The hall was packed.

I'd anticipated feeling out of place, Southern, weak, slow, confused and brainy-but-in-a-useless way.

Yep – spot on.

If I say 'the Hall was full of people', it'll sound like I'm not describing anything at all. What I mean is, it wasn't full of young or old or middle-aged people. It was full of all of the above. Grandparents gave tips to grandchildren, dads coached sons and daughters.

Bill nodded to a few people he seemed to know. I recognized Tom Harrington, former world Champion and MBE, from a photograph in Roger Robson's book.

I managed to introduce myself to Roger, but I could tell he was preoccupied by what was to come. One of the teams hadn't showed, so all his neat knockout tables of Wrestler A vs. Wrestler B were useless.

He went up behind some tables on a wide stage. Next to him was Jill Scott, who ran the C&WW Association. Bill and I found seats in the second row.

I looked about me, wondering who was going to invite me to try the wrestling. All four sides of the room, around the edge of the mats, were crowded. The people were chatting. There was excitement but no hype. Something was going to happen, they knew that. But they didn't seem to expect it to be anything they hadn't seen before. They were like parents waiting before a Year Three assembly.

The wrestling started.

I was excited. I had been looking forward to seeing this for months. But to begin with I had a strange doubleness to my vision. I'd read so much about wrestling by Georgian and Victorian writers, particularly William, that I almost expected to be transported back in time. Who were these spiky haired children sloping out onto the mats, beneath bright fluorescent lights? Why weren't the wrestlers whiskery men in homemade clothes? Everything *Wrestliana* described seemed, on the surface, out of date. William had never seen the Nike swoosh on a pair of shorts. He'd never seen shorts. And he'd certainly never seen boys competing against, and often losing to, girls.

At first, with the children chucking one another around, the wrestling was fun. But as the ages and weights went up, it became thrilling. The double vision went. I forgot all I'd read. This was happening, and happening *right there*.

As a spectator, I'd never been closer to any sport. Not only close enough to see it and hear it, but close enough to smell it. (When I later asked Roger's wife, Jill, if she felt she'd missed out by not attending, she said, 'Well, I didn't miss the B.O.') I could see the huge effort involved. I could hear gristle in the grappling, and bones clicking in the falls. Neck sinews stood out like tree roots, white faces turned pink. I flashed back to boarding school, The Other Boy, force, spit, losing. I remembered losing fights. That feeling of being squashed by someone else's not quite so squashy flesh. Blood in the cheeks and sometimes in the mouth. I didn't want that again. But maybe I had to face it.

If I was going to do some wrestling myself, to find out what William was on about, this was what I'd be up against. This was how much effort I would have to put in. There weren't any injuries, but backs flew twisting through the air and shoulders landed with a crunch. A man about my age, a grey haired ex-champion I recognized from Roger's book as Alun Jones, made a good show but lost. I could tell that the falls hurt him more than the youngsters, although he didn't want to let on. One wrestler got kneed in the nuts accidentally. Every male in the room winced at this – we knew what that was like, that feeling of being obscurely diminished for the next few hours. The young man came and sat on the corner of the canvas-covered mat, almost on my feet. His breath was ragged. Bill asked, 'Are you alright, lad?' The wrestler nodded. That was it as far as suffering went. No great show.

With William's descriptions of the various throws and chips in my head, I tried to understand what I was seeing.

I couldn't.

Everything happened too fast. At most, I could figure out the basics of what was going on. Well, *he* seems to be getting the best of *him,* oh no, now he's on his arse. The subtleties of footwork – chips and clicks – eluded me. I could spot the buttocks.

The rules of C&WW are simple: First wrestler to touch the ground with their knee or shoulder or any part of their body that *isn't* their foot loses. If there's any doubt, and the umpire and assistants can't make up their minds, the fall is called a 'dogfall' and wrestled again.

It's best of three falls. If a wrestler wins the first two, there is no third.

Because C&WW starts with the wrestlers already locked together, tight in a double bear-hug, there's never any of that awkward faffing around you get in judo or karate. No cagey bit where the opponents try to grab a hank of collar. Instead, the wrestling is all action. Some falls take less than a second.

The easiest way to understand what's going on, in slow motion, is to picture doing it yourself.

So, imagine you are about to wrestle.

You and the other wrestler are called onto the mats, you shake hands and the umpire then orders you to 'Take hold'.

You, you and your opponent, standing very close, both stretch your right arm forwards – below the other's left armpit, around their left flank. (In taking hold, the left arm is always above the right.) Your left hand also goes behind him, meeting up with your right hand just below his shoulder blades. But your left arm goes round naturally, as if hugging the other wrestler, whereas your right forearm is twisted as if you were looking at a wristwatch. This is so your fingers can fit together. The fingers of both your hands are formed into hooks, into J's, which interlock, an inverted S. If you break hold even for a moment, you will lose the fall. When the umpire is satisfied neither you nor the other wrestler has gained an unfair advantage in taking hold, they step back and call out, 'Wrestle!'

Whilst this was all going on, time after time, I was afraid of two things. Firstly, that Roger Robson would introduce me over the speakers, and I'd suddenly have the whole room looking at me – here's a living descendant of the famous William Litt, let's give him a big Bootle welcome! Secondly, I was scared that, right after this, the obvious thing for Roger Robson to say was, 'Why don't we see if the lad can wrestle?'

This didn't happen. A few people noticed me. I saw Tom Harrington looking questioningly in my direction, and perhaps asking the man next to him who the hell I was.

Some other glances came my way. Some of the heavyweights looked at me as they left the mat. I couldn't help but imagine how I seemed to a man who had just wrestled and won – sitting in my grey coat, bearded, scribbling in a black notebook. Probably like a weakling who's never been properly tested. Like a man who took one look at the world and got scared, and ran away into words. Like a London intellectual who's going to look down on anyone not similarly brainy (for which read 'up himself'). Like an easy victim.

But this was my paranoia.

For the most part, me being there made not one bit of difference to the evening.

Rothbury won.

I managed a chat with Roger after the prizes were awarded. He was pleased. It had gone well. There had been some high quality throws from the younger wrestlers.

'Do you know why they put the nuclear power station at Sellafield?' he asked, unconnectedly.

'No,' I said.

'Because it's as far from London as you can get.'

I didn't mention Scotland. I knew he was talking about something else.

★

I returned to London the next day.

Safely back home, I wanted to see more wrestling. Most of all, I wanted to see what C&WW was up against.

Like most people of my age, if you say the word 'wrestling' to me, I think of the TV star all-in wrestlers of the 1970s – Big Daddy, Giant Haystacks.

Simon Garfield has written a brilliant book about the rise and fall of the professional version of the sport, in its British version. He confidently titled it *The Wrestling*, because (in the UK) only this type of wrestling deserves the definite article.*

But for anyone under thirty, say 'wrestling' and what they're likely to think of isn't C&WW, or Giant Haystacks and Big Daddy, but WWE.

WWE (World Wide Entertainment) is what WWF (World Wrestling Federation) became when it lost a legal battle (over the letters WWF) to the World Wildlife Fund. The Ecological Panda laid out Hulk Hogan, The Rock, Ultimate Warrior, John Cena et al.

If C&WW is unbranded sport, WWE is brand as sport.† Much of the entertainment that hardcore fans derive from the week-to-week in-ring shenanigans of the wrestlers is, in fact, a blow-by-blow microanalysis of the franchise's (as they see it) decline, corruption, or resurrection. Bloggers presume deep corporate motives behind the way this or that *mano a mano* encounter has been scripted.‡

---

* Simon Garfield, *The Wrestling: The Hilarious True Story of Britain's Last Great Superheroes*, Faber, 2007.

† I am not being naïve; I am aware that this is equally true of Manchester United.

‡ And they *are* scripted – when Bob Mould, former singer of the American band Hüsker Du, went on hiatus from music, his new day job was writing these scripts for a rival franchise, WCW (World Championship Wrestling). He's happy to talk about it. Probably a lot happier than answering questions about why Hüsker Du broke up and will they ever reform? The scripting doesn't always cover moment by moment moves, but it will let the wrestlers know in advance who wins, and how.

In *The Wrestling*, about the nearest equivalent kind of wrestling in the UK, Simon Garfield summarizes it once and for all – it's not *faked*, it is *fixed*.

Or, to put it another way, 'The blood was real, but its production was often pre-planned'.[*]

I needed to see some of this stuff for myself.

Luckily for me, the biggest event of the year, WWE Smackdown, was taking place at the O2 Arena a couple of weeks after my visit to Bootle.

I hadn't been inside the O2 Arena since examining giant-sized reproduction pubic lice in the Body Zone, back when it was the Millennium Dome. Bootle Station Village Hall could fit in the foyer space between Five Guys and TGI Fridays. Smackdown was a sell-out, but still felt underwhelming – in an interesting way.

Among the things I expected, before I got there, was intro music that sounds a bit like Metallica but isn't and the high-calorie air of European and American sports venues and the arena to glow like a diamond encrusted tiara with raised phones and to feel isolated, grumpy, snobby, metropolitan, point-missing, swizzed, uninformed, bald. I wasn't disappointed. WWE was a lot more predicable than C&WW.

John Cena would be challenged; John Cena would – ultimately – triumph.

Cena is WWE's biggest current property, if you ignore frequent returns to combat by bona fide Hollywood film star Dwayne "The Rock" Johnson. Cena represents, as one commentator said, 'not only America, but everything that is good'. Cena is particularly popular among pre-teen boys, who wear T-shirts in his eye-pranging electric blue and banana yellow colours and chant his name. In appearance, he

---

[*] Simon Garfield, *The Wrestling: The Hilarious True Story of Britain's Last Great Superheroes*, Faber, 2007, p. 95.

is a strange mix of US marine, skater-boy, the class of gay man known as a Muscle Mary, and shucks just your average 250lb guy.

In the US, he is a straightforward hero. In the US, he does not – as happened when I saw him at the O2 – get booed as he walks on.

To my surprise, there were a lot of mixed reactions, all evening long. Bad News Barrett, a cheating Brit to the American audience, is our biggest international star – and his long body and bristle-haired head was received with cheers, until he started doing really sneaky things to turn us against him.

I had expected to be surrounded by hysterical grapple fans, but there was a lot of checking selfies and getting up to buy more Pepsi Max. Aggression was stirred when someone you were meant to hate made their bombastic entrance down the ramp towards the ring. The audience around me got particularly exercised over Sheamus, a redheaded, tattooed, Celtic-themed chap. 'Get a sun-tan!' they screamed. 'Where's your caravan?' And 'No-one likes the Irish!'*

The only really electrifying moment came when the boringly named Daniel Bryan made his entrance. He's smallish, long haired, and looks like a cross between a Status Quo fan circa 1975 and a brown rat. When he appeared, every single person in the audience – including me – jabbed their index finger up towards the lighting rig and chanted 'Yes! Yes! Yes!' I wanted this to go on for a lot longer than it did.

WWE is a made-for-TV event, which led to lots of drops in tension. Wrestlers who had been snarling at one another a moment before stood around, inches apart, waiting for the director to make a decision. When one bit of business was fluffed, there was a retake. All of the overheated commentary that is so central to the on-screen experience is missing – it felt as if I was watching with the mute button pressed.

---

* Oh God. Such a *stupid* thing for any Englishman to think, let alone say. When travelling, I've often wished that I was O'Litt – the welcome I'd have received, everywhere in the world, would have been warmer.

About halfway through, I realized all the bodyslams that didn't really hurt and arm-smacks that you could see missing by inches were making me yearn for something else. I was starting to yearn for real violence. I wanted to be in the front row for an amateur boxing match. I wanted to be where punches were punches, and a broken nose was a badge of honour for life.

Then I realized I didn't really want that at all. Where I wanted to be was away from all the branding, branding, branding, away from the hyped up emotions we Brits can't quite bring ourselves to feel.

Where I really wanted to be was back around the mats in Bootle Station Village Hall.

As we were walking out of the vast stadium, a boy said to his father, 'That was *awesome!*'

'What?' said Dad. 'Men in pants?'

9

ECKY THUMP

People laughed.

When I told them back in London that I was writing a book about wrestling, they found it funny. Part of this was the lack of fit between author and subject matter.

You?

Wrestling?

You?

The other part was that wrestling itself amuses a lot of people.

Perhaps it's because superhero movies have come along, and we expect a proper fight to involve the twisting of bridges, the pulverization of skyscrapers. The sight of two men attempting to grapple one another onto the grass is enough to send some people (particularly women) off into hysterics.

Leigh thinks it's funny because – to her – it's so obviously *not* about what it's about. 'If they want to kiss, why can't they just kiss?'

I wanted to take my subject seriously, just as William had. But before I went any further, I needed to address the tricky issue of men looking very silly.

Picture a muscular man dressed in white long johns. On top of these, he has on a pair of outsize underpants – they are home made, the material is black velvet. He isn't wearing trainers, instead he wears an ordinary pair of mid-length black socks.

All in all, your standard-issue Circus Strongman outfit.

This is what a Cumberland and Westmorland wrestler will wear for one of the big shows. It's 'traditional' costume, but doesn't go back to William's time.

The black velvet underpants (known as the 'centrepiece') were a mid-Victorian innovation – at first plain, though later on it became the fashion to embroider them with brightly coloured flowers around the groin area.

Much more recently, the wrestlers' names and images of wrestlers, cows and tractors have also appeared down there. The white long johns haven't changed much, though nowadays they are likely to be bought from the thermals section at Marks & Spencers.

William would have wrestled in his undergarments. They would have been plain and unremarkable undergarments. And, to us, they

Figure 12. No one has any problem making eye contact during the line up for the costume competition judging, Grasmere 2015. Except the chap in the middle.

would have looked silly – but not as silly as the Victorian mock-traditional costume does.

Bear in mind, Cumberland wrestling in the 1810s was sport before mass produced sportswear. This is the knotted handkerchief worn as sun hat, because baseball caps had yet to invade, and because it's not worth buying a hat you're only going to wear one week of the year. Not just the *holiday* week, the *sunny* week.

The film director Mel Brooks knew a great deal about men looking silly. He made a film called *Robin Hood: Men in Tights*. The title is probably the funniest thing about it. But the title is *very* funny, especially the colon.

Men in tights, men in pants, men in socks – they're funny, too. I can't analyse this, to any depth. Perhaps it is something to do with a man simultaneously struggling to maintain his dignity at that same time he's completely losing it, because of how ridiculously he's dressed.

Consider for a moment the difference between these two versions of a song from *The Full Monty*. The real, original version is 'You can leave your hat on'. Sexy, yes? Raunchy. Now reimagine that as, 'You can keep your socks on'.

This makes me think of *The Muppet Show*, and Sam the Eagle's appalled realization that underneath their clothing the entire population of the world was walking around *completely naked*.

Visit any European beach, and look down. Oh! those English legs – so much less purposeful than the German, so much less svelte than the French.

It may have something to do with the whiteness of the leg in juxtaposition to the blackness of the sock. There is just *something* wrong about the semi-undressed Englishman.

(The socks left on when the trousers have been removed are particularly funny, but not as funny as socks put on prior to engagement with trousers.)

The epitome of all this is John Cleese's 'sexy' strip, anticipating a romp with Jamie Lee Curtis, in *A Fish Called Wanda*. The Cleese character, beautifully choreographed, dances around the designer pad removing first his tie, then his shirt, then his trousers. But, because this is a comedy, the last to go are his short black socks. It is all the failed raunch of chartered accountants from Macclesfield, the mojo-not-workingness of Sussex solicitors.

But C&W wrestlers don't wrestle bare-legged. No, they wear long-johns. If I were stretching things here, I would suggest this – via the circus strongman – was the origin of the Superman costume. A two-tone lyrca outfit, with illustrational pant-area, is somehow far less creepy than a one-colour unitard.

Among the comments I've heard, around the ring, are, 'Is there a *shop* where you can buy these outfits?', 'Don't know *how* the mothers get the grass stains off the white' and, most frequently, '*Very* fetching'.

Former wrestler, and competition MC Alf Harrington, must have overheard some of this banter because later in the year, at Grasmere, I was to hear him offer (I wish he hadn't) this *apologia pro sua clobber*, 'I know it's slightly old-fashioned and out-dated, but it's part of who we are'.

Also part of this, and likely to cause amusement, is the more precise technical language of C&WW – most of all, 'the buttock'. Buttock is one of those English words, like sock, flange, wimple and prone, that reigns forever on a Golden Throne in the Eternal Halls of Silly. After a particularly good example, Alf Harrington may offer, 'Tidy buttock' or 'She got the buttock in there' – thus drawing attention, once again, to the traditional strips.

There are two main types of buttock – the cross-buttock and the full buttock.

In all of wrestling, there is no more magnificent example of masterful and controlled violence than a well executed buttock. The wrestler going down is inverted, his feet often flying higher than his head ever reaches.

Figure 13. Jack Brown full buttocks a challenger
with the ease of a World Champion.

Sophisticated north-western crowds adore a buttock. This may be the reason that, for thirty-seven years, Bob Horsley, the wrestling correspondent of *The Carlisle Journal*, chose to write under the pseudonym of 'Cross-Buttocker'. Researching old wrestling books, I often came across inadvertent snigger-triggers such as, 'The number of famous buttockers in the present day could be counted on the fingers of one hand'.*

---

* Walter Armstrong, *Wrestling*, https://archive.org/stream/Wrestling_897/Wrestling_
djvu.txt, retrieved 7 September 2015, 11:24.

C&WW is a serious but never a po-faced business. Every C&WW ring creates a halo of mirth. Most competitions begin with the youngest, smallest wrestlers, and their slab-faced seriousness, and the epic nature of their encounters, contrasted with their scale, makes everyone smile. This is especially the case when two physically mismatched opponents step into the arena – in the Under-12s, one sometimes seems twice the height and weight of the other. 'I think we'll call that "the Long and the Short of it", Alf Harrington may say. The crowd laughs, but is also prepared to be delighted, and to laugh again and louder, if Goliath is felled by a well-timed full buttock from David.

And often, during adult bouts, as well as shouts of encouragement and gasps at risky holds, there is laughter.

To someone arriving who has never seen Cumberland Wrestling beforehand, two men who have just 'taken hold' can look silly.

Theirs is an awkward embrace, as if both were keeping their genitals and buttocks as far away from the other as possible. Yet, also, it is a dance. Spontaneous choreography occurs when the wrestlers fall into a 1–2–3 1–2–3 waltz rhythm of sideways steps, or rhumba back and forth on camel's legs. Their chins, each of them, rest upon their opponent's right shoulder – like they were slow dancing at the school disco. The profile of one is fully visible behind the back of the other's head. They could not be further from eye contact if they tried. The view each gets is what the back of the other's head would see.

Although they are struggling against one another, the two wrestlers can appear very much as if they had mutually agreed to do an impersonation of an exceedingly pissed crab. Sometimes, they spin faster and faster, gallivanting around, and start to look like the *triskelion*, the three-legged Isle of Man icon. When the skill level is low, they are just like any other pair of blokes, pawing at one another in hopes of gaining an advantage.

There are other moments, when the wrestling comes (or seems to come) to a total stop. The most hilarious interlude, building and building the longer it goes on, is when the hank has gone in – when, that is, one wrestler has been lifted completely off the ground by the other (often larger) wrestler and, to prevent immediately being thrown, has succeeded in snaking one or both of their feet around their dominating opponent's calves. This makes the clinger-on exceptionally difficult to throw – like trying to chuck into the laundry basket a pair of trousers the left leg of which one is still wearing.

Roger Robson has a beautifully tender description of this impasse, and its purpose. The Wilf is Brocklebank; the Harrington is Tim:

> No-one could match Wilf's strength, but Harrington used to find
> a haven from the power by angling his body into the big man and
> nuzzling in at his chest. From that haven in the storm, he could
> sometimes catch out the bigger man if he made a false move.*

Has any other sports writer used the verb *nuzzle* with reference to heavyweights?

Sometimes it looks as if a mouse has got into the ring and, for want of a chair, the phobic has climbed up on the other man.

But it's a *very big* mouse.

Finding C&WW wrestlers funny isn't a recent thing. Here is the report of an article from *The Times* of 11 August 1925.†

> To an ignorant southerner wrestling is a peculiarly engaging specta-
> cle… it can be exhaustingly comical… a clumsy imitation of modern
> dancing, the gentlemen in embroidered tights and pink flush trunks.

---

* http://www.cumberland-westmorland-wrestling-association.com/2015_Articles/
NEWS-06-Feb-5th-2015.html, retrieved 7 September 2015, 09:59.
† 'The English Lakes: Fell Life and Sport', *The Times*, 11 August, 1925, 18 fn.

Figure 14. Look, it's right there – and it's looking
at me with its horrible pink eyes!

The introduction of the words 'ignorant southerner' brings us to something important.

I could have made this transition earlier, by comparing the comedy legs of John Cleese to the comedy legs of Tim Brooke-Taylor, one of the Goodies.

The Goodie I want to write about is Bill Oddie, born 7 July 1941 in Rochdale.

The Goodies, for those who don't know, was a massively popular TV English comedy show of the 1970s. I was the perfect age for it. I thought it was the best thing ever, or at least the best thing since The Monkees.

Like The Monkees, and like The Beatles in *Help!*, The Goodies lived together rather than with wives and children. They travelled on a bicycle made for three. They didn't have normal jobs. Instead, they spent a lot of time mucking around. To the 10-year-old me, this seemed ideal. I see them more clearly but less passionately now. Tim Brooke-Taylor looked like a pink-faced civil servant in a farce, always trying to re-establish his dignity, constantly humiliated, frequently stripped of his trousers. Graeme Garden, with muttonchop sideburns, might easily have been standing in front of a blackboard covered in physics equations. Bill Oddie, consisting of 10% brown beard and 90% mischief, was something far less conventional. If he belonged to the human race at all, it was as a time-transported caveman. Oddie was the most childlike, and the most loveable, of the three. He was also the most multitalented – writing and playing their songs, coming up with much of their weirdest material.

The 'I heart the 1970s' shows, that were so popular about a decade ago, were wonderful shortcuts to nostalgia. Our memories, influenced by repeated viewings, work like this, too. For example, here's an unfree association on sweet things: Wagon Wheels the size of your head, Space Dust, Blackjacks, Sweet Cigarettes. Here's a riff on kung fu: Bruce Lee, Elvis Presley's stage moves, David Carradine, glasshopper, hi-yah!, 'Henry, the mild-mannered janitor?', Monkey, The Water Margin, chubby beflared pre-teens trying to kick one another's teeth out. All to the soundtrack of Carl Douglas's novelty pop song 'Kung Fu Fighting'.

Playing off the martial arts craze, and more directly parodying the opening sequence of the TV series *Kung Fu*, Bill Oddie invented 't'age-old Lancastrian* martial art of Ecky Thump'.

Mention of this may help explain the title of The White Stripes' sixth album, *Icky Thump*. Jack White is an Anglophile, and loves *The*

---

* My father is Lancastrian, from Lytham Saint Annes, although his accent only comes out when he's dispensing wisdom, or discussing what's fur uz tea with his big sister Shirley. He's always played his Northern origins for comedy. Lytham Saint Annes is about as South as the North gets. But I'm still the son of a Northerner whose forebears were all from the North. And the older my father gets, the more Northern he seems to become.

Goodies. (I hereby make Jack White an honorary Englishman, by inviting you to imagine him with extremely white legs in red Y-fronts and calf-length black socks. I think he does very well.)

In his autobiography, *One Flew Into the Cuckoo's Nest*, Oddie has nothing to say about the invention of Ecky Thump. It's not hard to see what it's about, though.

'Eck' is a Northern h-dropping shortening of 'heck', which is a way of avoiding blaspheming when you say 'hell'. For example, 'Bloody heck' or 'What the heck?' So 'ecky' means 'hell-like' or 'hellish'. 'Thump', of course, means 'hit hard but with a slightly softish object'. You don't *thump* someone with a baseball bat, you smack 'em or whack 'em. A thump, even with a fist, has an element of concern to it. *I'm only thumping you now, mate, because I know we're going to make up later.* Putting all this etymology together, 'Ecky Thump' ends up meaning something like 'The Martial Art of the Single Hellish Blow, Not Intended to Wound Permanently'.*

The first Ecky Thump sketch was a straightforward, affectionate (or perhaps not so) take on Southern stereotypes of Northerners. Oddie – not a tall man, not a thin man – goes in quest of ancient knowledge, and winds up at The Mystic East… chip shop on Rotherham High Street. He is kitted out, once accepted into the Ecky Thump dojo, with an outsize flat cap, cotton shirt with rolled up sleeves, red necktie, braces, dark trousers, hobnail boots. In other words, he becomes exactly the kind of shorthand Northerner painted by L.S. Lowry. The kind of figures fondly remembered by Brian and Michael in their number 1 hit 'Matchstalk Men and Matchstalk Cats and Dogs'.

Ecky Thump first appeared in 1975.† It was part of a wider trend in TV comedy, abandoned now, to go at cultural stereotypes head

---

* By this logic, Jack White's 'Icky Thump' would mean 'The Martial Art of the Single Blow that Leaves Behind an Unpleasant and Quite Possibly Demeaning Residue'.

† *Kung Fu Kapers* (aka *Ecky Thump*), Series 5, Episode 43 (of 76). Aired 24 March 1975.

on – hence, funny Jamaicans who were funny because they were so Jamaican, funny Indians, funny Northerners.

Oddie details the special foods eaten, as part of the dojo's training regime, 'black pudding, chip butties, tripe and a piece of Parkin for afters'.

It's assumed that it's innately ludicrous that there should be a Northern martial art, or that there should be anything mystical or sophisticated about it.

But that martial art did exist – in Cumberland, Westmorland and surrounding areas. It was wrestling.

Some people will always laugh.

IO

ALL-ROUNDER

William Litt was known as a seriously odd human being.

I've already mentioned the contemporary, probably Robert Gibson, who wrote about him as an 'anomaly in nature'. This was said admiringly. The praise continued, 'for, while he shines in the *arena*, and was, at no distant date, the undisputed champion of Cumberland for a series of years, in all those exercises which require superior strength, courage, skill, and dexterity, his mind is so exquisitely delicate, that many of his effusions in *poetry* will continue to be read so long as genuine taste and feeling are cultivated...'*

These words from 1824 put William's championship years in the past, and his poetic years in the present. But they did overlap.

His most famous bout, with the cobbler Harry Graham, took place on 26 October 1811. His first published poem – as far as we know – appeared in the *Cumberland Pacquet* on 4 August 1812. I imagined William strolling from victory in the Cleator Moor ring straight down to the Whitehaven Literary Society, where he was an equally dominating presence.

The Memoirist, who attended these meetings, has already been quoted as saying, 'His conversational powers were... remarkable. His voice was singularly fine and powerful; and one accomplishment

<hr>

* *Cumberland Pacquet*, 12 January 1824.

he possessed above all men we have ever known, – he was, without exception, the very best *reader* we ever listened to'.*

I found this amazing, and inspiring. For a few years, William became a one-man example of *how to be both* – both physical and mental, athlete and poet, jock and nerd, body and soul or mind or intellect or whatever isn't body.

Such a combination, the ability to be a true all-rounder, is a difficult thing to achieve in western societies – particularly in England and America. We like to know where we stand with a man. They shouldn't be too good at too many things. What 'all-rounder' means, in cricket, is just that a man can bowl *and* bat *and* field, not that they can write a decent essay on the causes of the French Revolution *and* cook beef Wellington *and* play the flute.†

People are fine with Gary Lineker as a cheeky-faced football presenter who can take the banter as well as dish it out, but when he starts voicing his highly articulate political opinions, he gets told to stick to sport.

William was a strong man who wrote powerful books – this was something I needed to investigate.

How unique was this? Who were his competitors?

Name a man who performed at the highest level, both as sportsperson and as writer?

The pub quiz answers are quickly thrown out. Albert Camus – existentialist novelist *and* goalkeeper! Samuel Beckett – literary genius and appears in *Wisden*'s *Almanac* for his cricketing prowess! Dick Francis – wrote and rode thrillers! Terry Venables – thriller-writer

---

* 'Memoir of the Author', *Henry & Mary*, 2nd ed., p. xi.
† Being good at the waltz in *Strictly Come Dancing* is just about allowed, if you are shown wincing, falling on your arse and complaining to your dance partner that the training is *really* hard.

and footballer, too! Jack Kerouac – King of the Beats and college halfback! David Foster Wallace – novelist of vast ambition and sneaky sliced second server!*

The imbalance in each case is obvious. If the sporting achievement is high, the artistic level is low – and vice versa. Dick Francis probably came closest to being at the very top of both games. Anything resembling balance is clearly hard to maintain.

Balance was what I'd wanted to talk to Roger Robson about.

The day after the Academy Shield at Bootle, Bill Hartley had driven me up to Roger's farm. I was very aware we were travelling much faster than William ever did. This was, as Laurie Lee put it, a landscape 'bulldozed for speed', cut to pieces for the motorcar. Above the low hedges of the flat fields around us we could see the hills of Scotland, across the Solway Firth.

At the farm gate, a plastic ball was rolled toward us by Jess, Roger's sheepdog. She was after a game of football.

The Belted Galloways were in the next field along. If a maker of liquorice all-sorts were to design a cow, they would look like this – all gorgeous shaggy black apart from a cummerbund of creamy white.

Roger and his wife Jill invited us in.

The top of the front door hit a dangling light shade, making it swing back and forward on its wire. I wondered how long it had been like that.

---

* My Facebook friends, who helped with many of my askings, also suggested John Irving (novelist and wrestler), Arthur Cravan (poet and boxer), Morley Callaghan (poet and pugilist – k.o.'ed Hemingway), Ernest Hemingway (novelist and wannabe boxer and all-round nob), William Hope Hodgson (novelist and athlete), Sir Arthur Conan Doyle (writer and goalie), Owen Lowery (Judo champ and poet), Andre Gide (*literateur* and golfer), Howard Jacobson (novelist and table tennis player).

We went through, into the sitting room. I'd spotted a few wrestling mementos in the hall. Here, on the window-ledge, there was a metal statue of a particularly good throw.

Tea came out, and Roger and Bill spoke about how Cumberland wrestling compared to judo. They spoke of their own bouts, sussing one another out. They were presenting their credentials as fighters. I had none to offer. I stayed quiet.

After a while, I put my idea to Roger: William was a genuine all-round man, a real oddity. It was the crux – if Roger had said no, I'd have felt humiliated, wrong. But this is what he said:

'It's funny – what you're recounting there is *me*, because I'm a grammar school product. I went on to university, and so on – *but* my father was a mole-catcher, and, in the holidays, well, I would be going – Christmas, mole catching; Easter, lambing – hill-lambing. And I can remember, on one occasion, it was about two o'clock in the morning, I was lying in literally a feather bed, and I was reading James Joyce's *Ulysses*, and lying there reading, and at two o'clock I thought, "I better stop reading because I'm dipping sheep tomorrow morning, and I'll have to get up and out." And the wrestling was part of that. And I've never given up on the culture I came from, but I've been able to look at it from a different perspective, from having been removed from it a bit.'

I said, 'So, you were reading *Ulysses*. Did you have a bit of a reputation among the other wrestlers that you were a bit of a boffin?'

'I was always known as being, you know, a bit clever.'

'Doesn't that mean "too clever", when they say that?'

'It does when you say "clivver". "He's clivver, him."' Roger gave me a look. I knew who 'him' was, in that room. 'But, um. Not really. No, I was never aware of that.'

'I think, if they knew that you could prove yourself in their world,' Bill added, 'you could do whatever they did, and maybe better than they did, in some cases…'

Roger agreed, 'I'm my father's son, so...'

'It meks a difference,' said Bill.

'Y'know,' said Roger, 'one of the real prejudices I had, which *still* twitches me sometimes, is to hear public school voices: the voice of privilege. And I still squirm at that.'

With some fear, I said, 'I did go to public school. Do *I* have one of those voices?'

'Edging towards it.'

'Edging? – okay.'

They laughed and I joined in.

'You're getting there,' said Bill.

I was clivver. I was only a passing visitor there – a tourist.

With my accent, and my London ways, I stood out.

Roger was wary of me. William probably wouldn't have much liked me. In November 1812, he published his second poem.* It was a satire of the recent Lake District tourism boom. The title was 'The Lakes: A Serio-Comic Poem'.

When I got back to London, before I went to see the WWE wrestling, I read this poem again, very closely. It was the best clue to what William would have thought of me if I, or my nineteenth century equivalent, had been introduced to him.

I read and re-read 'The Lakes', following up the contemporary references I didn't understand, footnoting them, but feeling all the time that I was being rejected.

So I looked closer, and read harder, and one evening I got the very strange impression that William was sitting in front of me, and I was looking over his shoulder at lines still inky-wet on the page.

---

* *Cumberland Pacquet*, 18 November 1812.

He was at his desk, back from a convivial meeting with his friends McCombe, Todd, Ledger and Gibson, at the Whitehaven Literary Society, and was feeling moved to respond to the influx of Lake visitors.

I began to imagine that he even sensed me – as I quite often sense ghostly desk-presences. (*He* is here; *she* is watching.) For me, they are usually writers.

Is it uncanny? Is this unlikely?

Of course it's uncanny and unlikely – isn't all storytelling like that? It's an attempt to make dead language come alive. It's calling spirits forth.

With the first touch of dipped nib to paper, William was throwing his hat into the ring – the place where I, nearly two hundred years later, fought my inky battles. 'THE' he wrote 'LAKES'. His handwriting was slightly childish.

By 1812, he was no longer content to be a reader. He was trying to become an author. And I was standing there, ringside, silently roaring him on. Even if he was writing against me, I wanted William to write well.

He was trying to prove something. That he wasn't just a lunk.* He was – was he? – was he *really*? – a poet.

And he was going to do it by having a good go at all those tourists.

THE LAKES.
A Serio-Comic Poem

He was calling it 'Serio-Comic', I think, because it had a Serious message but a Comic manner. Conventionally enough for that time, he begins with a classical epigraph.

---

* One of my father's favourite words, usually coming in the form of 'You great *lunk!*' Quite often applied to men playing sport who have just done something immensely clumsy. A lunk stares at his palms, where the ball is no longer. The female equivalent is 'lummox'.

It's a bit of chopped up Virgil, lines from the *Aeneid* – the part describing the hero Aeneas's round trip to Hades.* When I looked them up, I found the poet Dryden had translated them as meaning—

If you so hard a toil will undertake,
As twice to pass th' innavigable lake;

And followed them with the words, 'Receive my counsel.'

A more literal translation would be: 'If it is your desire and passion to swim the lake, and you want to indulge in such a mad endeavour...'

In a way that his friends at the Whitehaven Literary Society would have appreciated, William was mischievously presenting the heavenly Lake District as a hellish place.

William began his poem by switching to something right up to date:

THOUGH Europe's *Lions* be seen no more,
Since *Bonaparte* has shut the Cage's Door, –

After his failed attempt to invade Russian, Napoleon retreated to Paris in the Autumn of 1812 – and Europe gloated for a bit, and awaited his next eruption.

Yet some we have at Home, of smaller Breed,

Literary lions, that is. People like me.

And these to *visit* Fashion has decreed,
To thee, fair CUMBRIA! now my Lyre awakes,
Thy cloud-roll'd Mountains, and thy glassy lakes:

---

* The lines, from Virgil's *Aeneid*, Book 6, lines 133–136 [137–139], one of the best bits, describing Aeneas's round-trip to Hades, read in full:

'Quod si tantus amor menti, si tanta cupido est,
bis Stygios innare lacus, bis nigra videre
Tartara, et insano iuvat indulgere labori, ...'

What William was saying was that his part of the world has suddenly become fashionable, and he was not happy. William personifies his native county (Cumbria, like Columbia), and addresses her with passion.

> Thou marv'leth much, I ween, at such a Train
> Of motley Idlers in thy wild Domain.
> Boast of thy pathless solitudes no more:
> *Stage Coaches* roll where *Carts* scarce climb'd before:
> Coxcombs and Clowns on spiral Footpaths mix,
> and Mountebanks on Rocks display their tricks.

'Cloud-roll'd' was a fine piece of observation. I was happy to see that appear on the page. But there isn't much time for beauty, because the poking fun at the tourists ('motley Idlers' — motley being the costume of fools) starts here. William addresses the God of the booze these tourists are importing.

> Unwieldy BACCHUS! thou coulds't little think,
> When steel-nerv'd Romans met — to eat and drink
> In Southern Climes, that Northward thou shoulds't roam,
> And find, near *Skiddaw*, a congenial Home.

William was always eloquent on the subject of drink. But he had another God to address:

> Source of the Beams which gild that Mountain's Brow,
> O Sun! withdraw thy tarnish'd Glories now:
> This Age that, yawning, worships Midnight's Name,
> Prefers sold *Candles* to thy unbought Flame.

There's so much to say about this. William's future novel, *Henry & Mary*, depended almost entirely on midnight scenes. And the Lakers – Wordsworth, Dorothy Wordsworth, Coleridge, De Quincey, Southey – were much given to midnight rambles. To be out at this dark time, torchless, risking twisted or broken ankles, and advertising that you didn't have to be up with the dawn, or out with your herd or your flocks, would have been remarkable, and probably laughable, to the locals. Like their ancestors, the farmers would have spent the hours between sunset and dawn around household fires or asleep. Going out at these times of day, without any real *need*, was a novelty. For the locals there was one good excuse for going out at night – to go courting. Young men walked across fells to make love to young women, sometimes with parental permission, sometimes not.

When I visited him, Roger Robson had suggested I read James Hogg's short novel, 'Love Adventures of George Cochrane'. Hogg, patronizingly known as 'the Ettrick Shepherd', was a Scottish contemporary of William. More famous as the author of the amazing diabolic tale *Confessions of a Justified Sinner*, Hogg was also keen on sports – he organized the St Ronan's Border Games, the first athletics meeting in Scotland. 'George Cochrane' has lots of wrestling in it. It's about a wrestling-obsessed farmer who makes his daughter's lovers fight bouts for the right to that evening's night-visit.

Hogg wrote, 'Perhaps my Edinburgh readers will be startled at this agreement; but it is a fact that every young woman in the country must be courted by night, or else they will not be courted at all; whatever is said to them on that subject during the day, makes no more impression upon them than stocks or stones, but goes all for nothing, or mere words of course'.*

---

* Ibid., pp. 170–171.

Cumberland farmers, seeing Wordsworth out late, might have assumed he was courting a canny lass rather than observing light-effects upon the lake-waters. They would most likely have thought him a bit daft, and been amused by his doings.

> Hark! how prevails the Din of Dice and Cards!
> Flee from the Jargon, 'ye Five-wandering Bards,'
> No more with Nature your high Converse hold,
> But *advertise* your Villas to be sold.

In other words, William was saying 'Naff off' to all the outsiders. Seeing him write this made me feel awkward, because I was one of them. I could hear the contempt in his word 'Villas' – it was a well chosen sneer. The proper houses, in Cumberland, were farms and cottages. William's choice of the word 'Jargon' is great. He seems to be presenting London as built out of a fearsome mix of jangling, new-fangled language. There's a daring, as well as some real venom, to his way of putting this.

I found the phrase 'ye Five-wandering Bards' puzzling, until I discovered it was a reference to the satirical cartoonist James Gillray's 1798 cartoon 'NEW MORALITY'.*

This fearsome image came from the *Anti-Jacobin Magazine & Review*, and is a manic Tory assault on all perceived sympathizers with the

---

* The full title is 'NEW MORALITY; Or The promis'd Installment of the High-Priest of the THEOPHILANTHROPES, with the Homage of Leviathan and his Suite'. In a typically crowded scene, against a background of classical pillars, Gillray shows – on the right – a leader of the French Revolution, preaching the Religion of Nature before an altar upon which stand female personifications of vengeful Justice, avaricious Philanthropy and washed-out Sensibility. Before him kneels a pack of propaganda-creating Jacobin sympathizers, the 'Five-Wandering Bards', who pour nonsense forth from a cornucopia of Ignorance. Behind them comes a chunky Leviathan with the face of the Duke of Bedford, ridden by politicians. In its wake, more fish-tailed sycophants surf along. A clear reproduction is here: https://upload.wikimedia.org/wikipedia/commons/a/a7/GillrayNewMorality.jpg.

Revolutionaries of France – 'The sect of MARAT, MIRABEAU, VOLTAIRE'. Some English traitors' names are given in full, others are dashed out but would have been known by all.

'Whether ye make the Rights of Man your theme, / Your Country libel, and your God blaspheme, / Or dirt on private worth and virtue throw.' This was William's politics – manly, patriotic, straightforward.

Chief among the 'creeping creatures, venomous and low' worthy of disdain are poets. The verse below reads: 'And ye five other wandering Bards that move/ In sweet accord and harmony of love / C____DGE and S__TH_Y, L___D and L__B and Co'.* William, in similarly rumbustious vein, cops this entire, and names the 'Co' to boot: Southey, Coleridge, Wordsworth, Lloyd and Lamb.:

> S—the-y and C——-ge, W-rdsw-rth, Ll—d and L—b!
> No more veg-musing, dine on Eggs and Ham;

I found 'veg-musing' very funny. And I liked the unwitting anticipation of Dr Seuss's 'Green Eggs and Ham'. I could see William starting to delight in the sound of his words.

> Your lov'd *Elysium* other wanderers throng
> And teize you to applaud their vapid Song.
> With Rhyme-clad Oaths, haste! quit your shelt'ring Elms:
> Search England's Maps for some more Desert Realms.
> Pack up your Manuscripts and fishing go—

What a wonderful line that was! How dismissive – although I knew I was one of the manuscript-makers being dismissed.

---

* That is 'Coleridge and Southey, Lloyd and Lamb'.

Where you may not be gaz'd at – for a Show.

This was very interesting, because the flood of tourists into the Lake District is usually dated a little later than 1812.* When William was writing, the very idea of a tour-ist was only just getting going. Wordsworth was playing his part in encouraging it, by anonymously publishing – in 1810 – *A Guide through the District of the Lakes*. Within a few years, with true irony, Wordsworth himself had become a stop on the tourist trail. Dove Cottage, quite unhermitagelike in its location, was on Grasmere's main road (and within sight and sound of the wrestling ring). There are anecdotes of visitors pursuing the despairing poet up into the once solitary hills. But they were the guests his verses had invited, come to admire the beauties he had publicized.

Then quick emerge, ye Cits, from London Dust;

That's what Bill and Roger had implied I was, with the Belted Galloways mooching in the next field. A 'cit', a city boy. William's geography here, and his genealogy, was deliberately off. To address Wordsworth (born in Workington, the next big coastal town north of Whitehaven) as a city-boy was just wrong. But William is more likely having a go at Wordsworth's Southern imitators. This distinction wouldn't have impressed Wordsworth, and may be one of the reasons they never got on.

'Tis hard (they cry) to live 'midst Tar and Oil,
And never in a *Wood* the *Kettle boil*; –
And then how sweet to lounge by gurgling Streams,
And dance – and frisk again in Morning Dreams

---

* Saeko Yoshikawa, author of *William Wordsworth and the Invention of Tourism, 1820–1900*, Ashgate, 2014, confirmed in an email that this poem 'is one of the earliest references to the Lake Poets in the context of Lake District tourism'.

And when we've seen whate'er is fine or frightful –
To tell those pert Miss GRUBS will be delightful.
"For the once noted MARY'S Form enlarges!
"How *low* the *curtsies*, – and how *high* the charges!"

This is great.* These were the kind of lines I love in Alexander Pope.
Pithy, balanced, knowing. William was succeeding – his poem had
started to fly.

In the next few lines, William showed himself remarkably up to
date on recent discoveries in earth science:

Geologists, [Gout]-fetter'd, – you, alas!
Cannot with H[U]TT[O]N over *Hardknott* pass;
Cannot gut *Bowfell* of his Fossil Stones,
Nor drag to light a *British Mammoth's Bones*.
Yet you may study Strate on your Stratum;

If you say 'pass' aloud, making it rhyme perfectly with 'alas', I think
you can hear an echo of William's accent.

I knew I was biased, but I thought that last line worthy of a Cole
Porter lyric.

---

* I don't really mean *great* great. William is not a great but forgotten poet, I am not
going to claim *that* for him. It's as a prose writer, of early sports non-fiction, that his
name will continue to be remembered, and his muscular sentences read. His lyric verses
are, at worst, competent and conventional. At best, as in 'The Lakes', they are pungent,
lively and heartfelt – but in a style that, by 1812, was very old-fashioned. William's
influences were those of a couple of generations back. They are now considered in-
betweeners, pre-Romantics, not major writers. His canon includes the poems he studied,
and probably learned by heart, at St Bees: James Thomson's 'The Seasons' (1730);
William Collins' 'Persian Ecologues' (1742); *The Works of Ossian* (1765); Goldsmith's
'The Deserted Village' (1770). And 'The Lakes' is influenced by an even earlier crowd.
Heroic couplets, as a satiric tool, were perfected by Alexander Pope (1688–1744),
although William's have a roughness and almost manic energy that puts them closer
to Jonathan Swift (1667–1745).

H[UTTO]N sells Proofs of any Postulatum;
Plutonian or Neptunian, 'tis the same;
H[UTTO]N will sell your Legs, and Eyes and Fame!

What William was writing about were the conflicting geological the-
ories of his time. Big questions about how the world was made, and
whether the Bible was right. So, I realized, he wasn't just a wrestler
and a literary man. He was keeping up on popular science, too. The
Plutonians were led by the Scottish scientist James Hutton. They
asserted that, as part of its ongoing churn, the volcanic earth lifts up
seabeds into landmasses and spews out rocks like granite. These big
and small features are eroded and swept downstream into the sea. Our
world was made in leaping fire, shaped by falling water. The Neptunian
theory, as you can probably guess from its name, had a less explosive
vision – one of sediments settling at the bottom of vast oceans, now
drained away. Noah's Ark could have floated above Neptunian mountains. By modern times, the Plutonian theory was victorious. Very
unusually for him, William doesn't seem to have felt the need to take
sides – although I'm pretty sure he'd have favoured the volcanic.

ARTISTS! prepare a Purse One Year in Seven
Come to your *mental* Home, your School, your Heaven,
Laden with what would break a Donkey down,
At break of Day set off on Foot from Town;
With Cloth Umbrella, and with Bomb-Proof Shoes,
And sneaking Kindness for a scornful Muse, –
Spouting your Scraps of Verse with Hat in Hand,
Defy the Grins of yonder Rustic Band.

J.W.M. Turner passed through Egremont in 1809. This glimpse was so
vivid that I was tempted to place William among the rustic grinners who

watched Turner shamble by. In itself, this was masterful word-painting. Who wouldn't smile at 'Bomb-Proof Shoes'? We were getting into nonsense verse territory.

But I felt increasingly awkward. I and my kind would definitely be the target here.

> Come, ye soft Dilettanti Painters, too;
> (Who Fame obtain by libelling all ye view)
> Condemn with half-clos'd Eye, and Pedant Phrase,
> Scenes on which Angels would delight to gaze.
> Welcome! ye half-grown Heirs of ill-got Money,
> Who eat, without preparing Pleasure's Honey;
> Ye, who no *views* can *take* – may *take* a *Fish*
> And tasteless else, – may criticize a Dish!
> Here dissipation holds her annual court,
> And gay REGATTAS offer varied sport;
> Here Swains, dead drunk, and hugging each his Brother,
> Lie heap'd like sausages one on another.

Now that was nearly genius, wasn't it? I was full of envy now. Sausages! It gets their shape, the colour of their skins, their clamminess. The rhythm was perfect, the words fell into place. But the final lines were approaching. James Hogg, in 'The Love Adventures of George Cochrane', writes, 'The great art in making poetry, you will observe, is to round the verse well off. If the hindmost line sounds well, the verse is safe'. Go on, William!

> Low in the Scale of Social Life descends
> The false Refinement that to Ruin tends –
> Then haste thee, PEACE! – to *Gallic Cities* give
> All who corrupt – *the Land in which they live.*

Bingo, as my father would say.

Should I go abroad? Do I corrupt the land in which I live?

After I had finished watching William write his best poem, I felt reassured and undermined at the same time.

Reassured, because he was clearly enough of an all-rounder to figure as a writer as well as a wrestler. A literary critic could descend into one of his poems, line by line, and find gems. I already knew that William's writings, particularly *Wrestliana*, had stood the test of time.*

Yet I felt undermined because William seemed to hate me. He hated what I was and what I stood for. Even though I was born so many years later, my politics were still close to the radicalism of the 'Five-wandering bards'. I think the French Revolution was a good and necessary thing, despite the bloodshed – perhaps because of the bloodshed.

More directly, when I travel to the Lake District, I am an artistic outsider. I'm not like James Rebanks, author of *A Shepherd's Life*, going back generations in the same fields. In comparison to him, I'm a rootless cosmopolitan – a 'cit'.

I came away from 'The Lakes' feeling I needed to understand William more as a man of his time, and to see how he related to other men of his time – men a bit like me. Men of letters.

The Wordsworths and the Litts almost certainly went back a generation. It's likely the two William's fathers knew one another. Both

---

* I was able to buy a brand new copy from a print-on-demand service in India.

were employees of the Lowther family, who will come to dominate this book, as they dominated all aspects of life in Cumberland and Westmorland.

Lowther Castle, the shell of which you can still visit, does not stand close to Bowthorn, where John and Isabella Litt raised their family. But the Lowthers – usually headed by an Earl of Lonsdale – controlled life in the north west of England more completely than the King did. They owned every parliamentary seat, they made all the political appointments. You were either their man or hardly a man at all. Added to this, they were rich – the largest private landowners in England.

William Wordsworth's father had been employed by James Lowther, 1st Earl of Lonsdale, as his solicitor, and Wordsworth's own fortunes will sketch the Lowther family – as far as they relate to our William – in adequate detail. James Lowther was known as 'the Bad Earl'. When Wordsworth's father died in 1783, the Bad Earl owed him around £4,000. The Bad Earl had spent much of this money buying political influence.

The Bad Earl's other obsession was with the daughter of one of his tenants. Infamously, he kept her corpse in a glass topped coffin, after she died.

The Bad Earl's son, confusingly called William and styled Viscount Lowther, was a lot less bad, and in 1802 honourably repaid his father's debt to the Wordsworth family – allowing the poet to marry and begin a family.

Later still, in 1813, when Wordsworth had moderated his radical politics, Viscount Lowther appointed him Collector of Stamps for Westmorland. This made Wordsworth financially secure, and politically subservient.

When Keats tried to call on Wordsworth during a walking tour of 1818, he found him out 'canvassing for the Lowthers' in the General

Election. 'What think you of that [?]... Sad – sad – sad – and yet the family has been his friend always'.

It is absolutely certain that John Litt became Commissioner for Enclosure because he was a Lowther man. And so when Wordsworth's father was himself out, canvassing for local elections, he would have been sure of a warm welcome and a vote at Bowthorn.

If the father's got on, the sons didn't.

In my first research binge at the British Library, I had managed to put William Litt and William Wordsworth in the same place at the same time.

I remember coming back home, after a day of spooling through newspaper pages, and announcing to Leigh, marking undergraduate papers on her laptop, 'They met. I can prove they met'.

It was at a Regatta on Lake Windermere. A newspaper report of 1824 gives us the occasion in full colour.*

> The grandeur of the mountain scenery, the splendour of the flags
> waving in the breeze, the firing of cannon, the melody of music, and
> the blaze of beauty and fashion, all conspire to render the Regatta
> most enchanting to the senses. – The grand acquatic procession of
> the barges and numerous row-boats of the Lake, was the most beau-
> tiful sight ever witnessed on Windermere. The other amusements
> of running, leaping, and wrestling, were admirably conducted. The
> famous Wm. Litt, author of "Wrestliana," was one of the umpires....
> The belt, with five guineas added, was won by Sandys, a Cumberland
> wrestler, after much skilful and manly exertion... – The young Duke
> of Buccleugh [17 years 8 months old] was of Colonel Bolton's party

---

* *Lancaster Gazette*, Saturday, 7 August 1824, reprinted from *Kendal Chronicle;* also
reported in *Calignani's Messenger*, Paris, Saturday, 14 August 1824.

at this exhibition, as was also Mr. Wordsworth, the poet... and nearly the whole of the fashionables of the neighbourhood, including a host of elegant females, were present.

But what did this paragraph prove? The two men had probably met before. Their intercourse on this occasion might have amounted to little more than a nod of the head.

Wordsworth was, basically, a right git to anyone he didn't respect – and he certainly didn't respect wrestlers.*

I found it very easy to imagine a likely encounter, given Thomas De Quincey's description of how Wordsworth 'behaved with absolute insult' to those he did not value. 'To everybody', in other words, 'standing outside of this sacred and privileged pale'. On these occasions, he 'did not even appear to listen; but... turned away with an air of perfect indifference; began talking, perhaps, with another person on another subject; or, at all events, never noticed what we said by an apology for an answer'.†

However, there was an intermediary – a man who would very much have wanted to bring the man of sport and the man of letters together. In fact, the entire Windermere Regatta had been organized and paid for by this man – his name was John Wilson, although he wrote under the pseudonym 'Christopher North'.‡

John Wilson had inherited enough money to indulge his taste for outdoor sports. The news report on the Regatta says, very fulsomely,

---

* It is also possible that Wordsworth remembered 'The Lakes' from its appearance in *Cumberland Pacquet* twelve years earlier. Anything short of adoration didn't do for Wordsworth; attacks like that were never forgotten.

† Thomas De Quincey, *Recollections of the Lakes and the Lake Poets*, Penguin, 1980, p. 376.

‡ John Wilson wrote as Christopher North, and Christopher North was not merely a pseudonym – there was a division of personalities, too. The division, as by now you'll expect, was about physical prowess. Christopher North was the superhero, John Wilson, the secret identity.

'We may compliment Professor Wilson on the complete success of his exertions in re-establishing this delightful spectacle...'

What goes around comes around. One of the reasons William was being referred to as 'the famous Wm. Litt' was because John Wilson had written a long rave review of *Wrestliana* in the very successful magazine *Blackwood's*. And one of the reasons the review was so positive was that, in the book, William had given credit to John Wilson for bringing about a revival in wrestling by providing decent prizes at the games he organized.

John Wilson was one of the writers around and about the Romantic movement who helped develop the ideal of the Sporting Gentleman. He finished his review of *Wrestliana* referring to the great motto of this ideal: *mens sana in corpore sano*.

Healthy mind in a healthy body.

I was starting to think it wasn't such a bad idea.

John Wilson was extremely strident in his own attempts to exist as both healthy mind and healthy body. And it's that stridency, his efforts becoming more and more ludicrous, that defines Wilson's character. There is more than a touch of the poodle-walking Norman Mailer about him.

As a student at Oxford, Wilson had thrown himself into as many scraps, against as many opponents, as possible. He was not just fighting for the sake of it, he was fighting to preserve an ideal. '"Straightforward" and "manly"; these are terms of the highest approbation in contemporary writing about sport of the non-antipathetic variety'.*

John Wilson believed that sport not only taught boys to be men, it taught men to be warriors.

---

* For a full unpicking, see 'John Wilson and Sport,' by John Strachan, pp. 215–225, in *Romanticism and Blackwood's Magazine: 'An Unprecedented Phenomenon'*, Robert Morrison and Daniel S. Roberts (eds), Palgrave, Macmillan, 2013.

The Romantic era, at its height in the year of the Regatta, gave birth to the idea of the poet as practically disembodied.* 'I wandered lonely as a cloud'.

The Romantics were not a healthy bunch. Byron, lame, was known as a dirty fighter. Shelley was more cloud in trousers. By the time we get to the second generation, we have Keats – who would probably have lost a stand up fisticuffs with Emily Dickinson. After this, there were a raft of poets who simply wouldn't deign to get involved – Swinburne, Wilde, Eliot. Attempts to bring health and straightforward masculinity back to English verse seem silly, and always fail. The dandy is a provocative chap, and may start fights, but will rely on others to step in and defend him. D.H. Lawrence would have wished for physical robustness, to match the strong mental health of his poetry. The famous naked wrestling bout in *Women in Love* is wishful. Lawrence was an ailing, dying man.

In other words, Wordsworth is where the nerds really take over.

De Quincey relates an anecdote† about himself and Wordsworth's sister Dorothy, out for a walk in the vale of Langdale, falling behind Wordsworth and Mr J—, a Westmorland clergyman. De Quincey has already mentioned that Wordsworth looked puny beside Mr J's, 'fine towering figure, six feet high, massy and columnar in his proportions'. (William Litt was also six feet high; De Quincey – fine one to talk – was around five foot tall.) As she looked at the two men, in front of her, Dorothy at intervals exclaimed to herself, in a tone of vexation, 'Is it possible? – can that be William? How very mean he looks!' and,

---

* There's a whole huge argument here – because it's always possible to go further back, and find antecedents. Someone looking for earlier examples of bodiless poets could mention Hamlet, wafting blackly and indecisively around Denmark. But it's very clear from a close reading of the full play, and not the caricature image, that Hamlet is a renaissance man – and could both duel and wrestle to the highest standards.
† Ibid., pp. 135–136.

De Quincey says, she 'could not conceal a mortification that seemed really painful'.

When I imagine the Williams, Litt and Wordsworth, in the same room or against the same background of green hills, the contrast is just as great.

Looking at Litt, Wordsworth would have seen a confident, rough, physical gentleman; looking back at Wordsworth, Litt would have seen a pretender, a celebrity, a puny specimen.

Turning to look at John Wilson, they would have seen a man desperate to be friends with both of them – and also to combine, in one person, the wrestler's virtues with the poet's.

But John Wilson's attempts to do this already seem strained. The cultural divide between Jock and Nerd was already opening up. In 'The Lakes', William had given his Jock's view of the Nerds. Wordsworth didn't think the sports he witnessed worth commenting on at all, even in his letters. Nerds wrote about hills and streams, peddlars and waifs, not strong, healthy, young farmers buttocking one another.

Increasingly, over the years to come, the two ways of being a man that John Wilson hoped to unite moved further and further apart. Being a true all-rounder became almost impossible.*

---

* It is very rare to find a man who can pass in changing room and bookshop. In the 1800s, William's physical and mental prowess gave him remarkable social mobility. He was, it was said by the Memoirist, 'Equally at home in the most polished and in the rudest society'. I imagine him exchanging knowledgeable wrestling talk with Lord Lonsdale and respectful banter with shepherds. By contrast, Graeme Le Saux is now remembered mainly for being 'the footballer who read the *Guardian*'. In his memoir, *Left Field: A Footballer Apart*, he wrote, 'Because I had different interests to the rest of my team-mates, because I didn't feel comfortable in the pre-*Loaded* laddish drinking culture that was prevalent in English football in the late Eighties, it was generally assumed by my team-mates that there was something wrong with me. It followed that, naturally, I must be gay'. The fans in the terraces responded accordingly. Choruses of 'Le Saux takes it up the arse', to the tune of the Pet Shop Boys' 'Go West', boomed out from both home and away supporters whenever he played. To be an intellectual sportsman is, naturally, to take it up the arse. Imagine what they would have sung if Le Saux had been caught reading Wordsworth's 'Daffodils'.

There are rare exceptions – Roger Robson, reading *Ulysses* and winning at Grasmere, is one. As I kept on researching William's life, Roger's dig at me for being clivver hurt more and more. And I couldn't forget William's satire of cits. I knew, if I were to stand any chance of gaining Roger's respect, and understanding William properly, I'd have to step into the wrestling ring.

That was probably a good thing, wasn't it?

Any man, as William would have said, needs a variety of occupations.

I I

SMUGGLER

Right from the start of my research, whenever I told people about William being a smuggler, they said something like 'Wow' or 'Cool'. They never disapproved, as they would have done if I'd said he was a burglar or a mafioso.

They often wanted to know more. They asked how I could be certain he'd really done it, if it was something that happened so long ago, and was secret and illegal. I usually answered that William's novel, *Henry & Mary*, was all about smuggling, and that William never wrote about anything he hadn't done himself.

If they were really interested, I'd tell them about a novel called *John Peel*, published in 1932 by a Cumbrian writer called J.M. Denwood. As part of the plot, the huntsman John Peel (made famous by the song 'D'ye ken John Peel') goes to William Litt for help. In case the reader was tempted to disapprove of what they were about to do, J.M. Denwood inserted this aside:

> At the time when Peel arrived at the man's estate, smuggling was rife along the Solway coast, and he and many of his friends, including William Litt, thought nothing of engaging in the traffic. It was extremely profitable, and a man lost no prestige by indulging in it. His self respect and dignity depended on his conduct towards his fellow-men, and not on his keeping of a law which, in the opinion of most of them, should never have been passed.

Our attitude today is still indulgent. I think there's something in the word *smuggler* that makes them seem like cosy criminals, and that's the *ug*-sound – as in 'snug as a bug in a rug', as in other comforting domestic objects, jugs, mugs, plugs.

Also, the English think well of anything associated with the sea. Even pirates are, paradoxically, domesticated by the fact they operate on the watery part of the planet.

It takes a modifier to give the word back some power of terror: *heroin* smugglers, *people* smugglers. How horrifying. This fear immediately flips back to cosiness, though, if we hear *whisky* smugglers.

The historians I read, whilst I was trying to discover what William was up to, disagree about social attitudes toward smugglers in the eighteenth and nineteenth centuries. Were they seen as Robin Hoods, or just as hoods? Some thought the common folk loved them for getting one over on the tax-grabbing government. Others, that they were brutal ruffians who terrified the local population into silence and compliance.

Although the public don't exactly see them as criminals, not on a level with smugglers, antique dealers still have the image of being a little bit dodgy. In lots of countries around Europe, old furniture is just that. When grandparents die, their houses are cleared, the contents sold, and the grandchildren get what cash they can in order to buy brand new chairs and tables to go in their new apartments. In Great Britain, we are much more likely to think something old is valuable, and that if a professional dealer is offering you £5, he's probably ripping you off – because your tin snuffbox is actually worth £500, or your dauby painting of a depressed cow would fetch half a million at auction.

Now that he has retired from the trade, my father is quite happy to join the many viewers watching TV shows like *Bargain Hunt* and *Flog It!*. He prefers the more upmarket version of this, *The Antiques Roadshow*.

Roadshow used to be family viewing in 99 Dunstable Street – with my Dad saying he'd known this or that expert when they were working as a porter at Sotheby's or Christie's. But the bow-tied charmers giving valuations on country house lawns are essentially trustworthy. The common view of dealers is a lot closer to the roguish wheeler-dealer that was Lovejoy, played with sexy charm by Ian McShane.

My father's business was legit. He never sold reproduction furniture as original. Most of David Litt Antiques' profits came from one of two things – buying furniture up North and selling it to London dealers, or buying furniture that the public wouldn't want, because it was in a bit of a state, and having it restored by cabinetmakers before selling it on, to the public.

Restoration might involve stripping paint off a dresser, sanding it down, and polishing it up to a lovely mahogany shine.

But what use to anyone is a set of six dining chairs where one has only three and a half legs?

If my father's cabinetmakers turned something you couldn't actually sit on without falling over into something useful and beautiful – and he didn't point out that this particular leg was not quite as old as the others...

Was that dodgy?

Pieces of furniture were brought back to life; because customers were allowed to believe they dated entirely from 1815, that they were 'lovely, original'. The job of my father's cabinetmakers was to make their work invisible, so that even another dealer wouldn't know exactly what restoration had been done.

A set of eleven dining chairs is worth no more than a set of ten. But a set of twelve are worth quite a bit more. One way of solving this problem is to take the whole set apart, and to distribute one new joint there, one new leg there. That's an old antique dealer's trick – and who is harmed?

No one could point to any particular chair and say, 'That one's fake.' Instead, a number of them have had some undetectable restoration work – and when the customer sells them on, they can go in the catalogue as 'original condition'.

In a sense, I suppose, my father was involved in a kind of smuggling – smuggling new bits of wood in amongst old bits.

My own associations with the idea of smuggling are all positive. One of my favourite books when I was about fourteen was called *Atlantic City Proof.** American prohibition was the background, and the plot consisted almost entirely of the coast guard almost apprehending the heroic smuggler one night, and the heroic smuggler outrunning them the following night with a bigger, faster boat. I loved the escalation; I'd never tasted rum. I must have read *Atlantic City Proof* about two or three times, and at that age I hardly ever got to the end of novels.

Back when I was thinking I might write William's life as a novel, the smuggling scenes were the ones I was really looking forward to. I knew my father wanted to read them. These would be the action sequences, just as they are in *Henry & Mary*. But if I'd been fictionalizing, I'd have been free to put William in peril he most probably avoided.

I was writing the chapters of William's life in chronological order. Earlier on, when there were fewer records, I'd found this a struggle. But after watching William write 'The Lakes', I felt I'd had some kind of breakthrough. I was a lot closer to him. I could feel what it was like to be in the room with him. The writing he'd left behind seemed designed to help me. The smuggling part of his life was the one for which he'd left the largest amount of material, but all of it oblique.

---

* Christopher Cook Gilmore, *Atlantic City Proof*, Penguin, 1981. Read it, it's a lot of fun.

In *Henry & Mary*, as you'll remember, the whole plot depends on Henry falling in love with Mary, the niece of a notorious smuggler, and falling in with his dodgy family, the Fosters.

In 1815, at a birthday dinner held in Lord Lonsdale's honour (I was soon going to be visiting quite a few of those), William met the very young and presumably very attractive Elizabeth Mossop, better known as Betty.[*]

Sixteen-year-old Betty was a barmaid, and the Mossop family were notorious smugglers.[†]

Not long afterwards, William married Betty.

If *Henry & Mary* is disguised autobiography, as I'm convinced it is, then William didn't take much persuading to join the family business.

In the novel, Henry meets and falls in love with and wants to marry Mary, but is worried his small fortune isn't enough to support them. One day, Mary's brother Walter – already a smuggler and the son of a smuggler – slyly tells Henry:

> In the course of a few nights a certain vessel will be off this coast on her annual visit to this channel. Her owner sells for ready money only; but for ready money he will sell so low, that, if fortune be favourable, it is easy to double your cash after every expense is paid. Our gang at this time is bold, trusty, and numerous, while the [customs] officers and their fellows are comparatively few and timid; and therefore the risk and difficulty is a mere bugbear.[‡]

Although he knows it is the wrong thing to do, Henry decides to invest in Walter's plan, and assist in carrying it out – with fatal consequences…

---

[*] Elizabeth Mossop, daughter of John Mossop and Hannah Southward, born in 1798 at Blacklands, Whillimoor, Arlecdon, and baptised – as was William – in Arlecdon Church.
[†] Betty Mossop's mother was landlady of The Ship Inn, Corkickle.
[‡] *Henry & Mary*, 1st ed., p. 258; 2nd ed., p. 147.

William was never caught smuggling. He was never shot and wounded by a customs man. Instead, he ended up making a mysteriously large sum of money – around £3,000 (money that certainly didn't come from farming or wrestling) – and then losing it by trying to start a legitimate brewing business.

But that is for later.

This is how I picture his first night.

The moon is muffled by clouds; no tinkle of silver scatters across the waves hitting the beach. Out upon the black sands, the men speak in whispers as they listen for the dip and creak of oars in rowlocks. These are stout men, in all senses of the word – hefty, undaunted. William Litt is among them. Why? Because it's useful to have some real muscle along? Because he'd heard all his life about the trade, and was curious to witness it himself? Because a friend asked, and he had nothing better to do that night? Because he needs the money to get married? Whatever the reason, he is among smugglers, doing what they direct him to do. He is young. This is his first step away from the path of rectitude.

Off shore, a lugger has dropped anchor. She has just come in from the Isle of Man, a West-East downwind run of thirty miles.

If you were to design a bay for smuggling, you could not do better than Fleswick Bay. On a map of the coast, it looks as if a giant spade has made a deep nick into the green whaleback of the land. It's to be found, or not found, one mile north of St Bees School, one mile south of Whitehaven. Well out of sight of town but close enough for quick access.

Those of her crew that row the first load towards the beach are armed with weapons that will in later years come to seem comic – cutlasses and blunderbusses. We've seen too many plastic cutlasses at children's pirate-themed parties to take them seriously. The very word 'blunderbuss' seems to suggest an affable uncle of a weapon, who'd pat you on the back with a sweaty palm. But a good shot from one of those beauties could take your arm off at the shoulder.

A few words of identification are exchanged, over the last few feet of water. Recent nights have been successful, but caution is profitable. The rowboat grinds into the sand, and the unloading begins. This is why William is here. He has invested his own money in this venture. He wants to ensure it is returned.

There are glugging wooden casks, of course – massy hogsheads, barrels requiring two lifters, hefty kilderkins, firkins you could cradle and pocketable pins. Making these is skilled work: a cooper, like Bill Hartley's great-grandfather will one day be, is seven years an apprentice. But if the joints are loose, the drink soon becomes brackish.

Inside the casks is French brandy, real cognac, Scottish and Irish whisky, Dutch gin known as 'Hollands'. They also bring off salt, tobacco, light and transparent French lace, anything subject to heavy excise duties.

This is not a small business. Every year, the crown invests hundreds of thousands of pounds to support the excise-men. But, for all this outlay, the excise-men only seize goods worth tens of thousands of pounds.

Horses have been provided for the occasion, with carts. These are quickly filled. The air smells of sweat and sea-salt. It is time to be off.

As usual, the smugglers judge it prudent to avoid the road. Instead, lanes are taken. Farm tracks between hedgerows, sheep standing quiet in the fields beyond. The men move inland, Eastwards.

Trusty scouts are dispatched in different directions. The smugglers have to be cautious. There may be watching eyes nearby, informers. Eight or ten resolute men surround the cargo. William is anxious, the axle-tree creaks like a crow.

Someone might spot them, run off to tell the excise-men, but farmers and their families are superstitious. Smugglers are fond of raising rumours of ghosts in churchyards and evil spirits that haunt old mansions. Better not to say anything, if you hear flittings in the night.

The men continue on through the night, making their way past Press Gill.* They go along Thistlegill, which William may have invented when he fictionalized his smuggling days in *Henry & Mary* – if he had called it 'Thorney Beck', all his likely readers would have known where it was. A gill is a ravine, a beck is a stream. The men feel the weight of the casks alongside them. It is good stuff, whisky – warmth amid snowfall, distraction from troubles, encouragement when there is pain; it helps. A hand touches smooth, gently curved wood; other hands feel smooth leather reins.

The outskirts of the parish of Cleator are reached. So far, they have encountered no difficulties. Ahead of them is Wediker, a high, dark ridge. They will be exposed when they reach the summit, but they will be closer to their destination: Salter Park.

Some of the men begin to relax, laugh; they are told to quiet themselves. William is enjoying this. If his investment is successful, his money will be more than doubled. He can smell the peat-reekie perfume of the kegs; 'athol brose' meaning mountain dew, also known as 'Scotch soup'.

As he strides confidently through the night, William is surrounded by pit-falls, old quarries, peat-holes, cattle-wells. There are a thousand places booty might be concealed, and never discovered. Not unless one of the party peached to the revenue officers.

The moon, which is not full, this gang are not *that* daring, comes out from behind scudding clouds. The breeze, already carrying the lugger back toward the Isle of Man, wraps tendrils around William's fingers – it is cool but warming, like whisky.

---

* This location was not searchable on Googlemaps: I had to ask Bill Hartley where it was. He told me it's now known as 'Priest Gill', and is between Hensingham and Moresby. And then Googlemaps found it, in a completely different place.

The smugglers crest the hill and descend into shadow, and the rest of their journey is uneventful. The booty is safely concealed. Men part with handshakes, words curt but warm. William is asked how he reckoned it. He realizes he has become one of them, and cannot unbecome. Not even when he writes in his novel *Henry & Mary* about smuggling being 'a pursuit so often attended with the most pernicious consequences'.* Not even when he self-condemns by saying, 'the business... had made him a very coward'.†

But, perhaps, like Henry, William did what he did for the purest of reasons – so he could marry the woman he loved.

---

*   *Henry & Mary*, 1st ed., p. 339; 2nd ed., p. 192.
†   Ibid., 1st ed., p. 282; 2nd ed., p. 161.

12

HUSBANDMAN

Like most children, I wanted to know what my parents were like before they became my parents.

My mother said very little on the subject, although she gradually let me understand (when I was old enough) that my father hadn't been her *only* boyfriend. My father, without meaning to, gave me quite a deep glimpse into one of his might-have-beens.

By the time these revelations happened, I already knew about my father's life after he finished doing National Service. A friend called David Sutherland, who was studying at Trinity College, Dublin, had said to him something like, 'Come on over, the craic's great, and they'll let just about anyone in.'

The young David, mostly – I expect – to please his mother, began a law degree. The craic *was* great. This was Dublin in 1958. He had digs in the Merrion Square house where Oscar Wilde was born.* He bought the writer Brendan Behan a pint – everyone did. After a year, he gave up on the Law and switched to German and geography. (This was easy for him – he already spoke German and had a photographic memory, so could remember maps at a glance.) He wrote a play. He began to haunt the antiques shops.

---

* Dad likes to give him his magnificent full name: Oscar Fingal O'Flaherty Wills Wilde.

One Trinity-era story has my father-to-be drunkenly attacking a privet hedge, along the front of college, only to find it pristine the next day. Further attempts to desecrate its infuriating perfection were only met by further miraculous moonlight repairs.

Another story finds him arrested on O'Connell Street for crawling on hands and knees, barking like a dog, or perhaps for being so drunk he thought this normal behaviour. The Dean of Trinity is brought to the police station, to bail out the disgraced undergraduate. When he appears in the cell, Dad looks up at the Dean and says, 'I see they got you, too'.

David Sutherland, the friend who enticed my father to Dublin, was rich – he drove an Aston Martin, and his father part-owned the company. I think there was a certain amount of whizzing very fast down country lanes. My father still has friends from this time, male and female. But he hadn't kept touch with ex-girlfriends.

My father met my mother, Helen Grindley, in digs – again – in St Albans, where she was working for the company that made the Contac 2000 cold remedy, and he was helping run an antiques shop. They were married almost immediately, within three months, so later on they could never tell me I was moving too fast, when I wanted to move straight in with a girlfriend.

They were, though, disappointed that I didn't get married – as both my sisters did. Once I'd met Leigh, though, a conventional church wedding was never going to happen. Leigh's bookshelves, when I first stayed over at her flat, were full of a scary number of feminist classics. She wasn't going to love, honour and obey *any* husband – not unless, she used to joke, I bought her an *extremely* big diamond. (That was never going to happen, either.) And so I am not, and am not ever likely to become, a husband.

I enjoyed my sisters' weddings. The dressing up was fun and the vows were moving, but the part that got to me emotionally – the part I was sorry I wouldn't be doing with Leigh – was cutting the cake.

This is because, growing up looking at my parents' wedding album, there was a great series of photographs of them cutting their cake.

In these few little moments, I could see their whole long, happy marriage. There's humour, there's a little bit of hamming it up, there's extraordinary tenderness and affection.

David Litt married Helen Grindley at St Paul's Church, Hereford, on September 18th 1965 – a Saturday.

William Litt married Elizabeth Mossop at St James Church, Whitehaven, on November 7th 1816 – a Thursday.

St James stands halfway up a hill, looking straight down one of Whitehaven's grid of streets – and, if this was how William approached the church, riding in a carriage on his wedding morning, he would have had plenty of time to put things in perfect perspective. The building, small at first, would have loomed up and up.

Nearly two hundred years later – in August 2015 – I stood at the top of the hill, looking back at my imaginary William. My day was a beautiful one of blue sky and light breezes, his may have been more overcast.

I felt melancholy. Weddings often make me feel like this. Everything about them is optimistic, and that makes me expect that everything's going to go wrong. But I was especially sad because I knew what happened to William and Betty, after their – I hoped – happy day. I knew how difficult their lives were going to be.

I had come up again to Cumberland, for a longer trip. This time, I was going to stay with Bill and Margaret, and go with Bill to visit again all the places connected with William. We had already been to

Bowthorn, where he was born, and Cleator Church, where he was Christened, and now we were here at St James's.

Like Whitehaven's other big churches,* Holy Trinity and St Nicholas, St James was shaped like a small briefcase with a whisky bottle still in its box standing at one end.

Bill was careful not to let my imagination run away with me. He knew the church well, and as we walked through the large glass doors and into the lobby, he started to point details out and say, 'That wasn't there then.'

The wall plaques for divines and parishioners who died years after William's wedding day – those weren't there.

But what *would* have been there, to scoop William in like elegant cradling arms, were the two staircases to the left and right. They are a little bit French chateau, and – in between them, through the door where the boxiness and straight lines resumed – awaited William's bride-to-be, Betty.

Bill and I walked through, me doing my best to imagine William's arrival. He must have been impressed, if not overawed. St James's is big inside – William and Betty could easily have had three hundred guests in the wooden pews on ground level, and another two hundred in the balcony, column-supported, on all three sides excepting the altar. I doubt there were that many.

Before I took the train up, I had done weeks of research, and now I was trying to give it some colour.

William, as he strode in to be married, was six feet tall and just past his thirty-first birthday. Up ahead of him stood the Reverend Richard Armistead.

If William could have glanced over his right shoulder, into the future where I was standing with Bill Hartley, he'd have seen us looking at

---

* Whitehaven, as well as a very pubby place, was also extremely churchy. Visiting sailors had lots of choice where to get drunk and almost as many where to repent.

Richard Armistead's wall plaque. This would have told William what was going to happen in the life of the man about to say, 'We are gathered here today, in the sight of God...'

The Reverend Richard Armistead would, like William and like William's own father John, become father to many children. The dates of their births and deaths start off appallingly close together – as if the first three poor little ones, who died so young, were experiments, necessary to set up the last three, who lived into their sixties.

In my research, I had found out a lot about the man who married William and Betty. Much more than I could use. Richard Armistead began his ecclesiastical career in high style. He had only been 24-years-old when he was appointed to St James. But he had impressed the Bishop of Carlisle. He was ordained in the 'magnificent' St George's chapel at Windsor Castle and 'received the Sacrament afterwards in the King's private chapel'.* Afterwards, he 'had repeated opportunities of seeing the whole Royal Family both at Chapel and on the Terrace... and of associating with very distinguished characters in an easy, familiar way'.

That was twenty-six years before William's wedding day, and the Reverend Richard Armistead had done nothing in that time to make him anything but respectable. Which made the choice of William and Betty's two witnesses slightly curious – if I wasn't making too much of it, which was definitely possible.

The first witness was Hannah Walker, who Margaret Hartley had told me was William's first cousin (his father's eldest sister's daughter). Margaret knew very little else about her, apart from that she had married a Henry Sharp in 1789. And that her age for William's wedding, was 54-years-old. She seems to have been illiterate, as she signed the register with 'her mark', a firm X.

---

* Letter from Edward Wilson, M.A. (1739–1804), canon of Windsor, dated 12 July 1790, quoted in Shuffrey, William Arthur, *Some Craven Worthies*, London, 1903.

I could only assume that Hannah Walker was a woman William liked and trusted. If William had wanted, he might have chosen a grander or more influential person.

The other witness I knew more about, but he was an even more curious choice. Robert Hogg was — if not on William's wedding day, then very soon afterwards — a proponent of a much hotter, harder Christianity than the Reverend Armistead. By 1821, he had become minister to a rival congregation within Whitehaven, United Presbyterians, numbering around three hundred.

I thought he was very odd company, this Hogg, for easy-going, drinking, gambling William. In 1823, Hogg even wrote an extremely puritanical *Appeal to the Christian Public on the Evils of Theatrical Amusements*.*

Reading all the evidence, but even more standing in the large space up by the altar of St James's, I get the idea of William's entire nuptials as a piece of theatre. The staging, the cast, everything was set up to give the reassurance that these are respectable goings on. No rush job, no shotgun in sight.

For me, the capping theatrical moment comes when William signs himself as 'Husbandman'. This seems to have been mischievous; not only a pun on his newly married state, but also a play — half despairing — on his status. He couldn't properly sign *wrestler* or *winner of 200 belts*, and couldn't yet sign *writer* (and it's unlikely he ever would have done). He might, though, have put *brewer*.

In William's poem 'Freedom', published four years before his wedding, on the 18th of November 1812, he observed that he had been prompted by Napoleon's recent defeat to write 'Heroic verse!!' even though he was only 'a drowsy brewer.'

---

* I haven't found a copy, dammit.

A letter dated 14th December 1812 or 1813 – from John Gibson, who was to become the publisher of William's books – gives some more information. 'William Litt,' it says, 'has taken Russell's brewery'* and a few days later that he 'has began the brewery business and does very well'.

So, William could have signed himself as brewer, but perhaps he was not yet certain of that identity. 'Husbandman' makes his social position absolutely clear. A husbandman was not a gentleman, an inheritor of land. He was not even a yeoman, a renter of land. Instead he was a free tenant farmer – the exact meaning being 'master of the house'. (Even this was not true of him: William was master of no house; after they were wed, he and Betty went to live with his parents at Netherend farm, where their children were to be born.) But husbandman was, I think, a cover – as we know, William had other, less respectable, identities.

What about the most important person there that day, what about the bride? How did she look as she signed the register? Was she happy?

As I stood in St James, after months of looking for clues, I still had no idea.

All I'd been able to find out about Betty, apart from when she was baptized, married and how many children she had, and where she later lodged at the time of the national census, was that one day, years later, she was to be blinded – and was to spend many more years bringing up her children alone.

The thought of her fate made me feel even worse than the thought of William's. But all this was far in her future. On the day she said 'I do', she was very young – only 17- or 18-years-old.

---

* This was a few yards from the Whitehaven waterfront, on Tangier Street. It is now the Deep Tan Sun Centre.

The dinner in honour of Lord Lonsdale's birthday where she'd met William, on December 29th 1814 or 1815, had been held in a large hall opposite Hensingham church, and reported at length in the *Cumberland Pacquet*.

In his vivid poem, 'Arlecdon Filly Fair', probably dating from the 1840s, the Cumbrian writer William Dickinson explicitly warns young men off marrying young women they've met in such alcoholic circumstances:

> An' ye who want a prudent wife,
> A partner for your future life,
> Seek not amang thur haunts o' strife
> > For sec a blessin',
> For those wi' modest virtue rife
> > Will oft be missin'.*

Was William and Betty's marriage as happy as my mother and father's? I didn't know. I thought so. But all I had been able to do was build up speculations on top of the dates of births, deaths and marriages that Bill and Margaret had found in church records.

There were certainly plenty of births – William and Betty's first child, William, was born exactly one year after they married, and their second, John, eleven months after that.

Other babies followed pretty regularly. But did this give me a glimpse into the conviviality of William and Betty's bedroom, any more than William's parents' eight children gave me a glance into theirs?

Not really.

Similar speculations came from the dates of death. William's father, John, died on the 19th of October 1817 – after 'a long and severe illness borne with entire resignation and uncommon fortitude'. He was

---

* 'Arlecdon Filly Fair', *Uncollected Literary Remains of William Dickinson*, William Dickinson, 1888, p. 156.

73-years-old, and his death certificate gave his occupation as 'Gent.' It was a title he had for some time only been clinging on to.

In May 1817, William had been – along with his older brother John and another man – one of the witnesses to his father's will. It is a gentleman's will.

> My children all having been previously assisted at their outset in life. Unto my dear wife Isabella Litt I give and bequeath all my Real and personal property whatsoever and wheresoever that I may die possessed of, out of which I order all my just Debts and Funeral Expenses to be paid.

But John Litt's finances, like his health, had been collapsing for several years. The *Memoir of the Author* says, William's father's 'large speculations had latterly been less than usually successful, and [he had] become involved in a heavy chancery suit'.

John's partner in mine ownership, Jonas Lindow, Spade-Manufacturer, was declared bankrupt in March 1815. It's also possible that John also had investments with John Drape, a Whitehaven stockbroker who went bankrupt one year after Jonas.

Around this time, the lease on Litt's pit was given up. Bowthorn and Netherend were eventually handed over to other tenants.

Mine owning wouldn't have suited William. William describes himself, around the time he wrote *Henry & Mary*, as being:

> ... dressed in a white flannel suit, nothing the *whiter* for its frequent visits to the regions below – I mean no allusion to any other world, but simply the lowest parts of *this* which can boast of much company – the bottom of a Coal Pit.

Let's pause for a moment to think what kind of man would visit a coalmine wearing a white flannel suit.

Bill Hartley and I came out of St James, back into the sunshine.

I imagined William on that spot – looking down on Whitehaven and out over the sea, Cumbrian November sunshine, meaning grey.

By marrying, William had ceased to be one thing but hadn't yet become another. I don't think he quite knew what to do with himself.

I found him very sympathetic, at this moment. I was happy for him, but I pitied him, too – because I knew what he had coming. By this time in his life, though William couldn't have been aware of it, he'd already gone from being a winner to being an also-ran, and soon he would be a loser.

But that's too grim an ending for what was probably a very happy day.

Just as William poetically associated mothers with love, he associated weddings with happiness.

In the poem I've already quoted, 'The Bells that Hang in the Old Church Tower', he sketched a country wedding very like the delightful episode that begins D.H. Lawrence's *Women in Love*. It's one of William's liveliest, most energetic pieces of writing, and will have to do for his own account of the moment of leaving the church:

> I hear their chime – their merry chime –
> And my thoughts float back to the golden time,
> When the heart was gladsome, it knew not why,
> And pleasure beam'd in each youthful eye,
> As we watch'd the simple country maid,
> In her snow-white bridal dress array'd,
> Borne on her lov'd one's arm along,
> Through the midst of the idle merry throng,
> Her warm blush starting at each rude jest...*

---

* *Cumberland Pacquet*, 12 February 1839.

13

MIRTH

In August 2015, I went for a drink with Jane Hartley, Bill and Margaret's daughter.

She's a few years younger than me, with strawberry blonde hair, fine bones and lively eyes. She teaches art but would like to do nothing but paint.

We didn't go to just any pub – this was research. We went to The King's Arms, Hensingham. The King's Arms is the pub where William Litt, in 1831, was victualler, or 'person who is licensed to sell alcohol'.

This was where, on one of his antique buying trips, my father had proudly announced to the landlord that he was the great-great grandson of William Litt, former proprietor.

Quietly, he'd been told, 'I'd be careful mentioning that name round here, if I were you – that man owed a lot of people a lot of money when he left.'

The implication was, keep talking, mister, and some of those people might try to get some of that money back, off *you*.

I had a pint of lager, Jane had a glass of white wine.

Jane tried mentioning our family connection to the young man behind the bar, but he was more interested in the game of pool in the other room.

We took our drinks and sat down near the door.

'Well, cheers,' we said, deadpan.

Empty apart from us, the lounge bar was a place completely without atmosphere – Sky Sports on the television, walls painted magnolia and, on the way to the loos, a single black and white photograph of the pub a hundred years earlier. I wrote in a notebook: 'felt like a pair of gerbils in a cardboard box'.

My lager tasted of orange, Jane's wine of lemon.

Bill and Margaret's bungalow is a short drive away. And, all his life, Bill has never lived more than half a mile from where we sat.

Jane grew up here, too. But she always wanted to get away. A few years ago, Jane fell in love with a man she met on a plane, and moved to Greece to be with him. Now – the relationship over – she was back, and she wasn't happy. Pubs like The King's Arms were not where she wanted to be. The Athens lifestyle suited her – I'd seen photos on Facebook. She was missing the sun.

To cheer us both up, Jane told me the anecdote of how Bill fixed the family TV with a long finger of wood. She spoke of both her parents with very fond exasperation. She didn't understand why they lived so much in the past.

I understood.

I was at the wrong angle, but from where she was sitting, Jane could look over the roundabout at the Sunday School building. This was a large, practical barn with a steep shingled roof and big wooden doors at the near end. You would not notice it, passing through.

As we'd driven back from St James's church, earlier that day, Bill had pointed the Sunday School building out. That was where he'd been an apprentice to John Gill, cabinetmaker, undertaker.

'I served part of my time with him,' Bill said, then told me he quite liked making coffins.

But Bill and I also both knew that, upstairs in a fair sized room decorated with flags, this was where William had attended, and spoken at, and been the star of the birthday dinners in honour of Lord Lonsdale, the Earl of Lowther.

As you already know, it was at one of those dinners (though not in the Sunday School) that William met Betty.

Bill and I had read the long write-ups in the *Cumberland Pacquet*. Everyone who attended seemed to be having the most wonderful fun.

I asked Jane if she'd like another glass of wine – perhaps a different kind.

The Lowther birthday dinners were not meant to be simply *fun*. Their whole point was political. This was about checking and ensuring loyalty. This was about maintaining power. And in this, they were a great success, gaining in popularity every year until 1829.

At their height, these dinners brought together over two hundred men. Hensingham was the biggest of them, which may be why William started to attend there rather than the Black Lion Inn, Whitehaven. (Or possibly it *became* the biggest gathering because it was where William was.)

On the 29th of December, flags went up on public buildings in Whitehaven, and then up the masts of ships in the harbour.

The most powerful local men would forgather in the early afternoon; dinner would be served at around three and, on some occasions, 'the party did not separate till time's iron hand pointed to the commencement of the succeeding day'.

After the wines and viands of Mr and Mrs Hartley* – always excellent – were consumed, the 'same standard' toasts were given. First,

---

* Yes, the family providing the food and drink were called Hartley – although Margaret and Bill aren't exactly sure which branch of the family they're from. Sometimes I almost suspect it's actually Bill and Margaret themselves, and that Bill has successfully made a time machine out of wood.

'the King', then 'the Duke of York and the Army' and 'the Duke of Clarence and the Navy', then – the most important one – 'the health of the Right Hon. the Earl of Lowther'.

Cheers always resounded.

After this, speeches would be made and other, sometimes slightly more frivolous toasts offered. In 1822, these included 'Lady Eleanor Lowther, and may her infant daughter be well battened', 'The Wooden walls of Old England' (meaning the Royal Navy), 'Success to Trade and Commerce', 'Improvement of the Agricultural Interest' and 'May the British Constitution and the World Fall Together'.

In all likelihood, this last was what everyone present believed – that Great Britain was not only the greatest but also the most important country in the world. William had already made this very point in his thunderously patriotic poem 'Original Song'. It begins with Napoleon's defeat:

> The long Night of Tyranny fast wears away,
> And Europe, awaking, salutes the new Day;
> Her Blood-dream is gone, and she turns with a Smile,
> To the Day Star of Freedom o'er Britain's green Isle.

And, after twenty similarly throbbing lines, it concludes with a proud hope for the future:

> From each gallant Heart may the warm Wish ascend,
> That the Patriot's Flame through the World may extend,
> That all Sects and Parties may now be combin'd
> Since the Cause of our Nation's the Cause of Mankind.

That cause, of course, was Freedom with a capital F.*

---

* These verses of patriotic thunder date from another Public Dinner, in the Assembly Room, Lancaster, 29 December 1813. There is a great generosity to William's wishes. He says, 'let Victory's Trench be Hostility's Grave / And the Foes whom we Spare be

England in William's time reminds me far more of America today than England – their pride in their Armed Forces, their confidence in manifest destiny. William speaks more like a president than a humble constituent.

As Jane and I came out of the King's Arms, the evening still light – we'd decided we'd rather not stay for a second drink – I looked across at the Sunday School hall. I'd read so many words about what happened there, and part of me wished I could time travel back to the 1800s, to see it all for myself.

But God, if I'd travelled back as the French Revolution-supporting radical I am, I would have found these long, long jingoistic evenings unbearable. Endless toasts to titled toffs. Public pledges of loyalty. Mass celebrations. Eugh.

I knew I wasn't alone in my queasiness. In an online archive of digital newspapers, I had found an amazing speech by William's first son, William Jnr.* He gave it on the evening of the centenary of the birth of the great Scottish poet Burns, January 25th, 1859, in Shrewsbury. William Jnr was Vice-President at the Burns' society.

He said, with exquisite point:

---

the Friends whom we save'. These are sentiments of a national confidence we lost long ago. After the Second World War, we were too exhausted to give ourselves a similar boost. And now? Would William have voted for Brexit? I don't know. He proudly says,

This the Triumph of Britain, who opens her Brest,
That the famish'd may feed, that the weary may rest:
The Night-Fire of Hope, both to guide and to warm;
The Life Boat of Europe amidst the wide Storm.

Is Britain now the 'Life Boat of Europe' or rather some pirate vessel sailing Westwards, away from the voices of the drowning?

* He wasn't really known as 'William Jnr', but I think this is going to be the simplest way to distinguish the many Williams. For example, William Jnr had a son called William (William Jnr Jnr, my great-great-uncle).

Public dinners we know are common enough everywhere, and they are particularly common in our own neighbourhood, where every scion of an aristocratic family who happens to be born, or to live to cut his eye teeth, or, which is not always a consequence, to get married, furnishes an excuse for such a gathering. I hope I am not speaking irreverently of these things when I say that the motives which draw men together on such occasions are easily understood, and are not always of the most disinterested character. (Hear, hear.) But what is to be said of a meeting like this to-night (cheers), where there can be no fawning on those in power, no profit derived from flattering the titled or the rich, but where a mere sentiment, and that, too, a sentiment so remote as the birth of a Scottish peasant, in a mud hut, a hundred years ago, can call together such an assembly as this I have now the honour to address. (Great cheering.)*

I winced when I read this. For – just as with William's account of hare coursing – every line seems a blow aimed directly at his father. All that fawning and flattering, William Jnr seems to be saying, all those speeches and songs, and what did it get you, Dad?

But William too, as I was aware from the *Cumberland Pacquet*, had been cheered to the echo. He sat in the midst of mirth.

As Jane drove me back to her parents' bungalow, I had the feeling I'd missed something – not just that evening, but more generally.

In my hours of research, everything had started to shine.

At about eight o'clock on the 29th of December, 1824, Mr Rigg rose and observed that there was a gentleman in the Sunday School room

* 'A Hensingham Gentleman's Speech at Burns's Centenary in Shrewsbury', *The Whitehaven News*, 3 March 1859.

to whom the attentions of the company were owed – he meant Mr Litt, (Approbation followed.) He proposed Mr Litt's good health, and thanked him for his excellent song. The toast was done with much approbation.

William's drinking song, to the tune of a song called 'The Life that is easy and free,' gives us the mirthful scene.

> Mark the prospect before us! how glorious the sight!
>> See – our table abounds with good cheer!
> A scene so inviting should make us unite
>> And remember the cause why we're here.
> 'Tis to welcome the day that to LONSDALE gave birth,
>> – Aye – and many more such may he see!
> While foes to all discord, and brothers in mirth,
>> We still will be jovial and free.
>>> Then fill up a bumper and let it go round; –
>>> To this maxim you all will agree: –
>>> That when LONSDALE we toast let shrill echo rebound,
>>> That free tribute to worth, three times three!

After Mr Rigg's toast, William stood up to speak, and spoke for some time. He spoke, feelingly, of the public and private virtues of Lord Lonsdale. He was listened to, liked.

'Gentlemen,' said William, in conclusion, 'I again thank you for the loud and flattering manner in which you have been pleased to drink my health, and in doing myself the pleasure of pledging yours in return. I can only observe, that any trifle which it is in my power to contribute towards the hilarity of the meeting, will always be at its command. (Applause.)'

★

William has just said his final word. He's still on his feet. There he stands, smiling, in his long black tailcoat and his clean white shirt, his best waistcoat, his pale neckcloth and his sandy-coloured breeches.

Let's freeze-frame him here – hold him still for a few moments. A 39-year-old, father of three boys, former wrestler, future exile. Author of last year's *Wrestliana,* and this summer's *Henry & Mary.* He is simultaneously at his height and past his best.

He's a fine man, isn't he? Probably a better man than I am.

Imagining him like this made me wonder – where would I stop time, if I could pause myself like I've paused William? Which instant, of all my instants, was best? Was it halfway through that first kiss that turned out to be a last kiss, or that other kiss that was only the first of hundreds? Or in the huge embrace of my father on a Cornish beach or with my mother's dry hand on my feverish, day-off-school forehead? That ball on its inevitable way across the bumpy Alameda School football pitch, and into the corner of the goal, beyond the keeper's desperate reach? That word from Mrs Hetherington, my English teacher, about that poem I'd shown her – 'Superb'. That midgy evening in the Worcester College quad, when that girl looked at me as if I had a halo? That climax to that song by that singer at that gig? That undressing and being undressed. That tent, that room. That being naked and being accepted. That club, that field. That sideways glance at Leigh's pale hands, in the restaurant the evening I met her. That secret, shared beneath hotel sheets. That second after they'd announced my name as the winner of the short story prize. That moment when I first held Henry in the delivery room. That first glimpse of George, swimming up still in the caul – up through the blue water of the birthing pool. That glance around the dining table, at the happy faces of my friends, who were well fed, still young enough to be hopeful. That minute after Crystal Palace went one–nil up against Manchester United in the FA Cup Final and I jumped up and down with all the other Eagles fans at Wembley Stadium. That relief when I realized the mourning for my mother no longer required absolutely all of me, and that joy still did exist. Or that leaning back from the desk, a story finished. Or that leaning in to the desk, a story just reaching the second page.

That time when I won.

14

SHOWS AND SPORTS

After the graves in St James churchyard and the King's Arms, and Bowthorn, Cleator Church, Michael Moon's bookshop in Whitehaven, and the site where the wrestling was held at Carlisle, and Arlecdon Moor and its haunted churchyard – after the historical visits with Bill, I went to join Roger and Jill Robson for the wrestling.

I wanted to see more of it. The Academy Shield in Bootle had given me a glimpse. Now I needed to try and understand what William got from it.

Weeks earlier, Roger had sent me the Wrestling Diary, and I had picked this week in August. It was the high-point of the season, starting with a medium-size show at Ennerdale, then Grasmere, the showiest show, and finally the biggest battle, the all-weights Championship at Keswick.

Roger and Jill had offered to put me up, to drive me around and to be my guides, to feed me and explain what was going on. That whole week, my biggest expense turned out to be keeping them in ice-creams.

Staying overnight in their spare bedroom, with the Belted Galloways outside the window, I fell in easily with their summer routine.

They always tried to arrive at the shows early; early enough to secure front row seats. Their Black Skoda Octavia would be parked on something between a mud-bath and a lawn. The people checking tickets said hello.

As we walked down the grassy hill into the Ennerdale Show, Roger tipped me off. 'If you're looking for the wrestling, look out for a small tannoy system.'

For the rest of the week, the grey duck-bills of the speakers were where we headed, time and again – past Tombola stalls, tables with home-made cakes and jam.

Jill Scott from the C&WW Association would be there, accepting entries from the regulars and the first timers.

Once at the ring, camping chairs were planted, coffee was fetched, and people came up to see how Roger and Jill were.

Roger was still wary of me, the clivver London lad, but I think he was a little won round by the fact I'd come back for a longer look.

Sometimes, he introduced me to other wrestling enthusiasts as the descendant of William. Most of them asked if I was going to give wrestling a go. They knew that anyone who wanted could put their name down. Slightly boozed up farm lads often tried their luck, in jeans and socked feet.

'Not yet,' I'd say. 'I'm still in training.'

'Well, we'll look forward to it,' they'd say.

I wasn't looking forward to it.

The more wrestling I saw, the more I was convinced I'd get injured – perhaps seriously – the moment I got in the ring.

I watched closely.

Jill always took photographs for the website. 'Although sometimes, I get too involved,' she said, 'and forget.'

Roger made notes for his written reports, and shouted advice to his nephews and niece, who often took part. 'Keep your right shoulder up!'

The most constant voice was Alf Harrington's. A former All-Weights Champion, he MC's the bouts through the small tannoy system. It wasn't hard to imagine him speaking at one of the Lonsdale dinners.

'I think we've got the sunniest part of the day for the wrestling,' he said at Ennerdale, 'and the cleanest part of the field.'

It's true. If you didn't have the tannoy, you could find the wrestling by looking for the only pristine circle of green in a sea of brown. Thin blue ropes looped around metal poles keep off the Wellingtons and hiking boots.

'Amazing how uninjured wrestlers are,' said Roger. 'A dry year, these rings are like concrete.'

What else did I learn?

The wrestling starts before the wrestling starts. It starts when the wrestlers first see one another, or when they hear who has entered the competition, or when they hear rumours about how hard so-and-so has been training all winter.

There isn't much warm-up – some discrete hip-thrusts, left and right, whilst chatting to the girlfriend or a mate.

Just as experienced rugby union fans know that the first scrum down is a defining moment of the game – where we see which pack gets the shove – so wrestling aficionados watch how the wrestlers make their entrance.

Some wrestlers, you can see, are defeated the moment the other wrestler comes in view.

Stepping into the ring, each time, is a kind of coming out – 'My name is X and I self-identify as a wrestler'.

Talking to people about this book, London people, they often conclude – as Leigh does – that wrestling is all homoerotic. It *has* to be about men finding an arcane way of touching one another, because otherwise they're not allowed to do it – or think about it. 'Oh, why don't they just start snogging?' is the attitude.*

---

* This is a shortcut way of understanding the world; everything a secret history. I used it myself. In 1987, at university, it was my key to everything. What else could explain Margaret Thatcher's bitter rage against mankind? Or Scargill's love for the working man? They must *want it*.

As I watched bout after bout, I thought about this, in relation to William. Was that what all his love of wrestling, and of the press of crowded rooms, and close male friendship was about – was there a simple key to that? Was William gay?

I could only answer, no. Reading the sentences of *Wrestliana* as forensically as I could, it isn't desire I find. William loved fame, he loved being with men, and he loved to win. If you believe that for any man to wish for victory over another man is, at base, because they want to bugger them, then wrestling, chess, all sport, is gay.

In that case, William was gay. I'm gay. Mohammed Ali was gay. And the category of gayness becomes meaningless. Because you'd also have to argue that a strong desire *not* to participate in competitive sports also reveals essential gayness.

Whatever was going on, in terms of desire, was complex. I didn't doubt that some male C&W wrestlers fantasized about having sex with one another. The community they belong to isn't one in which announcing you were gay would exactly be easy. But striding out into the ring, dressed in a floral embroidered centrepiece, to the titters of the first-timer viewers, is – in itself – a fairly major statement of *I don't care what you think, this is who I am.*

One of the most interesting things anyone said during my August visit, and it was just an aside, came from Jill Robson. 'Some of them,' she said, meaning the younger wrestlers, 'have overcome a lot just to get in the ring.'

Given the costumes, and the uncool old folk you get to hang out with, wrestling is unlikely to do as much to enhance your reputation at secondary school as, say, having 1,000 followers on Instagram or being able to get hold of high quality drugs.

That summer, I saw boys entering the ring as if heading for the headmaster's office, and leaving as if they'd been caned, or told they were the new head boy.

Some wore the proper costumes and had trained all winter. Others, egged on by dads and uncles, went in wearing Minions T-shirts – and got swiftly dumped by the lads in long johns.

Whatever their age, the two wrestlers aren't alone in the ring. There are three others – the referee and two judges.

The judges are ex-wrestlers. Roger would often be called up to take a turn. They kneel or sit, one to East and one to West, whilst the referee circles the wrestlers like a sheepdog trying to keep a nervy flock in check. But the match is also policed by the crowd. There are wise heads, perhaps a little puffy about the right ear, who will shout 'Heads out!' or 'Broke hod!' if they spot infringements.

Younger wrestlers know, if they still want to enter the ring when their bodies have aged and got injured and said *no more*, then they too will come to refereeing. It's second best by a long way, but it's still near the action. As a former fell runner said to Roger as we entered Grasmere showground, 'I'd give a town clock to go again'.

There's a tennis coach who is often on the public courts in Brockwell Park. He's grey haired, squat, with a very loud voice – and some of the kids he trains are extremely good. Their racquets don't just go flatly through the ball but describe the kind of butterfly curlicues of Rafa Nadal. As they step forwards to take the ball early, the coach always cries out the same thing, 'Now *explode!*'

In all sports, there are explosive moments. But most of them follow on from a period of sizing up the opponent. This is true for boxing, karate, fencing, Graeco–Roman wrestling.

When the umpire of a Cumberland & Westmorland wrestling bout shouts 'Wrestle!' they might as well shout, 'Explode!'

Although the grappling may, a few moments later, become extremely canny – especially if one wrestler has been lifted off the ground and has replied by putting a solid hank in, wrapping his legs like snakes around his opponent's legs – the first instants are often decisive. Some bouts are over in less than a second.

The explosiveness of it is partly what makes C&W wrestling so thrilling. Here are two competitors going, in one moment, from tensed preparation to absolute effort. Unless one of them, as in the case of brothers or a dodgy deal, is 'lying down' for the other, you are witnessing a wrestler doing their utmost. They reach immediately for the very limit of their strength, because if they don't they will lose.

A golfer, a tennis player, even a 100-metre champion, can have a lazy style – not a C&W wrestler. If there's a muscle or a sinew, it will come into play.

Some wrestlers' greatest excellence is during the capsize, when the both of them have begun to topple – they can pull a man round from on top of them to beneath them in a few hundredths of a second. This makes it a very demanding spectator sport because, to understand it, you can't watch slackly. Your alertness needs to climax, your focus

Figure 15. In some photographs, only moments from the end of a bout, it's still hard to tell who's going to win.

needs to be greatest, during those final moments of turn and tussle and twist. One and a half spins can happen whilst you blink. Even the judges often miss what's happened.

There's the loser, too. If you're watching carefully, you can see the look on a man's face, going down in the third fall, his eyes six inches from the approaching grass – already, he has relaxed into full knowledge of his defeat. Unless his opponent's knee touches before his own shoulder or hip does, it is over for another year. There is real tragicomedy in this moment – I have not lost yet, although I have already lost.

Roger had advised me to watch Andrew Carlile, as having one of the neatest styles around. Carlile, confusingly, was the coach of the Carlisle club. Roger said he might be persuaded to give me a lesson or two. That would mean getting in the ring with him. I looked him over when he came into view. Andrew Carlile was shorter than me, but all muscle.

I was meaning to speak to him at Crosby Ravensworth, but he lost in an early round and headed home a few minutes later. When I told him, Roger said he could put us in touch.

I watched the other wrestlers, trying to work out which I'd least like to face. In comparison to most of them, Andrew Carlile looked merciless but also friendly. He didn't look as if he'd kill you by accident.

Asminder Asmindersson of Iceland looked as if he'd be perfectly at home stepping into the battle scene of a saga. He wrestled in a tartan kilt. When I saw him at Ennerdale Show, the first I attended, I thought I might as well go straight back to London – no one was going to beat this monster for the rest of the season.

But then I saw Fraser Hirsch of Scotland, also kilted, take Asminder Asmindersson on, and beat him. When the two of them landed, the horizon seemed to wobble a little bit. Jill Robson caught the moment just before.

Figure 16. Frazer Hirsch fells Asminder Asmindersson. Oof – just oof.

Smaller and more gymnastic, Richard Fox of Hethersgill amazed me every time I saw him. He could work himself up into a state of fearsome intensity. In between falls, he paced the ring in figures of eight. One of his eyes had a grey glaze to it. Here he is, roaring as he downs Asminder Asmindersson.

Figure 17. The roar of victory, like a boiling kettle thrown from an F16 just breaking the sound barrier.

One of the great wrestling dynasties is the Brocklebank family of Warton, Lancashire. Their grandfather, known as 'Big Wilf', was a Heavyweight Champion, as was their father, Harry.

I'd already seen Ben Brocklebank, tattooed and holding hands with his girlfriend at the Academy Shield. His costume had the most flamboyant design of any I saw – a scorpion on his right knee, a viper on his left, a tiger on his chest. His wrestling style too was all or nothing. He regularly put down bigger men, but never showed any sign of pleasure.

His older brother Graham, usually wearing a bright orange vest, seemed much more vulnerable. Every twinge of pain was in his face, for all to see. But, when the falls were one apiece, he could get as worked up as Richard Fox.

The biggest of the Brocklebank brothers, Thomas, gave a greater sense of 'Let's go to work', of putting his bulk into action in a calculated manner.

I thought about what sitting round the Brocklebank dining table must be like, and how much food must go on it.

Figure 18. Ben Brocklebank looks as if he's out for a stroll. Graham Brocklebank looks as if he can feel every bone in his body.

★

By the time we reached the All-Weights Championship, at Keswick, I'd spent a week at ringside and was starting to pick out the chips and throws more clearly.

I knew the styles of the different wrestlers, and I'd seen most of them at four or five different shows. I'd seen Graham Brocklebank fight on with an agonizingly injured shoulder at Crosby Ravensworth, then appear with it strapped in blue tape to win at Grasmere. His face says it all.

I'd seen Richard Fox tumble away after felling his early round opponents, easily as a boy doing a forward roll down a hill. I'd seen Asminder Asmindersson, who continued to terrify me, but who seemed to have been figured out by the British wrestlers.

The one wrestler I hadn't seen was Robert Leiper, a Northumbrian farmer, who hadn't competed more than a couple of times all season. He looked bizarrely similar to Superman – broad shoulders, narrow waist, chiselled jaw. He reminded me of my father.

Roger Robson later wrote in his weekly match report:

> For me the highest point of a wonderful week of wrestling came in the third round of the All Weights Championship at Keswick when Richard Fox battled back from a fall down against the massive Icelander Asmundur Asmundursson. In the deciding fall you could see what Fox was up to as they circled round. He was sidling towards his favourite chip, and sure enough he struck with the full buttock and the Icelander flew high in the air and then thumped to the ground.

But then Richard Fox went out, and so did Asmundur Asmundursson, and the final for the World Championship came down to Robert Leiper versus Graham Brocklebank, shoulder still giving him trouble.

Figure 19. The Champion of Champions – Robert Leiper –
came down from the hills, won, went back to the hills.

Leiper won.

Tom Harrington called it 'the best heavyweight championship in twenty years'.

And after it's over? It's noticeable how embarrassed the celebrations are. Most of the wrestlers, although they have been through it all hundreds of times, have to be called back from trying to leave the ring to have their hand lifted high – to show everyone watching who has won.

Usually, the winner's head is down, his body language says, 'I'd rather be anywhere else.'

I saw no triumphalism – yes, the odd fist-pump, but nothing like 'I'm the champion of the whole fucking world' (which, when they become world champions, they could quite legitimately claim).

Perhaps the celebrations go off elsewhere, in the pub, back on the farm – perhaps they are wild and egotistical but private.

Congratulations from family members often goes no further than a pat on the back or, maybe, some significant eye contact. There's not a lot of whooping goes on at Crosby Ravensworth or Grayrigg. The point has been made. You've won. It's something you can think about, quietly, when other things aren't going too well.

By the end of the week, I think I'd seen some of what William saw.

When the wrestling is good, the edge of the ring is the most exciting place in the world.

15

Wrestliana

According to William wrestling is not only the most ancient and respectable sport, it is also 'infinitely superior to any other amusement at present prevalent in the world.'

That is what *Wrestliana; or, an Historical Account of Ancient and Modern Wrestling* set out to prove.

Although this was still early in the history of sports writing (which is why his book is so collectable*), William wasn't arguing with himself.[†]

Wrestliana is a countermove to another book. *Boxiana*, first published in 1812, was a bestselling compilation of pugilistic lore, anecdote, opinion and statistical fact. The author of it, the man William was matching himself against, was a famous journalist called Pierce Egan.

Born in 1772, Pierce Egan lived in and wrote about London. His mode is urbane, his tone, knowing. He's clivver.

William's book is not a counter*punch* – using that language would be granting the upper hand to Egan's inferior sport. Instead, *Wrestliana* is William's attempt to overthrow *all* other sports. But boxing was the

---

* A first edition of *Wrestliana* is so sought after that you would have trouble getting one for less than £1,000.

† Almost two hundred years after its publication, *Wrestliana* is a much sought after volume – not just by specialists in wrestling and martial arts, but among general collectors of sports books. The copy I and my father bought, in 2009 from an antiquarian bookseller in Suffolk, so there would be one in the family, cost us £500. The original price was 'Two Shillings and Sixpence'.

main competitor, in terms of popularity with the common people across England.

And so William begins by proving wrestling's priority in terms of antiquity and, even, divinity, over boxing.

He doesn't do this just vaguely, he takes Pierce Egan on point by point. In *Boxiana*, Egan says he isn't even going to try to write an early history of pugilism. Its origins are clouded in darkness. And whether the first man, Adam, boxed is completely obscure.[*]

William immediately moves in to take advantage. Adam? A mere mortal. In the Bible, in the 32nd chapter of Genesis, there is proof that Jacob wrestled with an angel. William takes a lawyerly delight in this:

> That the Patriarch's antagonist was a being of a superior order, and sent by Divine authority, no Christian has ever yet disputed. That it was... a wrestling match between them, is universally admitted. It cannot therefore be denied, that [wrestling] is either of divine origin, or that a Being more than mortal has participated in it.[†]

William then seizes upon Pierce Egan's concession that, in *Boxiana*, he is not going to try to prove that pugilism dates as far back as the Greeks and Romans.[‡]

It was wrestling, William says, that helped Greece extend from 'a few petty states' to 'the most powerful Kingdom at that time in the world'. This fact, he magnificently proclaims, is 'universally acknowledged by all historians and commentators who have ever treated of the subject'.[§]

The first two falls seem to have gone to William.

---

[*] Pierce Egan, *Boxiana*, 1813, pp. 1–2. But whom could Adam have sparred with, apart from Eve? Even with all his wiles, the armless Serpent wouldn't have put up much of a fight.

[†] *Wrestliana*, 1st ed., p. 8; 2nd ed., p. 2.

[‡] Pierce Egan, *Boxiana*, 1813, p. 3.

[§] *Wrestliana*, 1st ed., p. 10; 2nd ed., p. 4.

Judging the books by their covers, Egan is the winner.

Put a copy of *Boxiana* alongside one of *Wrestliana* and the latter seems a very scrappy, provincial production.

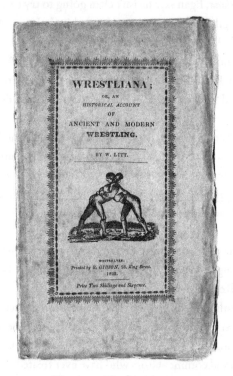

Figure 20. The first edition.

Egan's hardbound three-volume work has illustrations, William's none but the familiar wrestlers-with-disconnected-heads plate that had appeared for years in the Cumberland Pacquet, and that I've put as the frontispiece of my own *Wrestliana*.

Yet, despite looking much shorter and more pamphlet-like, *Wrestliana* was – once it got going – by far the more ambitious work.

After his brief dedication* and introduction, Egan was happy simply to compile a dictionary of famous boxers – a very long and, to me, quite boring list. William wanted his argument to run from first page to last, and with a strong narrative to boot.

The middle chapters of *Wrestliana* take the form of a series of match ups, Wrestling vs. Boxing, Wrestling vs. Hunting, Wrestling vs. Football.

As with William's ten undefeated years on Arlecdon Moor, Wrestling is victorious each time – and emerges at the end as last sport standing.

William has a particular hatred of the violence of boxing, and gives a wince-making description of the epic bout between Jack Carter and Tom Oliver, held at Gretna Green on October 4th 1816. This went to the thirty-second round, after which the defeated Oliver was hustled

---

* One of the most startling things about *Wrestliana* is its dedication, or rather its lack of dedication. Here was an easy way for William to ingratiate himself to the Earl of Lowther, yet he didn't take it. Instead, he replaces a conventional dedication with something very much like the studio chat skits that begin hip-hop albums. William first gives a cameo of himself at work on the proofs for his book. 'But our old acquaintance, Tim Twistwell, a knowing kind of *chap*, and something of a wrestler, looking in upon us and observing we were busy writing over the first sheet for the press, desired to look at the Preface'.

There follows a bluff argument.

'Preface!' says William, 'truly I mean to write none.'

Tim Twistwell makes various attempts to persuade William to be more backward in putting himself forward. 'Thou has not taken sufficient pains to acquire information.'

'"Too much pudding will choak a dog,"' William says, 'Tim, I know enough without it to illustrate my own opinion of the subject; and except in the historical department, where quotations are both amusing and instructive, my own knowledge will be sufficient.'

William concludes his victory by asking, 'Thinkest thou there is one man in the kingdom who has won as many prizes as I have and can write better?'

'No!'

'Then be content, good Tim, and in lieu of a Preface, I will publish our conversation.'

Figure 21. 'The Fight Between Carter and Oliver at Gretna Green, October 4th, 1816' by William Brown. An amazing painting. Half the sky is summer, half is apocalypse.

away in the company of surgeons who declared that 'in consequence of the vast quantity of blood he had lost' it was 'highly dangerous that he should be bled'.*

Because we know William saw this, and because there is a painting in existence of the event, it's possible he is one of the men standing around the ring. They are all dressed the same – top-boots, black jackets. If William's there, he is anonymized.

William's writing, in describing the brutality of this boxing match, and throughout the rest of the book, was energetic, muscular, quick-witted and good-humoured.

But the reviewers – and there were quite a few reviewers – did not agree.

---

* Ibid., p. 40.

John Badcock, writing in the *Annals of Sporting and Fancy Gazette*, a publication advertised on the back cover of *Wrestliana*, questioned William's scholarship. He also referred to Mr Litt very much in the same patronizing way as James Hogg, 'the Ettrick Shepherd', was commonly granted notice. Neither man had been to Oxford or Cambridge, or even Edinburgh or Glasgow, so – in Badcock's view – they could hardly be called *educated*. Hogg's self-education might be startling, in flashes, but could not give the clear, even light of consistent culture. William was also described as a naïve rustic who knew a bit but was fundamentally unsound.

To William's defence came Christopher North, the public person of John Wilson – whom we saw between William and William Wordsworth at the Windermere Regatta of 1824. And North's review was in a far more significant publication than *The Annals of Sporting and Fancy Gazette*.

In Haworth Parsonage, the four Brontë children read it side by side, in eager pairs. Coleridge considered suing it for libel. A bad review from it was thought to have killed Keats.

Popular, notorious, ground-breaking, spirit-breaking – *Blackwood's Edinburgh Magazine* (known as 'Maga') was one of the most influential publications in British history.

And so, for *Wrestliana* to receive a rave review from Maga's star reviewer, running to over eighteen double-columned pages, was a very big deal.

I'm glad it was a big deal because, apart from his victory against Harry Graham and the ovation he received at the 1824 Lonsdale dinner, this was the high point of William's life.

The same magazine, and the very same reviewer, that had written of Samuel Taylor Coleridge, 'A man who abandons his wife and children is undoubtedly both a wicked and pernicious member of society...',* said of William that he was as honest, upright, and independent an Englishmen as ever floored or threw.

Even more expansively, Christopher North's review gave *Wrestliana* this opening-line puff: 'Our literature is rich in British Sports, and this admirable little volume will be a valuable addition to the most bang-up library'.

Some of the reasons for Christopher North's high praise are political, and some personal.

Blackwood's was a Tory magazine, set up in direct opposition to the *Edinburgh Review*. If William's politics had been radical, he could have expected a slating, however good his book was.

It also helped that John Wilson himself liked William personally, and had wrestled against him. But most important was that he was the right sort of chap saying the right sort of thing.

The default setting of Christopher North in *Blackwood's* was murder–death–kill.[†] He could also mercilessly ignore what he didn't like.

To confirm this – there was no equivalent outflow of praise for William's novel of the following year. As far as I can tell, *Blackwood's* didn't once mention it. And this effectively ended William as a writer.

But *Wrestliana* was a different matter. It gave Christopher North the chance to do what he liked best of all, opine. And North's favourite subject, the core of his public persona, was sport – particularly, fighting.[‡]

So, let's have a fight.

---

* 'Some Observations on the "Biographia Literaria" of S.T. Coleridge', John Wilson, *Blackwood's Magazine*, October 1817.

† In the 1980s, there was a fashion for American newspapers to headhunt British tabloid journalists. Why? Because they could do the *Blackwood's* style better than anyone else. They wrote to a purpose and with a vengeance. Facts were merely the opinions of the unimaginative. All of this attitude could be seen to start with John Wilson, John Gibson Lockhart and James Hogg in 1820s Edinburgh.

‡ John Wilson had written a very long article on boxing, in 'Maga', in 1819.

Mr North vs. Mr Fancy, the rave review vs. the stinker.

Seconds out!

Mr North tries to assert himself early on, but seems then to back away. He speaks well of wrestling, declaring himself a 'Littite' in believing that it is superior 'as a British field-sport, to pugilism, cock-fighting, horse-racing, foot-ball, running, leaping, and single-stick', yet flinches by saying 'our opinion remains wavering between the comparative merits of the science of the Fist, of the Back-Hold, and of the Quarter-staff'.[*]

Mr Fancy wades in; he has no such doubts. Boxing is 'the primest and, indisputably, *most manly* exercise in which man can possibly engage'.

Mr North staggers back, and Mr Fancy follows in with the hard blow that 'instead of *wrestling* being distinct or superior to' boxing, it is secondary to it, wrestling forms part of the match but only 'after science is exhausted'; wrestling 'terminates the rounds as the pell-mell fag-ends of a grand procession put the finish to a state raree-show'.

The referee intervenes, and Mr North takes a standing count. He insists, though, that he's still up for the fight – and returns with an unexpected uppercut. 'There is,' he asserts, 'none of that bluster about William Litt which there certainly was about Napoleon Buonaparte'. A slightly strange comparison, but the point is that, had William come second at the Carlisle meeting, 'he would have entertained towards his conqueror none of those petty feelings of spite and envy with which the exile of Helena regarded the victor of Waterloo'.

Mr Fancy counters with an accusation of rank cowardice. William is a 'shocking stick' – ooh! – who has handled the subject of boxing

---

[*] *The Annals of Sporting and Fancy Gazette*, March 1824, p. 268. Other quotes that follow are nearby.

'*currishly*'. Ow! 'For, after flooring the whole system… he turns about upon his heel, like a fellow who floors another in the street, and runs away to some well-known haunt'.

Back comes Mr North, 'Mr Litt is a person in a respectable rank of life, and his character has, we know, been always consonant with his condition. He is, in the best sense of the word, a gentleman…'

But Mr Fancy is having none of that. Litt 'returns again and again to the subject of boxing or pugilism, mixing and confounding these and the terms of art in the manner common to novices, flats and yokels'.

Mr North will not allow this. At the 'last grand northern meeting' (Carlisle, 1823), William – to the gratification of the thousands collected round the ring – was 'honoured by the especial notice of the most powerful noble family in England', the Lowthers, of course. Take that, Fancy boy.

Mr Fancy's response to this attempted knockout is a sly kidney punch, William 'showeth forth his non-knowledge in every fresh recurrence to the thing'. The thing being, boxing.

Mr North – a bit stunned that this is where the fight is going – shifts back a bit, and tries to regain control. William, he says, 'possesses a clearer head and style' than Macvey Napier, author of 'Dissertation on the Scope and Tendency of Lord Bacon'.

The 'mode of execution' of *Wrestliana*, Mr Fancy jabs away, 'does not rise above mediocrity' and 'is full of localisms and obscurities'.

The two fighters now move onto the ground of *Boxiana*. Mr North lands this one-two combo. 'We love pugilism and Pierce Egan, but in some respects they must yield the palm to wrestling and William Litt'.

Surprisingly, Mr Fancy seems to concede this equality, but returns with a dangerous swipe, 'and as to *"eloquence,"* and all that sort of thing, both these gentlemen seem much upon a par'. But wrestling, William's 'favourite sport of "tumble down Dick"' is no match for the glory of pugilism.

Mr North attempts to conclude matters with 'we thank Mr Litt for his well-written, candid, manly, and scientific' volume.

As he backs towards his corner, the bell for the round having gone, Mr Fancy counsels Mr Litt to 'avoid controversy, and round off his flowing style'.

Not likely.

Mr Fancy! – God, don't you really just want to clobber him? – to smack the lah-di-dah little tosser right in the gob?

Which is, I'm pretty sure – though in slightly less demobbed 1950s language – exactly what a lot of men feel when they hear *me* speak. Not because I'm necessarily going to be super-articulate. A lot of the time I'm a shoe-inspecting mumbler who, Leigh complains, always messes up any story he tries to tell. But I did go to public school and then to Oxford, and they're still there in my voice. I sound clivver.

In 1997, the actor and television presenter Stephen Fry was interviewed by Anthony Clare on the radio programme *In the Psychiatrist's Chair*. His point was this: the British public associate eloquence with insincerity.*

Clare asked, 'And you can intellectualize almost anything?' And Fry, in a magnificent statement worth quoting in full, said:

> Yeah, but also it's a problem of being in this culture now where, you know, feelings seem to be presented as an antithesis of logic and reason and to me part of the real beauty of humanity and the world is reason and is thought. It is one of the most beautiful things we have and one of the most moving and most profound. Yet *we live in a culture in*

---

* Anthony Clare, *In the Psychiatrist's Chair III*, Chatto & Windus, 1998, p. 140. It's interesting that, for no particular reason (apart from what this whole book is about), Fry spends a lot of time discussing his attitude to sport – as non-participant and as fan.

which people generally think that if something is well expressed it's less likely to be true than if it's badly expressed. That a fumbling for words is an index of sincerity and truth and a mastery linguistically of expression of feelings, however complex, must be regarded as an example of precisely that. That I'm describing something that means a lot to me emotionally but doing it in language that is not chaotic. And people distrust that, and perhaps rightly and perhaps I distrust it myself.' (Italics mine.)

The fact that Fry had been able to speak about his depression with coherence, and the occasional sub-clause, made people believe it wasn't that serious. The full force of an emotional point is only ever made by inarticulacy. What he'd really needed to do, to convince them, was cry like a baby.

True feeling, supposedly, drives out language – only tears, screams, gestures (hugs, fist-pumps) and flying fists will do.

Mr Fancy's parting advice is foolish – if you take away William's flow and his controversial opinions, you leave him very little.

Judged by Mr Fancy's metropolitan standards, William's prose *is* poor; judged by our contemporary standards, his liveliness and vulnerability are far preferable to the strut and sneer and quote and carp of 1823 Oxford-educated prose.

William is not at all concerned about being *correct*, he just wants to be *right*.

Fine abstract sentiments, William would have argued, are all very well for fine abstract subjects – what I'm about is the practical. You're not in the library, man, you're in the ring – and this man's there, against you. He wants to put you down. How do you take hold? What do you feel, his chest pressed against your chest? When he tries a chip, what then? What use are words now?

In reading the bad reviews of *Wrestliana*, I hated to hear William put down. I found myself skimming ahead through each new paragraph, willing the writer to say something positive about him. And if they didn't, I got angry.

He's a better man than you, I'd think. You great Georgian *ponce*.

Clearly, even apart from Christopher North, William got many more of his contemporaries on his side. James Hogg wrote to the magazine's editor, William Blackwood, after reading that number of *Blackwood's*:

> My dear Sir… The maga is excellent. No dross… Wrestliana is the very thing for me. Wilson must come to the Yarrow games this year…[*]

Wilson may have gone to wrestle, William didn't.

I needed to.

When I read *Wrestliana* once again, in the Spring of 2016, I wasn't looking at it abstractly, or as a literary critic.

It was my training manual.

[*] Hogg letter to Blackwood, 18 January 1824, quoted in *The Collected Letters of James Hogg 1820–1831*, edited by Gillian Hughes, Edinburgh University Press, 2006, p. 196.

16

ACTUALLY WRESTLING

23 March 2016

All the way up, on the train, I read and reread the practical bits of *Wrestliana* and thought about how — in five hours, then four hours, then three — I could be riding in an ambulance.

I knew fairly certainly which injuries I feared most. I'd constructed a sliding scale.

At the very top, there was quadriplegia — a broken neck and me in a wheelchair, unable to hug my children, scanning websites for advances in robot exoskeletons. Then there was the fractured lower vertebra, keeping me away from my desk, perhaps forever. There was the ruptured knee ligament. In the days before, I had started to notice how many of the men I saw were limping as they walked. I started to walk with an imaginary limp myself, because I thought a knee injury the likeliest. I flashed forward to the serious painkiller addiction that would follow. Next, there was the broken collarbone and the dislocated shoulder. By the time I got this far down the list, I was staring to bargain. 'Okay,' I thought, 'I'd settle for that.' Badly strained wrist, yes, that would be fine — as long as it was the non-writing hand. Can we make it the left wrist?

Usually, when I travel by train, I like to look out the window and drift off. I play Nick Drake songs and make notes in a black notebook.

This time, as the clock ticked down toward my A&E appointment, I went urgently through *Wrestliana*, searching for 200-year-old tips. What did William say about avoiding being thrown?

> ... the defendant should feel his feet firm upon the ground, slack his hold, and bear forward with his breast against the assailant's.

That seemed plain enough. What was his best tip for knowing what the other wrestler was about to do? He stressed:

> ... the judgement formed by feeling with the chest, and breast, what kind of assault is most likely to prove effective...

A little later on, William – after repeating tips about the chest – confirms this:

> ... it is the *feel*, and not the *sight*, which generally regulates the movements of a good wrestler, especially at the commencement of a contest...

I felt like I was listening to Yoda: 'The chest you must feel.'

When I began to lose attention, I thought about Asminder Asmindersson, hitting the grass of Ennerdale.

I re-read William's words more intensely.

Roger Robson met me at the station. I was carrying my suitcase down off the stairs from the opposite platform. Roger gave my upper arm a squeeze. 'Some muscles there,' he said. 'We'll see what use you make of them.' I could tell he was looking forward to this.

Jill collected us in the black Skoda.

After a quick trip back to the farm, to deal with a flood in the barn and to feed Gules the bull, and to eat a dinner I wasn't sure I should have, we drove to Currock House.

Every Wednesday evening, from October to April, the Carlisle Wrestling Club meets here. The coaches are Andrew Carlile, Alun Jones and Tom Harrington. There is a monthly points competition.

Through some gates at the side is The Small Room. It is slightly bigger than a tennis court. Blue mats a couple of inches thick, and thirty or so people sat watching the youngsters.

Most of those getting ready to take part were young farmers. A call had gone out on Facebook. This was the last chance to have a go, this year. They were shy, jokey. One of the boys wore a T-shirt that read, 'Forget farming, let's do carpentry – we'll get hammered and then I'll nail you.'

We warmed up. This meant running in a circle on the blue mats, then turning sideways and keeping going, then touching down left and right hands, left and right knees, and that was it. There weren't even any groin stretches.

'Warmed up?' Andrew asked.

Everyone harrumphed yes.

Along the far wall were school benches – the long, low, pine sort, with robot-nipples of rubber sticking up at both ends. Three in a row.

Andrew Carlile asked us to stand in a line, smallest at one end, and oh my God I hope I don't have to wrestle *him* at the other end.

I ended up in the middle, two female young farmers in orange polo shirts to my right.

We sat down, and Andrew and Alun showed us some basic clips.

Theory and practice. I was very aware how difficult I find having something physical demonstrated to me, and then actually *doing* it. For example, depressing the clutch when about to change gear whilst checking the rear-view mirror as you're going round a roundabout. I failed my driving test first time, and didn't retake it for fifteen years, because I knew I'd fail again.

The shortest pair of wrestlers, from the bottom end of the bench, were called up. Andrew asked the next wrestler to be ready to come on straight away. No messing.

Then, soon, far too soon, although I'd successfully delayed it for months, I was called on the mat.

I felt amazed horror: You're really doing this. You haven't wimped out.

But there was only about a second for that – before the handshake, before I was remembering right arm over, left arm under.

The two girls beside me had been beaten by a young man who was shorter than them. So I was against him.

We put our arms around one another. I'd seen it so many times, during the previous summer. I'd demonstrated the hold to Henry and George. But it still felt extraordinarily weird being in a tight hug with someone I'd never even spoken to. I could smell his hair, his ear wax.

I concentrated on my chest and his chest. Trust William, I thought. Young Farmer #1 vs. Not-Young Writer.

Chest.

Feel the chest.

Somehow, without really knowing how, I had won – and, crap, after a handshake and another handshake, I had to go again.

I was a bit disappointed – if I'd lost, I'd have been able to sit down and think about what I'd just done.

Also, I could have looked across at Roger, to see if he'd give me a smile or a nod.

I didn't celebrate in any way, not even inside. I don't think I was even relieved. It was a job of work. I'd finished it, which meant I had another job of work in view.

Figure 22. That is me on the left, bringing all my weight to bear.

Figure 23. I am taking this seriously. I hope you can
see that I am taking this very seriously.

Young Farmer #2 – Tom Dent – was ginger-haired and compact. He'd sat to my left because he was taller than me. I think we were about the same height, but after a moment's eyeballing, I'd let him be taller.

Chest.

I felt him. He was very solid but quite stiff. I must have felt mushy and middle-aged to him. I'd been at a desk when he'd been freeing lambs from barbed wire fences.

But I got my leg outside his, pushed, pushed again, and down we went – him beneath.

Two in a row.

This time I really wanted to look at Roger, but didn't. I could feel the attention of the room. It was warm, amused. With my bald head and tummy, I was a bit of a surprise.

Handshake and handshake.

No time.

Young Farmer #3 was taller than me – dark haired with wide shoulders.

I was aware of muscle and a will that, through that muscle, was more likely to move me this way, that, and down. This body had been to the gym.

Crunch, for the third time I hit the blue mat – hit first.

It felt a bit like being slapped with the flat of a spade, playfully. Whack, across the shoulder blades.

Handshake, and go and sit down, puffed.

The ginger-haired young farmer, Tom Dent, was sitting where he'd been before.

'I think I have to go there,' I said, and he had to slide to the left, down the ladder.

When two men say 'Hello,' one of them loses.

In one round, I'd moved two places up. I was no longer shoulder-to-shoulder with the lasses and the 14-year-olds.

It had been years since this much adrenalin had sluiced round me. I remembered being in the delivery room for the birth of Henry. Fuck, this is really happening. Fuck.

I was afraid of an adrenalin backlash. I might start shaking badly.

I had won.

At the time, it's just something that has happened, only later – when you walk away from it – does it become a victory.

I was afraid what little would be left of me, when the adrenalin tide went out.

The muscles across my chest, on the right, felt tight. Was this a heart attack?

A couple of minutes later a young farmer, taller, dislocated his shoulder and had to go off to hospital – much sympathy he got from his mates.

('That's unusual,' said Roger later, 'that hasn't happened all season.')

'I didn't see anything bad,' said Tom Dent.

'I'm not doing this again,' said the next but one along. He'd pranged a bollock. His jeans were too tight.

We were all embarrassed. We'd been closer to one another than to any other strange man (except, perhaps, when hugging drunkenly) – it is embarrassing. You do want to get away.

Your face has been rubbed against their shoulder. Anyone would blush, if only on the right cheek.

Afterwards, after I had won twice more, and lost twice more, I went and sat down next to Roger.

'You did well,' said Linda Scott, who I'd met during the summer.

Roger said nothing.

When I'd got my breath back, I got Andrew Carlile to show me what I'd done wrong. Mainly, I had put one leg across another, as if attempting a judo throw. Then we went through some basics. When we took hold, he felt like an iron climbing frame.

'A world champ,' Roger reminded me, from off the mats. 'He's the reigning 11st champion.'

That made him about two and a half stone lighter than me.

At one point Andrew twisted his spine to show me how he'd shift position to take advantage of me being off-balance. He turned slightly faster than he'd meant to, and his shoulder hit my shoulder like a punch.

I got a glimpse of what it would be like to be against him – the sheer muscular intensity.

No possible way I could compete.

Too weak, too slow.

I thought that was it – we'd shake hands and go home. I was disappointed that Roger hadn't said anything. But it turned out there was a bit of club business. Some cups were to be awarded. These were Points Trophies, for the best performances over the whole season.

At the Academy Shield in Bootle, I'd been worried that Roger was going to announce me in front of everyone as William Litt's ancestor, and then force me to wrestle.

Now that I had wrestled, I didn't have to worry about that second bit any more. And, after quickly asking if it was okay with me, Roger loudly announced to everyone in the room who I was and why I was there.

I was glad to hear William mentioned.

Then I got to shake the champions by the hand and give them their trophies.

★

I spoke to Alun Jones, ex-champion – winner of everything but the All-Weights World Championship.

He was bulky, matter of fact. I'd seen him lose at the Academy Shield.

'How'd you enjoy it?' he asked.

'I'm not sure,' I said.

'See how you feel tomorrow,' he said.

Tomorrow, when I woke up at Roger and Jill's, I felt okay, a little achey – and then I sneezed.

One or two muscles didn't scream.

I felt it in the chest. The muscles below my arms were torn in both directions. My upper back, particularly on the right, felt as if someone had tried to break a champagne bottle on it. My right calf was very sore, because I had pushed off from it more powerfully than for years. I'd taken a small chunk out of my left thumb. I had broken blood vessels streaking out of my armpits. There was a tiny scar on my cheek.

But I hadn't been badly injured. And I'd beaten a couple of younger, fitter men.

I was sure that, if I hadn't read *Wrestliana*, and learned from William, that they'd have humiliated me.

William had been a good coach.

Alun Jones had said, 'I had to give up.'

'What gave first?' I asked.

After a grunt, Alun Jones said, 'Everything.'

17

DOGFALL

When I came back to London and carried on writing William's life, going through it stage by stage, I began to feel him coming apart.

I read that in the 1820s, he was reputed to be 'wrecking his fortunes through attending wrestling and race meetings'.[*]

As merely attending wrestling matches is not expensive, this seems to mean that William was drinking a lot and losing bets.

In quite a few of his writings, especially those for the newspapers, William offers a wager. It seems to have been his default response when he disagreed with someone.

> And therefore, ye gentlemen of Keswick, we offer to your acceptance one bottle of Ginger beer, and one piece of the largest silver coin in this kingdom – for we will not bet gold – on the *heel*, not the *head* of this Patlander [William means an Irish person], against any light-footed native swain, not only of your own far-famed vale, but of the County which boasts your beauties as one of its most attractive embellishments.[†]

---

[*] *Cleator Moor, Notes, News and Views* [by "Denton"], 'Henry and Mary Again', *Cumberland Pacquet*, 21 March 1929.

[†] *Westmorland Gazette*, 7 August 1824. See also the *Carlisle Patriot*, 24 November 1824, 'I challenge him for a bottle of port, or porter, that Mr. R himself corroborates my assertion'.

From William's point of view, just having an argument didn't prove anything. You could carry on forever. But offering a wager invited a challenge. You think I'm wrong, show us your money. If no one was man enough to take up this challenge, the point was made.

Around this kind of behaviour, a whole economy was established of what nineteenth century men knew to be right and proper. Just as in the British legal system, abstract law-making had no place: precedent could only be set by adversarial trial.

William loved laying down the law. What I found throughout my research was that, in the moments he came off the page most livingly, William was often in the role of referee or judge – even before his retirement.

On the 10th of June, 1808, William had been in attendance at the Lamplugh Club – this was according to William Dickinson, in his collection of local stories called *Cumbriana*. It was an occasion for great mirth, following the pastor's sermon. The young ones from Harras Moor and Distington were kind of half bickering about their bull-dogs and terriers. Some of the young lions from Whillimer couldn't keep out of it. A fight was clearly in the offing.

> An' rare wark theer wad ha' been if Will Litt heddent sprang in amang them an' sed they suddent feyt, an' he whangt them aboot like as menny geslins: bit he duddent git them fairly partit till sum o' them gat gay bleuddy feasses. T' meast o' them was willin to giv way ta him, for they o' knew it was neah single handit job to cum crossways o' him, an' it o' settelt doon ageann.*

---

* William Dickinson, *Cumbriana, or Fragments of Cumbrian Life By the Compiler of the Glossary of Cumberland Words and Phrases*, Whittaker and Co, 1875. This is a rough translation: 'And there would have been a big old ding-dong if Will Litt hadn't waded in amongst them and told them not to fight, on top of this he whanged them around by their necks like a bunch of goslings: but he wasn't able to pull them apart before he'd bloodied up some of their ugly mushes. Most of them were more than willing to clear out of his way, because they knew you couldn't take him on solo, and so everyone simmered down again'.

Jump ahead to the late afternoon of the 29th of December 1830, and we find a middle-aged William attending one of the Lonsdale birthday dinners. His mirth is interrupted by the suggestion from the floor that, breaking with the accustomed way things have been done since his father helped set them up in 1807, the Chair would supervise proceedings rather than the Vice-Chair. Although it seems a minor point, William immediately bristled, in strong defence of tradition:

> MR. LITT and some others expressed themselves hostile to the proposed change. They could see no ground for the innovation, and they could not consent to any deviation from the original custom at the meeting, and under which it had risen to its present magnitude and importance.*

William and his backers were successful. '[F]eeling... was so warm in favour of the old custom' that the motion was withdrawn, and the subject dropped.

William had won, on both of these occasions. But it was something that was to become rarer the longer he went on.

If William was losing money, it was because he was backing losers. What is also strongly implied by the report is that – at a certain time – William began merely 'attending wrestling' rather than participating as an umpire.

I thought I had discovered why.

In 1824, a few months before the Lonsdale Dinner, William became involved in what Bill and Margaret have christened 'the "Athleticus" Controversy'.

---

* *Cumberland Pacquet*, 4 January 1831.

William had written an account of the wrestling at Carlisle on September the 14th for the *Cumberland Pacquet*. He took his usual combative tone, inviting challenges, but this time someone did decide to step up and gave him what for.

The correspondent, who called himself "Athleticus", wrote a letter taking issue with some of William's proposals for the efficient running of an open wrestling competition. He also publicly attacked William both as an inflator of his own reputation and as an incompetent umpire.

> [N]otwithstanding the vaunted achievements of the champion of Arlecdon Moor, there are those now living old enough to remember his being thrown in the Carlisle ring by very ordinary wrestlers, when in the zenith of his fame.

William replied to this with ferocious exactitude.

> I never wrestled but *twice* in the Carlisle ring, and never saw it when "in the zenith of my fame". The first time was in 1811, when, as I have stated elsewhere, I was thrown by Joseph Bird, who was surely no very *ordinary* wrestler. When taking hold, Bird got below my breast, and pinned my right arm close to the elbow, down to my side; and a person, *ignorant* enough surely! insisted, that because he found by pulling my left arm over his back, that he could make my fingers meet, I should either take hold, or be crossed out, I foolishly chose the first, thinking that I might perhaps better myself after. I was mistaken…*

(What an incredible memory William had, for the smallest physical details of a match that took place years before.)

---

*   The *Carlisle Patriot*, 20 November 1824.

"Athleticus" gave an unflattering description of William's demeanour in the ring.

> [W]hilst the wrestling was going on, it was observed in the crowd, that Mr. Litt was evidently displeased with some part of the proceedings; because he did not appear to take that interest in, or pay that attention to the sport which his situation as umpire demanded... he wandered about the ring with an apparent indifference, and seemed to pay less attention to the duties of his office, and altogether showed less anxiety about what was going on, than many of the spectators in the crowd evinced from the common motive of curiosity.*

William not paying attention to the wrestling, his great love? I felt desperation here, felt it in my chest.

Later on in his life, there came a greater modesty, and some accommodation with his diminished state. William's body had passed its climacteric. But in 1824, he seems to have been frustrated. The accounts of the day's wrestling at Carlisle suggest that the larger than usual crowd was drunk and disorderly. Behaviour at ringside was reprehensible; no hush fell.

I can understand William's annoyance. His own efforts, both in the ring and with his pen, had helped increase his beloved sport's popularity. Now, surrounded by the curious and the mocking, he saw the quality of the contest suffering.

If *I* were wrestling, he must have thought, these clot-heeds and carles† would have paid bloody attention.

Not possible – not any longer – he couldn't toss off his coat and join in.

---

* The *Carlisle Patriot*, 16 October 1824.
† A clot-heed is a 'blockhead' and a carle is a 'vulgar man'. Alexander Craig Gibson, *The Folk-Speech of Cumberland*, J.R. Smith, 1869.

Litt men, we suffer in the knees, our lower backs weaken. My father walks with a stick and has trouble making it off the sofa.

If there's any genetic carryover, from William to me, he too grimaced as his vertebrae popped and clicked.

How he must have ached in soul, for an impossible return to his triumphs, and ached in body, as the price of their achievement.

When Henry visits Mary, at the very end of the novel they share, we get – real or imagined – a sense of physical and psychic devastation.

> The pleasing visions of hope, and the presence of her whom he loved, – pleasures which could impart happiness even in anticipation – no longer animated a breast then in the arena of health, strength, and activity; but now – his prospects forever blasted by the final and lasting eclipse of that sun which gilded them, – emaciated in form, and altered external appearance, he seemed no longer the same [man] whose unrivalled prowess, and unshaken courage, made him the pride of his friends and the terror of his enemies.*

This is a description of my father, after my mother's death.

He was defeated by it.

For all of my family, the last two weeks were made worse by my mother's strength. She had ovarian cancer, that's what was killing her. She became a skeleton. But she was fit. She was a rambler, and said she wanted to be cremated in her hiking gear – boots, waterproof jacket.†
She'd walked coast to coast, from St Bees to Whitby. She'd done the Pembrokeshire Coast path. Her heart was strong, and it refused to stop beating. She fought against dying until each breath was a great struggle.

We were all exhausted, but especially my father.

The facts must be repeated.

---

* *Henry & Mary,* 1st ed., p. 368; 2nd ed., pp. 206–207.
† She was.

They had been married for over forty-five years.

She died on his birthday.

13 February 2012.

There's a piece of advice I often give my creative writing students.

'Write about what you don't want to write about.'

Because, chances are, if you start to confess something embarrassing or shameful or painful, it will be worth hearing, reading.

Remember pub-conversations: how, when you decide to tell people your considered opinion, they tend to look elsewhere (the men) or look intensely at you in a way that shows it's causing them effort (the women). But when you happen to say, 'I did this really awful thing...' or 'I'm so embarrassed...', they perk up and genuinely pay attention.

I sometimes say to my students, 'Picture yourself on a tube train. You're overhearing the piece of writing you've just given me. Imagine it's no longer words on a page but a woman whispering audibly to another woman. Would you stay on a stop beyond your stop, in order to hear the end of what she's saying? If she's giving her opinions on this or that, probably not; if she's slyly owning up to having slept with a friend's boyfriend, probably; if she's being forced to confess something weird and appalling she did involving an octopus and a Porsche, you'll be hoping you're on the Circle Line.'

It is hard to take your own advice, to become your own student.

I know what I don't want to write about. I don't want to write about being a loser.

Once, when the term was fashionable – that is, the years after Tarantino's *Pulp Fiction* – I was often called a 'cult writer'.

I objected to this. A true cult writer, I said, was one whose books had – at some stage – all gone out of print, been ignored. My books, I used to say, hadn't had such a tough time. *Adventures in Capitalism* was reviewed everywhere. *Corpsing* got into the bestseller lists. I'd got half a dozen foreign publishers and had sold the film rights. My books were in the shops, and so I couldn't be a cult writer.

Well, now, I'm a cult writer.

I've been one since about 2011, which is when I was dropped by my publisher. My books no longer sold enough for my publisher – under great financial pressure – to continue to put them out. My editor said he wanted to keep supporting me, but couldn't. The phrase *bean-counters* was not used, but it was around and about.

After this, I wrote three novels. I thought they were some of my best writing. None of them got published. My other books went out of print. My mother died. My father's health got worse. I left my old agent and then my new agent left me. I wrote a comic about two dead boys, and – after a year – the comic was cancelled.

I began asking myself a very basic question: Why do I need to write? Why do I need to put myself through this?

Perhaps because it was an addiction. I'd sat at the desk so long, for so many words, that I didn't feel comfortable, didn't really feel I existed, anywhere else. Perhaps because my creative writing teaching job depended upon continuing to produce at least two books every five years – and upon my job depended my ability to pay my way. Perhaps because I was deluded enough to believe a comeback was always possible.

Boxers, not wrestlers, are the sportsmen famous for misguided come-backs. Like Mohammed Ali's last-but-one fight in 1980. And Joe Frazier's, aged 38-years-old. But I have always thought there was a deep misunderstanding here, by the sneerers. What motivates an ageing boxer's hopeless comeback is exactly what, when they were young, enabled their greatest victory. Without the one, there would never have been the other. To understand it properly, you have to reverse time and make what happens later the cause: The true sign of a future champion is that, one day, they will make a hopeless comeback.

I was not going to stop writing. I was foolish enough to believe – perhaps because I'm like a boxer – that I could go beyond where I'd already gone.

After the 'Athleticus' controversy, William seems gradually to have retired from umpiring.

And it was when William lost his place at the centre of the action that he began to get into trouble. Perhaps he was too easy to provoke into a foolish assertion, and an unconsidered wager to prove it. Local pride would always have made him back a Cumbrian contestant against one from Westmorland – even when his lad was clearly the weaker of the two.

Yet in *Wrestliana*, William had made a great distinction between wrestling and boxing. 'Professed pugilism is gambling,' he wrote.[*] The interest of boxing to many attendees is 'the sum they are to gain or lose by the event'.[†] More awful still, each boxer was 'the hireling of the gambling opinion' and 'degrades himself to the condition of the game-cock, the race-horse'.[‡]

By contrast, 'Wrestling has never yet (at least in this county) become a subject of gambling speculation. The trifles sported by the spectators are never an object of much consideration'.[§]

---

[*]   *Wrestliana*, 1st ed., p. 39; 2nd ed., p. 24.
[†]   Ibid., p. 22.
[‡]   Ibid., p. 23.
[§]   Ibid., p. 28.

This distinction holds true today. It's no accident that the biggest boxing matches take place in Las Vegas whereas the most important wrestling occurs at the Olympics.

Boxing matches, as William presented them, originated in a bet. 'I will back my man against yours,' says the owner, just as the previous week he'd backed his ratter and the week before that, his grey mare. Wrestling matches, as part of county fairs, were completely different. They were a tournament, not just a contest. The contestants entered freely, weren't professionals, and could walk away uninjured even should they lose.

But, it seems, that William as a spectator was losing more than he ever did as a participant. This isn't the way it usually goes.

During the 2014 Brazil World Cup, a lot of which I watched on TV with Henry and George, I became very aware that most of the ads, when not for lager and junk food, were for in-game betting. The disembodied mockney head of a digital Ray Winstone incessantly manifested itself, cajoling us the viewers – as if we were his mates – oi!!! – to g'wan and gert more involved in the game, to gain from it, by putting a couple of quid on which player would be next to score.

Can we do that, Dad? No. But can we do that? No. But why can't we do that?

A more recent ad features a good-looking chauffeur, who often ferries sportsmen from hotel to venue, telling the viewer that this driving bit isn't when he gets closest to sport, no, that's when he's down his local greasy spoon, checking odds on his mobile (like you can do).

To gamble on the result of any sport is to tie your own fate, in a minor way, to that of the team or person you're betting on. If you don't bet, and your guy or your side loses, you are disappointed but that's it; if you backed them, then when *they* lose you, too, become a loser.

This might seem so obvious as not to need stating – but the intimacy of sportsman and sport's fan, through gambling, which the betting companies spend such vast amounts of money establishing, is false.* There's an absolute difference in kind between what a boxer loses by losing a fight and what someone who's had a punt on that fight loses. This is true even if both the boxer and the punter lose their house and then their family. The punter, whatever happens, has only lost money – and the loss of the money has caused his other losses; the boxer, though, as well as losing whatever money he laid on himself, has lost his ability to pursue his vocation, and had lost all or part of his livelihood, has lost his status within the world he inhabits, his backers, his motor functions.

The retired sportsman who opens a pub and loses all his money – it's a cliché. William, in his defence, was there towards this cliché's very start. And he did it on a grander scale – it wasn't just a pub, it was a brewery; it wasn't just a few pounds, he blew £3,000 in around a year on his bad investment.

To realize the size of this achievement, you probably need to know something of the drinking scene in Whitehaven, circa 1824.

Just when I needed to find out about this, I was – completely by chance – introduced to an expert. His name is Dr James Kneale, and he works in the Department of Geography at UCL. He's a psychogeographer of pubs. I met him because a friend of mine invited us both to be part of a public event at Stanford's Bookshop, on Longacre, near Covent Garden. Afterwards, we all shared a pint and a pizza in the nearby Nags Head.

When I heard what James did, I began to ask him questions about density of pubs. Whitehaven, it seemed, at one hundred people per pub

---

* Similarly, sport has nothing whatsoever to do with sweet fizzy drinks, despite the fact that sport has everything to do with sweet fizzy drinks.

(1 ppp) was a stupendously boozy place. Ports usually are. James said he had some figures he could let me see.

He did.

Whitehaven didn't have the highest ever recorded people per pub, but it was – James said – 'still looking pretty sozzled'. The whole of London, in 1856, had 156 ppp, and the City of London had 72 ppp. But these figures, unlike the one for Whitehaven, only counted people over 15-years-old. James concluded by saying, 'Whitehaven may not have the record, but it's pretty close'.*

William does seem to have been able to organize a piss up in a brewery, but it was a piss up he lost money on.

It is hard to work out the exact chronology of William's business failures. All the accounts agree: He invested his money in a large brewery. 'A collapse, and loss of nearly all the capital employed, followed in little more than twelve months.' (Remember the word *collapse*.)

More intimate with the events, and more sympathetically perceptive, the Memoirist says,

> He received a fair share of patronage; but, as he refused nobody who thought proper to favor him with an order, it was not always of the most profitable kind. Suffice it to say, that his book debts soon became very heavy; and he discovered that it was certainly not as a manufacturer of ale and porter he was destined to make a fortune. He therefore abandoned the business altogether, having lost nearly the whole of his investment in little more than a twelvemonth, and returned once again to the more congenial occupations of the plough and the pen, with an occasional bout in the wrestling ring.†

---

* James Kneale, private communication, 30 April 2015.
† Ibid., pp. viii–ix.

I believe William had a mania to be liked. If he had a fatal flaw, this was it. He couldn't, not for one moment, stand to see a man think the less of him. And this is a terrible basis upon which to do business.*

William the brewer suffered from being the same man as William the ex-wrestler. Propping up the bar is a very different thing to standing behind it, serving and taking money.

His business failing, William had no purpose. A quieter life beckoned. One, it seems, of waiting in vain for Lord Lonsdale to reward his loyalty – to notice the fawning and flattering.

The Memoirist describes William's life at this time, and also explains why William – unlike Wordsworth – was passed over. It is a sad paragraph, that covers years of wasted hours:

> He lived for the most part at Hensingham, holding some parochial offices, and expecting some long-promised consideration at the hands of the party always paramount in Whitehaven [i.e., Lonsdale], and to which he had rendered important services.†

In 20 June 1826, William is to be found on a list now among the Lowther Papers of 'them as constables'. (The list notes his authorship of *Wrestliana*, further down another constable is parsed as 'a large man'.) By 1831, as well as being 'victualler of the King's Arms, Hensingham', he was 'acting overseer and collector of king's taxes'.‡

The Memoirist speaks up for William, but at the same time dooming him:

---

* The very definition of 'it's just business' being – I may like you, but I'm still going to screw you and, conversely, I may hate your guts, but I'm still going to make you rich.

† 'Memoir of the Author', *Henry & Mary*, 2nd ed., p. x.

‡ For *his* loyalty, Wordsworth had by this time been made very comfortably off by Lonsdale's rewards. He had been put in charge of distributing stamps for both Cumberland and Westmorland.

He was not, however, of the stuff that sycophants and successful place-hunters are made, and certainly should not have hoped, if he did hope, anything from their gratitude. Do we not all know that it is on what Thackeray calls the genus "muff,"* as witness not only Whitehaven but everywhere else, that noblemen mostly shower their favors and their honours? And nobody will venture to say that William Litt was of this class. It is, however, too long a story to enter upon here, and there can come little good of raking up the ashes of things long forgotten. Pass on to the end.†

To Canada.

---

* Webster's *Dictionary* gives, 'A stupid fellow; a poor-spirited person. [Colloq.] "A *muff* of a curate." *Thackeray*.'
† 'Memoir of the Author', *Henry & Mary*, 2nd ed., p. x.

18

IMMIGRANT

I boarded a flight to Montréal on April the 22nd, 2016.

I had been reading and writing about William for eighteen months – and all that time, I'd known I would have to go and see where he lived the final eighteen years of his life.

Setting off, I still didn't have any idea why William chose Canada, rather than America or South America, as his new home. My best guess was that he knew people there, or thought it was the place he'd make most money.

Even though I'd written a whole book of short stories about a made-up Canadian band called *okay*, I'd never been to Canada before.

The most important part of my trip would be paying a visit to where William was buried. I hoped to find his grave, to pay my respects.

But for months and months, I had completely failed to locate the churchyard where William lay – dozens of times I had looked in records online; nothing. I knew the name of the church. It was called Saint-Stephen's. And there were several Saint-Stephen's churches in Montréal, but none of them near to where William died, in the Parish of Saint-Anne, on Isle Jesus.

With the date of my flight only a couple of days away, I became manic. The whole trip could be pointless. I sent out twenty emails to archivists, realtors, local history groups – and one of the people I contacted put me in touch with Vicki Onufriu.

Vicki, who grew up and went to High School in Laval ('Happy memories?' 'No.') is a young historian who has been studying the Protestant families who attended the churches of that region. She says she had been stuck in history as a spreadsheet – births, marriages, deaths in long columns. When I emailed her copies of William's 'Letters on Canada', it was – for her – a voice from a whole scattered cemetery of previously silent graves.

She was delighted to be in touch.

She had been trying to track down descendants of the people buried in those graves, but had only ever seen William's name written as 'Lett'.

We agreed to meet the Monday after I arrived in Quebec, and together to visit the parish of Saint-Martin, where William had been buried.

Vicki said she knew the exact place.

As the plane banked over Montréal, I strained my neck to look out the window. How hilly was it? How tall was Mount Royal? What would William have seen when he arrived? What would he have felt?

I have immigrated only once. You've already heard a little about it. On the 15th of April 1990, I left England (after leaving Scotland) and moved to the Czechoslovak Socialist Republic, which changed its name, a few days later, to the Czech and Slovak Federative Republic.

I wasn't simply going there to work: England disgusted me, I wanted as little to do with it as possible. Margaret Thatcher was about to begin her tenth year as Prime Minister.[*] The Poll Tax, which had

---

[*] On 4 May 1990.

been introduced in Scotland on 1 April 1989, was coming to England the same silly date, one year later. (We joked, the English teachers that I met in my first months, that we were Poll Tax exiles. It was cheaper to buy a coach ticket to Prague than pay up.)

When I set out for Prague, I thought I would never live in England again. I had left once already, when I went to live in Glasgow. What was England to me? England was Oxford, and Oxford was smugness, inwardness. I wanted to be a writer, how could I write in England? I was so full of hatred for the whole disgusting enterprise zone it was becoming that I wanted to be anywhere else.

I was going to an old city, an established place; William arrived in a country that wasn't new but that was still essentially defining itself. Would Canada become English- or French-speaking? Protestant or Catholic? Loyal to the Crown of England or to whomever was ruling France or, even, independent of all outside influences?

By the time he died, William had seen two parts of a country join into one, as Upper and Lower Canada unified, in 1848; I witnessed the splitting of the two parts of Czechoslovakia, as the Czech Republic and the Slovak Republic fairly amicably separated on 31 December 1992.

Absurdly, and fittingly, I arrived in one country,[*] lived in another[†] and left a third.[‡]

All of this, my mini-exile, is nothing. When William sailed for Canada, he was 46-years-old and had seven surviving children. Hannah had died, aged five months, in 1828. The youngest of them, also called Hannah, was a baby when he said goodbye to her. His oldest child, William Jnr, was 14-years-old.

---

[*]   The Czechoslovak Socialist Republic.
[†]   The Czech and Slovak Federative Republic.
[‡]   The Czech Republic.

The family explanation for William's departure, passed on by my father, was that he'd 'fallen out with the local lord'.

A far more extreme reason is given in *Wrestling and Wrestlers*. It is 'banishment'.[*] The authors actually say 'forced banishment', but what banishment isn't forced? The emphasis is telling, though; it suggests physical threats.

Depending upon how well-informed these authors were, this suggests that some time, early in 1832, Lord Lonsdale or his underlings sent William a clear message: *Clear off, and don't come back! Or else...*

William may have left in a hurry, but he did not go secretly. There was no midnight flit.

Bill Hartley reads a lot into the scene of William's departure. 'His wife's parents were living in the Olde Castle Hotel, and the morning he went away he knocked them up to say "Goodbye."'[†]

Bill reckons that William, far closer in age to his mother-in-law than to his wife, was also far closer to her full stop. Perhaps she was the woman he would miss most, in his new land.

The account, given by Mrs Cubby, William's granddaughter,[‡] in an interview reprinted in the *Cumberland Pacquet* in 1929, is the most kindly disposed towards William. She said he had 'decided to go abroad', rather than been forced. He did not desert his family, who were then living in Main Street, Hensingham. Instead, 'he went abroad with the intention of founding a private school, and left his family well provided for'.[§]

The Memoirist is sympathetic, but suggests it wasn't a free decision. William was 'induced' to emigrate by the 'gradually-increasing

---

[*]   *Wrestling and Wrestlers: Biographical Sketches of Celebrated Athletes of the Northern Ring*, Wordsworth Press, 1893, p. 70.
[†]   *Cleator Moor Notes, News, and Views* [By "Denton".] 'Henry and Mary Again', *Cumberland Pacquet*, 21 March 1929.
[‡]   She was Nanny Litt's daughter.
[§]   *Cleator Moor Notes, News, and Views* [By "Denton".] 'Henry and Mary Again', *Cumberland Pacquet*, 21 March 1929.

embarrassment of [his] circumstances, and the difficulties that every-where seemed to hem him in at home…'*

More urgent still, a Whitehaven native recalled years later, that William left 'on some differences arising between him and the overseers of Hensingham, by whom he was employed'.† This is getting closer to falling out with the local lord.

I decided William jumped rather than be pushed, perhaps pushed very hard – under a cart.

The first confirmation that William had left comes in the form of a minor disgrace. On 7 May 1832, a small notice in the *Cumberland Pacquet*, chronicler of so many of William's triumphs, announced that he had been 'replaced as Assistant Overseer' after he had 'absented himself from this situation'. No further monies were to be paid to him.

He was a free man.

To sail the Atlantic at that time was to risk your life. That time, for William, as far as I could tell, was March 1832.

William's advice to those about to cross the Atlantic – given in his 'Letters on Canada' – suggests he was well prepared, and didn't find it an extreme experience.‡

Shop around for a ship, he wrote.

---

* 'Memoir of the Author', *Henry & Mary*, 2nd ed., p. x.
† *Whitehaven Free Press*, 'Random Recollections and Stray Passages in the Life of a Native of Whitehaven, containing Remembrances about Whitehaven some 60 to 70 years ago. Commenced 6th May, 1857, and brought to a close, 8th August 1869.'
‡ The Letters appeared in the *Cumberland Pacquet* eight long years later.

Common prudence will teach any person of ordinary understanding, that if he has the choice of two or more vessels, a little inquiry will readily determine his selection…

Pack sensibly.

As for the provisions, his own taste and circumstances will evidently be his best guide…

Food:

In general, a couple of hams, with a sufficiency of potatoes and biscuit; some flour, oatmeal, eggs, sugar, and tea – if the latter be principally herbs he will find the beverage less sickly; and whatever trifling dainties he may fancy will assist in mitigating the nausea of the sea-sickness, or refreshing him after it…

The one cautionary note I found, which suggests William himself made a misstep, came at the end of his notes for travellers.

During the voyage, any unnecessary familiarity with the seamen beyond common civility, will sometimes subject him to liberties and references he had better avoid.*

I pictured a scene on deck – 'Think you're a bit of a fighter, do you?' – the impoverished, ex-wrestler William, being mocked by sarcastic tars; in the worst version, one of them has just decked him.

He was already a long way from home.

*

---

* All travel advice comes from Letter No. 2, dated 'Island of Montreal, June 2nd, 1840'.

Like Timbuktoo, Canada was something a byword for out-of-the-wayness. Thomas De Quincey, a genius of hyperbole, wrote of 'the farthest depths of Canada', where he imagined 'many a young innocent girl... looking now with fear to the dark recesses of the infinite forest' and reading Shakespeare, 'the infinite poet'.*

When I first heard that William spent his last years – the mid-1800s – in Canada, I imagined that he was moving *away* from things; that he would almost immediately have found himself sat in a small log cabin, reading Shakespeare, watching the seasons turn: I was quite wrong.

At the funky-looking Pointe-à-Callière Museum in Montréal, they have a theatre where a *son et lumière* show is projected half hourly down onto an excavation of some of the city's earliest buildings.

I paid a visit.

The digits of the years were projected for the small audience. They raced downwards, through the glacial periods, and then upwards through the time of the Native Canadians. With the arrival of the French, the dates began to slow. There was more of a written historical record. Certain events were dramatized. But they were mostly the signing of treaties.

When 1832 came up – the year of William's arrival – the show reached its high point.

Bright red and orange flames were projected onto the stones. The soundtrack played angry patriotic shouts.

Québec was entering its most unstable, violent era.

I enjoyed it. This was the stuff of my research, being brought to digital life.

---

* Thomas De Quincey, *Recollections of the Lakes and the Lake Poets*, Penguin, 1980, p. 144.

Necessary background: In 1832, Canada was not yet a single country but, as I mentioned earlier, was divided into Haut-Canada and Bas-Canada – Upper and Lower. This, confusingly, didn't mean north and south. Upper meant further up the St Lawrence River, so mainly Westward; that is, the area above America's Great Lakes. Upper Canada was wilder, more dominated (in terms of population, if not political power) by the French-speaking *Canadiens*. Lower Canada, where William was headed, was a lot more developed.

Just outside the Pointe-à-Callière Museum was the Laval Canal, already completed by the time William arrived.

When the writer de Tocqueville saw the farms and fields along the banks of the St Lawrence river, they reminded him of the French countryside. 'All trace of wilderness is vanished.'[*]

That didn't mean it wasn't dangerous.

By the time William's ship docked, the British authorities in the Canadas had been working for several months to prevent the arrival of cholera.

Unless his captain was sneaky enough to avoid being delayed, William made landfall thirty miles east of Québec City, on Grosse-Île. Here, he entered quarantine – mixing on the small, hilly island with passengers from other boats.

Their voyage across the Atlantic, depending on winds, would have taken six to nine weeks. Passengers who had travelled in steerage were always exhausted, and – if their ship had been delayed beyond the usual – might be starving.[†] Quarantine regulations required new

[*] *Tocqueville Au Bas-Canada*, edited by Jacques Vallee, Les Éditions du Jour, 1973, p. 88.
[†] George Bilson, *A Darkened House: Cholera in Nineteenth-Century Canada*, University of Toronto Press, 1980, p. 7. An extraordinary book.

arrivals be examined for signs of cholera; vomiting, diarrhoea. They then had to clean themselves and their baggage, and wait several days before continuing upriver.

One visitor, a couple of years earlier, wrote of her first sight of Montréal, 'all the buildings are roofed with Tin, which causes it to glitter in the Sun, like a City of Silver'.* Beneath these light-effects, the walls were grey stone. The tallest building, the Roman Catholic Church, 'rises with an air of grandeur, to a height which appears almost gigantic'.

Closer in, her positive impression might have changed. Here was a city perfect for the spread for water-borne diseases. Open sewers ran alongside roads and paths; garbage lay in piles.†

Flooding was frequent.

Despite the quarantine, the 9th of June 1832 saw Montréal's first recorded death from cholera. Ahead of this, there had been official denials; confirmation of the worst was terrifying. A French-language newspaper, the *Canadian Courant*, reported that 'a panic of an almost indescribable nature [took] hold of the whole body of citizens and [...] deprived them of presence of mind to an extent exceeding anything of a similar nature which had ever been witnessed in Montréal'.‡

The paper also passed on a recipe from 'a friend in Edinburgh – pour out one bottle best brandy onto a quarter pound of rhubarb, place over a slow fire for ten hours, then add 120 drops of spirit of lavender and laudanum'.

Newly arrived immigrants, such as William, were the object of deep suspicion. Food became scarce because the farmers were too afraid to

* Francis Ramsay Simpson's diary, from 1830, quoted in *the small details of LIFE: 20 diaries by women in Canada, 1830–1996*, edited by Kathryn Carter, University of Toronto Press, 2002, p. 46,

† Details from Paul-André Linteau, translated by Peter McCambridge, *The History of Montréal: The Story of a Great North American City*, Baraka Books, 2013, p. 84.

‡ George Bilson, *A Darkened House: Cholera in Nineteenth-Century Canada*, University of Toronto Press, 1980, p. 24.

come to market. Many people, in fear, fled the city – taking cholera with them.

I could not discover how just-off-the-ship William made his way through this, and whether his early days in Canada involved friends and somewhere to stay, or, instead, confusion and sleeping rough and hunger.

Of course, I was frustrated not to have any private letters from William, to give me details. In one of his public 'Letters on Canada' he mentioned 'the risk every person must incur who leaves the place of his nativity to sojourn in a far distant land'. This sounded quite casual. The risk wasn't a sweating, screaming death.* So perhaps William did whisk past it all, riding a borrowed horse out into the countryside, but equally, perhaps – unemployed – he helped to hurriedly bury the dead, without ceremony.

Whatever happened, he must – at least to begin with – have regretted his decision to decamp to this dangerous, chaotic land.

Deaths from cholera were soon occurring so often that the churches stopped ringing their bells, so as not to increase despondency. On the 17th of June, one hundred died; on the 19th, one hundred and forty-nine. But that day was the peak. By the time it was over, around 3,400 would have lost their lives – almost one in seven of Montréal's inhabitants.

More were coming to replace them, however. 1832 was the busiest year yet for emigration. 66,339 made their way to the North American colonies from the United Kingdom. As compared to 28,808 the following year. Only one other year, 1847, had a higher number.†

---

* Letter No. 4. William's use of 'sojourn' is telling. Eight years after arriving, he was implicitly describing his stay as temporary.
† http://www.theshipslist.com/Forms/EmigFromUK1815_1870.shtml, retrieved 17 December 2015, 13:28.

From Ireland particularly, thousands *were* sailing. Many of those struggling to survive around William had not been there much longer than he had. One fifth of the population of Montréal had arrived, from abroad, within the previous five years. The majority of the city – already the largest in Canada – was British in origin. But the different nations had formed their own ghettos. In the West were the Scots and English; South West, the Irish; and the *Canadiens*, French-speaking, held on to the East.[*]

The surrounding countryside was French – French-speaking, Catholic, and extremely angry about seeing their country stolen from them by immigrants. Among the *Canadiens* was where William would end up living, but not immediately.

The 'next news' of him 'came from Hull, near Ottawa – where he stated that he had decided to make Canada his destination'.[†] This is interesting as it suggests he might have intended moving on to America, but took a look around Canada, liked what he saw and decided to stay. It also may be plain wrong; there's no other mention of William travelling as far as Ottawa. All other records have him sticking in Montréal.

The writers of *Wrestling and Wrestlers* suggested his plans when he left Whitehaven were firm. William set off intending to 'retrieve his broken fortunes in taking the cutting of canals, and works of a like description'.[‡]

The Memoirist agreed that he hoped to join in with this industrial boom. What job middle-aged William thought he might do is unclear. He had no qualifications as a hydraulic engineer, and no aptitude as a business manager. Did he really want to engage in extremely hard manual labour? Probably he thought he would find something in a growing city. He was mistaken.

---

[*] Details from Paul-André Linteau, trans. Peter McCambridge, *The History of Montréal: The Story of a Great North American City*, Baraka Books, 2013, p. 73.

[†] *Cleator Moor Notes, News, and Views* [By "Denton".] 'Henry and Mary Again', *Cumberland Pacquet*, 21 March 1929.

[‡] *Wrestling and Wrestlers: Biographical Sketches of Celebrated Athletes of the Northern Ring*, Wordsworth Press, 1893, p. 69.

In 1825, the rapids on the St Lawrence river – an awesome sight when I visited them, a whole horizon of white water – had been bypassed by the construction of the Laval shipping canal. But if William was hoping to join in a major new building project, he had – with typical bad timing – arrived in between one boom and the next. It was only in 1843 that work began on enlarging the canal.

Very bluntly, the account of his life in *Wrestling and Wrestlers* has it that, 'A breakdown again occurred'.[*]

What kind of breakdown could this have been? One of those nineteenth century episodes people wrote about in their diaries, 'William has had a complete break down in health?' Or was this a euphemism for an alcoholic relapse?

After convalescing, for a time – how long is unclear – William tried journalism. The Memoirist says, 'he fell back again, as in England, on his literary abilities. Writing for the press, however, is a still more precarious source of income in Canada than at home...'[†]

Back home, I'd spent several days at the British Library, scrolling through contemporary issues of the *Montreal Gazette*, looking for the initials 'W.L.', before I came across this sentence in an authoritative reference work on the history of publishing in Canada. It said, 'the practice of the time was not to sign articles, or to sign with only a pseudonym...'[‡]

After reading that, I'd given up looking for William's contributions. It was most likely impossible that I would ever find anything William wrote for the Canadian press. Probably he wrote very little. Probably, most of the little he wrote wasn't wanted.

---

[*] *Wrestling and Wrestlers: Biographical Sketches of Celebrated Athletes of the Northern Ring; to which is Added Notes on Bull and Badger Baiting*, Wordsworth Press, Carlisle, 1893, p. 69.

[†] 'Memoir of the Author', *Henry & Mary*, 2nd ed., p. x.

[‡] *History of the Book in Canada: Beginnings to 1840*, Volume I, edited by Patricia Lockhart Fleming, Gilles Gallichan, Yvan Lamonde, University of Toronto Press, 2004, p. 237.

Wrestling and Wrestlers said of William's attempt to live by journalism, 'This failing, he became a teacher'.[*]

When I moved to Prague, with no qualifications beyond an English Degree (2.1), it was to be a teacher. I had got a job 'doing TEFL' — that's 'Teaching of English as a Foreign Language'. In those days of the Wild East, totally unqualified teachers were welcome; now, you would need to invest several thousand pounds in training yourself before you'll be employed.

My employer was Milena Kelly – a remarkable and extremely energetic woman. (In her forties, she had a baby and was back at work three days later.) She had gone into exile after 1968, grown up in America, and had returned to Prague around the time of the revolution. A few weeks after this, Milena went on Czechoslovak television to talk about her ambition: to start the country's first private language school. In the days after her appearance, she received over five hundred letters from people desperate to learn English. These ultra-keen bods became the first cohort of Angličtina Express students. (You might translate Angličtina Express as 'English for the Impatient'.)

I began by teaching four hour-long classes of them, one after another, at the Archbiskupské gymnázium on Namesti Míru (Peace Square). And I did, I think, what any unqualified teacher does – I tried to make my students love me, so they wouldn't rebel and kill me.

My ethos was simple: if they are laughing, it probably means they've understood the joke. I may not have a teaching qualification, I thought, but I *have* watched *Good Morning, Vietnam*. I treated the first couple of classes as a way of trying out material – they were the slightly dour, straight-from-work people. The seven o'clock lot, however, had often

---

[*]   Ibid., p. 69.

spent a brief while in the pub before arriving. They were a very good crowd. I became friends with several of them, and went out with the niece of one of them, Magdalena.

William also became a teacher – what kind?

His friend, William 'Leander' Todd, had set up a private school in Church Street, Whitehaven, in the Autumn of 1825. His advertisements in the *Cumberland Pacquet* show the kind of curriculum William, with his similar education, might have offered his students.

> [H]e purposes teaching the English, Latin, and Greek, Languages, grammatically; Book-keeping, Geography, the Use of the Globes, Arithmetic, and the various Branches of Mathematics.[*]

A couple of years later, he noted that he also taught 'the Principles of Composition, Versification, the Classics, &c'.[†] It is hard to imagine that, on a fine day, William didn't take his pupils outside and get them wrestling.

After a few unsettled years, the Memoirist says, 'a more certain and easier mode of life was offered to [William] in the profession of a teacher, which he accepted'.[‡]

To me, it seemed likely that he had a guarantee of work from one of the richer Protestant families on the northern coast of Isle Jesus, about fifteen miles from Montréal. Despite spending several days looking at state records, I couldn't find any mention of him owning

---

[*]   *Cumberland Pacquet*, 6 September 1825.
[†]   *Cumberland Pacquet* and Ware's *Whitehaven Advertiser*, Tuesday, 24 June 1828.
[‡]   'Memoir of the Author', *Henry & Mary*, 2nd ed., p. x.

a house there, or leaving property of any sort. I imagined him as a lodger, hopefully beloved.

William eventually came to live in the quiet, waterside Saint-Rose parish on Ile Jesus. It was a divided place. The Protestant and Catholic communities lived with as great a separation as they could manage. They spoke different languages, attended different churches. They even had different diets – the Anglophones cultivated potatoes, the Francophones grew wheat and said spuds were only fit for pigs. Of course, their children were not educated together.

William may have taught in a schoolhouse, but with fewer than a hundred adult Britons living on the whole island, his classes must always have been very small. I pictured him as more a private tutor than a headmaster.

This was the last of William's identities. Plough-boy, wrestler, writer, smuggler, husbandman, umpire, brewer – he had passed through all of them. When he died, he was set down in the parish register as 'William Lett, schoolmaster of the Parish of St Rose, County of Terrebonne & District of Montreal'.*

William did not speak well of his new occupation. Teachers in Canada, he said, 'are in no danger of starving; – and when they have acquired some knowledge of the country must just do the best they can, for I do not remember any schoolmaster who personified that imaginary rhodomontade of Thompson's "Delightful task, &c." which is very fine in every thing but *the realisation*'.†

What William was alluding to here were the lines in James Thompson's 1782 poem 'Spring' – a poem William probably had to learn by heart when himself a schoolboy:

---

* Ancestry-Quebec Vital Registers-Records & Church Register [Droin Collection] 1621–1967; Burial-Laval, Anglican Saint Vincent de Paul, Reg. [Photo Au Graffe De Montreal 1051–1052].

† Letter No. 3.

243

Delightful task! to rear the tender thought,
To teach the young idea how to shoot,
To pour the fresh instruction o'er the mind,
To breathe the enlivening spirit, and to fix
The generous purpose in the glowing breast.[*]

In other words, William meant, this is the sentimental view. For most teachers, *the realization* is less soft-focus.

I teach.

I can't support myself, as I used to, just by writing books.

I teach creative writing.

Like sports punditry, any kind of teaching is taken as a byword for failure. 'He who can, does. He who cannot, teaches'.[†]

But of all subjects, creative writing is the one that comes in for the hardest time. A regular arts news story is 'Can creative writing be taught?'

In the combative spirit of William, I recently came up with what I thought was a good answer for this. I was being interviewed and was feeling feisty.[‡]

I would like to end this forever. I invite anyone who doesn't believe creative writing can be taught to read the work of three creative writing students from the Birkbeck MA. First, to read the work they submit when they apply, and then to read those same students' final

---

[*]   James Thompson, *The Seasons*, 'Spring', T. Hurst, 1802, p. 44, lines 1149–1153.

[†]   George Bernard Shaw, 'Maxims for Revolutionists: Education', *Man and Superman*, Constable, 1903, p. 30.

[‡]   http://onlinewritingtips.com/2015/11/13/author-interview-toby-litt/, retrieved 22 January 2016, 10:45.

dissertations. You will see what attending a creative writing MA has taught them. You will find their work has got a lot better. If you want to, you can also compare their progress, over the same period, to the writing of someone who was accepted onto the MA but wasn't able to take up their place. This is a serious, open invitation.

'Creative writing' is a university subject; it's not the same as 'writing', although – if the teaching is honest – there should be a large overlap, and it's certainly not the same as 'great writing'.

Great writing cannot be taught. The only way this would be possible is if one were able to encourage a student to write in a particular way, then time-travel say a hundred years into the future, to see whether people had come to believe that student was a great writer.

We can't go forwards in time, but we can go back. *Henry & Mary* is about as self-tutored a novel as you could find. As my Dad said, it's 'a bit hard going'. But most of the fiction written most of the time by most wannabe writers is hard going. Most writing, unsurprisingly, is bad.

At my most negative, in thinking about what I teach, I believe that creative writing courses in the last forty years have merely raised the level of mediocrity.

At the beginning of each term, I tell my students two things: *There are no short cuts* and *There is no wasted effort.*

I was in the pub recently, with a group of students, and one of them took me up on *There are no short cuts.*

'But isn't doing a creative writing course a short cut?' he asked.

For a moment, I was stumped. Then I realized I did have an answer. There really aren't any short cuts. You have to do your bad writing (expelling the black bile, as I like to describe it). You have to go through every bit of being clumsy and clunky that you have to go through – and you have to do that on your own time. You have to make bespoke mistakes. No one else, no teacher, can do this for you.

However, studying creative writing can speed up your progress. Partly because you're writing a lot more. Partly because you're writing for a group of committed, exacting readers. And partly because you'll have a teacher to help you stop loving yourself quite so much.

I find the best students the hardest to teach. 'Keep going,' I end up saying. 'I'd like to read more.'

I like teaching; I believe it is mostly worthwhile.

But that's not to say I don't occasionally dream of reading Shakespeare and watching the seasons turn from my log cabin.

19

REVOLUTION

William was always taking sides.

As an Englishman living in Quebec, he could not help but side with the English-speaking minority.

Canada is usually thought of as a peaceful country – forests, lakes, geese. But by the 1830s, *Canadien* resentment of British rule had brought them to the point of revolution. And William was there to see it.

The eight letters, all addressed 'To the EDITOR of the CUMBERLAND PACQUET', were written in a great rush between June 1st and June 11th 1840.

I had brought copies of them with me to Quebec. I reread them in my hotel room.

In the letters, William covers the laws governing rents, marriages, and wills; the use of the plough, the scythe, the spade, and the flail; soil types; crop yields; butter yields; whether or not to plant particular vegetables; the price of a good milk cow; the best design for a one-horse sledge; how to counteract the effects of frostbite; differences in national types between the English, Irish, Scots, Americans and Canadians.

A far more famous report on Canada, written for the British Government by Lord Durham in 1839, describes the English- and French-speaking populations as 'two nations warring within the bosom of a single state'.

William laid out his own political journey when he wrote, 'After one year's residence in Canada I became convinced that a great change in the manner of living among the French population must necessarily take place, and my anticipations have already been verified...'*

Elsewhere, he described the *Canadiens* in a way that suggests the exasperation of close acquaintance. It was one of his liveliest bits of satirical writing:

> ... the national feelings and habits of the Canadians make them difficult to deal with in a busy time... for no people can surpass the Canadians in the choice of time for making a bargain. Though submissive and anxious to work when you are indifferent about him, the moment you are busy, or in a strait, the same person will be the first to harass you. He will dictate what diet he must have; you must increase his daily wage; you must advance him money, or he cannot work; it is an holiday; or he will leave you, which he is certain to do if he is in your debt, even if he starves for a few days; and when the hurry is over he will come back as confidently as if nothing had happened...

Here is an Englishman, describing the French. He even added, 'commonly, from four or five years of age, the pipe is their constant companion, and smoking often trespasses upon their hours of labour'.

William continued by criticizing the accounts of 'the Canadian character' given by 'non-residents' and 'gentlemanly' witnesses.

> They have seen the poorest amongst them bowing and accosting each other with more politeness and ceremony than is usual with gentlemen in England; and their limited intercourse with them has

---

*   Letter No. 4.

been characterised by apparent frankness, obsequiousness, and smiles. Now all this is undoubtedly true. These therefore speak of them as a well meaning, polite, honest, hospitable, and open-hearted friendly race of people. Now let me reverse the picture.

Brace yourself.

Consult the old country people [the Brits], settled amongst them in the country, who have had the experience of daily intercourse and business with them for years, and have been obliged to employ them both in the house and on the farm; and what will these people tell you?

Really brace yourself.

They will, I believe, almost universally maintain, that they are a mean, selfish, deceitful, and with very few exceptions, man and woman, a general race of liars and thieves.

But what does William himself think, from his own experience?

Being for some time, and during the two years of the rebellion, a resident among them, many of the prominent traits of their national character were too obvious to be mistaken. I considered them selfish, cunning, and impressed with the idea that every emigrant from the United Kingdom was a trespasser upon their rights; but...

At last, the *but*.

... but these qualities and ideas are the natural consequences of a total want of education, and prejudices fostered in youth, and more encouraged than checked by spiritual teachers, whose interests are diametrically opposed to the introduction of Protestant settlers. I believe that a great majority of those employed by the old country farmers [Brits] were addicted to pilfering, but the uncertainty attendant upon civil commotions might have some influence upon their actions, as well as opinions.*

This is far more liberal than one might expect, given William's earlier effusions about how easily we beat up the French at Waterloo.

William had grown up around Protestants. He disliked Catholicism. That was not going to change. Particularly not as, in this vivid scene, he directly links the Canadians' widely reputed ineptitude at farming (refusing to leave their fields fallow, pursue crop rotation) to their religious beliefs:

> One [*Canadien*] considerably above the common level was thus addressed, when sewing Wheat two years ago upon the same field for the fourth time, with one furrow, and no improvement [of the soil] whatever: – "Your Wheat has failed the last two years; why do you not try Oats, and lay it down with grass seeds?" He immediately replied – "I did think of that; but I consulted the Priest, and he said it was sinful to doubt the goodness of God, who would order every thing for the best!" I myself witnessed, for two successive years, the reverend Father riding along the concessions, at the head of the parishioners, to discharge the flies for destroying the Wheat.

Of course, the harvest failed once again, and 'a great many fields were not worth cutting, and the crops were left to rot upon the ground'.

---

* Letter No. 6.

The Priests, William averred, were keen to encourage the sewing of wheat because they received dues on the crop. They were to blame for the 'deterioration of the land, and the wretched husbandry which has so long prevailed among the Canadians'. He then, unexpectedly, switched into the radical language of the French Revolution to say, 'and it is surely time that the cultivators should shake off a thraldom so besotted and degrading...'

Earlier in the same letter, he said that 'many Canadians show evident signs of shaking off their apathy, and joining in the march of improvement'.

From a lifelong Tory, this 'shaking off' was the radical language of uprising. Why? Well, a first attempt at a Canadian revolution had already taken place.

When I got my scraps of evidence, and stitched them together, I was able to place William close to one of the most dramatic, and violent, episodes in Canadian history.* But – more than that – I knew from his own words that he had seen one of the main revolutionaries speak.

Typically, William came at this sideways. He was criticizing the *Canadiens* for refusing to eat oats, the native breakfast of Cumbrians. He continued to detail the inferior diet of the French-speakers:

Potatoes were no great favourites with them, and, as for oatmeal, the old country people were [they thought] pigs for eating it! It is a fact, that persuading them they would be forced to eat it, was an affective topic with the patriot leaders to induce them to rebel.

---

* In Letter No. 8, William wrote that he lived on a shared farm in 1836. In Letter No. 6, he said of the Canadians, 'Being for some time, and during the two years of the rebellion, a resident among them...' And in Letter No. 5, said, 'When I resided a few miles from St. Eustache...'

Then he gets to it, the closest Canada has ever come to revolution, and their great revolutionary hero:

> I once heard Dr. Chenier, who fell at Eustache, address a great number of habitans at the church door after service – in the French of course – at considerable length on this subject. The peroration was uttered in these words: – "And what, my countrymen, are those with whom you will have to contend? Do they not live on *oats* like horses and pigs? And do you think they can stand before brave Canadians, who live upon *bread* and *pork*?" These words were highly applauded; the argument was considered unanswerable; and they departed, swearing they would never live like pigs, and complimenting each other upon the implied bravery of well-fed Canadians…

Any Canadian today would know Dr Jean-Olivier Chenier. He is a martyr of the glorious, failed revolution.

I visited the statue to him, in Montréal's Viger Square. In oxidized bronze, he strides forward, pointing toward the future with his right hand whilst carrying in his left hand – nothing. The long-barrelled rifle has been broken off and not replaced. The statue's message has been changed, by this vandalism. Progress through violence, it used to imply – the tip of the rifle being ahead of the pointing hand. He exemplifies will and force, heading in the same direction.

When – in the last of his 'Letters on Canada' – William referred to 'the late rebellion', he was drastically underplaying the events. They had been bloody; they had been brief; the British forces had terminated the armed uprising with extreme prejudice.

After a *patriote* victory at St Denis, and a loss at St Charles, Dr Chenier and his forces were tracked by the forces of Commander-in-Chief John Colborne to St Eustache. The date was 14th December 1837. A contemporary painting shows the British soldiers on the left, disciplined, lined up, the *patriots* falling back, chaotic, in mufti, on the right.*

Around eighty of the *patriots* barricaded themselves in St Eustache church – a very high, handsome building with two towers. Today, its frontage is pockmarked in seven or eight places where cannonballs hit, ineffectually. These are the delicate reminders of two hours' British bombardment. After this, impatient, Colborne created a diversion by torching nearby streets, sent troops round the back to set fire to the sacristy and then waited.

Dr Chenier did, indeed, 'fall' at Saint Eustache – he jumped from a rear right window of the blazing church and was cut down fighting. The place where he died is now a parking lot.

Subsequent rumours, still the subject of angry debate in Quebec, had it that his body was desecrated – his heart dug out and placed on display, for several days, in a local pub. Whether true or not, this remains a point of disgust at the British.

What is not debated is what the British troops did. They pillaged houses then burned them down. When they moved on to St Benoit, very little of St Eustache was left – only the houses known to belong to Protestants.

In his final Letter, William said exactly this, 'The late rebellions in Lower Canada have caused much misery in the disaffected districts… It often happens in such cases that the greatest rascals escape, and comparatively innocent individuals suffer'. This is what has happened, he asserted, around where he lived. 'Many of the simple habitans were sued for the property they were ordered, and in some degree forced

---

* 'Back View of the Church of St. Eustache and Dispersion of the Insurgents – Dec. 14, 1837', by Charles Beauclerk (1813–1861), https://en.wikipedia.org/wiki/Battle_of_Saint-Eustache#/media/File:Battle_of_Saint-Eustache.JPG.

Also 'Front view of the Church of St. Eustache Occupied by the Insurgents. The Artillery Forcing an Entrance – Dec. 14, 1837', http://habitantheritage.org/yahoo_site_admin/assets/docs/Beauclerk_Charles.12254023.pdf.

to take, and nearly beggared. Others were imprisoned, their houses burned, and property plundered; and in all this there was perhaps not much *injustice*. But what is the case with many who bore commissions among them, and who laboured for years to excite the less knowing to insurrection?' Men like Louis-Joseph Papineau, a rebel leader who had fled to America. 'Why, after concealing themselves for a while, they have now returned, and are in the full enjoyment of their property, without being called upon to contribute one farthing more than the loyalest men in the province towards repairing the damages they caused; and this certainly is *unjust*'.*

If William lived near St Eustache, with a Protestant family, then after this violence they would have found themselves surrounded by hostility. If he lived with a Catholic family, his house may have been burned down. This most likely explains why William wrote in the Letters of living in that part of Canada in the past tense. It may also explain why we have none of his writings or possessions from that time; they may have ended in flames set by British troops.

Although clearly not on the side of the *patriotes*, William was sympathetic toward their sufferings. I got the sense that men he knew and liked, perhaps farmers he had traded with or lived beside, were feeling this injustice.

Towards the end of his final letter, his final publication of any sort, although he was to live for another ten years, William asked and then answered the question his Cumbrian readers must have had. '..is it advisable for able bodied labourers with families, or farmers with small capitals, to emigrate to Canada? I answer yes!'

And why? Had all this talk of liberty infected him? After a life of Toryism, is it possible Canada had got to William?

---

* Letter No. 8.

I think so.*

His final Letter was a kiss-off. In his typically boat-burning way, he decided to let loose. Goodbye to the old world. Sod you, Lonsdale. Sod you, Dad.

> [One] can purchase, and be the owner of as good a farm at the end of six years, for a less sum than he would have to pay in rent and taxes in England, where he would be perhaps poorer than when he commenced; while in Canada, he would be master of his own property, with full liberty to hunt, shoot, or fish, without fearing any man, and therefore surely a more independent gentleman than any farmer in the United Kingdom.†

Liberty! Independence!

This was almost William's last word. It reminded me of his son's disgusted remarks on the Centenary Burns' night. That dinner had been a place where, like Canada, there would be 'no fawning on those in power, no profit derived from flattering the titled or the rich'‡.

How many things I could read into that phrase 'without fearing any man'! After all this time, William is finally confessing to having been kept in his place by the Lowthers.

In Canada, he would be 'a more independent gentleman'.

This was as close to republicanism as William ever came.

★

---

* It's ridiculous to compare William to Rimbaud as a writer, or as a man, but I can't help but think of Rimbaud in Africa when I think of William in Canada – that complete departure both men made, from who they had been before.
† Letter on Canada, No. 8.
‡ 'A Hensingham Gentleman's Speech at Burns's Centenary in Shrewsbury', *The Whitehaven News*, 3 March 1859.

There was a limit, though. My image of William in his log cabin was right in one way – wherever he lived was probably made of wood. But it was also wrong. He was no frontiersman. When he wrote in order to put his fellow countrymen off taking on the 'bush', he became energetically disgusted:

> Respecting Cumberland and Westmorland men emigrating, with a design of taking up Bush lots, I advise them *not to do so*. It is work they know nothing about, and quite at variance with their habits and manners; – a wilderness swarming with mosquetoes – felling trees – digging among stumps – breathing an overshaded atmosphere, with squirrels, skunks, foxes, wolves, and bears for neighbours, and half starved, will entail nothing but misery upon them. My advice certainly is, not to think of it!*

A word here or there in the Letters glanced back to William's Cumberland dialect. In Letter 6, grain was described as less 'pubble' that elsewhere – what a lovely word! The definition given in *The Folk-Speech of Cumberland* is 'plump'. An Old Saying is used as example. 'At Michelmas a *pubble* goose – at Kersmas, standin' pie'.

Letter 7 described a particular style of threshing wheat as done 'cat under't lug'. William seemed to be reaching out, to say he still belonged. He referred to 'my own… county', still meaning Cumberland.†

When I leave Henry and George, even for a few days, I think about what it would be like never to see them again. Perhaps William did keep in touch with Betty, writing monthly letters, sending what money he could. But he was far away from his sons and daughters.

---

* Letter on Canada, No. 8.
† Letter on Canada, No. 4.

As William Jnr grew up, and started to train as a vet – William wasn't there. As his other children sank lower in society than he or his father had done – William couldn't help.

There was a harsh poetry in scientific fact. William observes: 'The 21st [of June] is the longest day; the sun rises twelve minutes past four, and sets forty-eight minutes past seven. On the shortest day, the 21st of December, the sun rises forty-one minutes past seven and sets nineteen minutes past four'. During winter 'the thermometer ranges from twenty-two to thirty-six degrees below zero'.*

Writing of sheep farming, William notes the flock will always have to be housed at nights to secure them from the wolves.

The exiled Cumbrian's melancholy came through strongly in one line. 'Twilight is always much shorter in Canada than in England'.

But William's Canadian twilight was to last a full decade.

---

* Letter 7. How did William know this so accurately? I think I have found an explanation.

20

EXILE'S RETURN

What proof is a poem? Of anything?

As far as can be proved, by non-poetic evidence, William Litt sailed for Canada in March 1832, and never returned. He died eighteen years later and was buried on Laval island without seeing his wife or any of his seven surviving children again.

William, in this version of his life, remained a stranger to his adopted village and his native fells.

But as I neared the end of my research, chasing up the last few references, that wasn't what I came to believe. I had a strong suspicion that at some time, probably in early 1839, William *did* return from Canada, and was for a short while reacquainted with Cumberland and reunited with his family. My evidence was circumstantial.

The United Kingdom Census of 1871 lists 'Elizabeth Mossop' as a widow who had been 'Blind 34 years from accident'. (I will pause, to say how sorry I was that I couldn't make anything more of this – there was a novel, at least, in this detail; but it was one I wasn't able to write, and not just because I didn't know what really happened.) This gave a date of 1837 or 1838 for the blinding. Here, then, was a possible motive, to explain William's return. He felt compelled to come back and make sure his family was coping with this disaster.

Another piece of evidence was that, soon after the time he would have been in Whitehaven, the *Cumberland Pacquet* began once again to publish William. Several poems and then the 'Letters on Canada' appeared.

I imagined a meeting with the newspaper's editor. In 1839, that was still Robert Gibson, the friend who had edited and published *Wrestliana* and *Henry & Mary*. During their reunion, William either proposed or was asked to write something of utility to his fellow countrymen, at least to those who were considering emigrating to the New World. With a handshake, William was welcomed back into the pages of the *Pacquet*. At the very least, the money would have been welcome.

'The Bells that Hang in the Old Church Tower' was published in the *Cumberland Pacquet** with the initials 'W.L.' and above the words 'Hensingham, 1839'.

Another poem, 'The Sky is Clear', also by 'W.L.' was located even more specifically: 'Hensingham, Feb. 15, 1839'.

I wondered for a while whether 'W.L.' might have been William Litt Jnr. But that seemed unlikely. He would only have been 21-years-old. Would he have written this way?

At this point, I suddenly realized I was the right person to be trying to figure this out. Some of my research – reading about William Pitt the Younger and conditions in Cumbrian mines – had made me feel like a very amateur historian. But reading these poems, and trying to get stuff out of them, was something I'd been doing since O level English.

Unless he was creating a very sophisticated impersonation of his father, I don't think William Jnr would have written of the bells:

> I hear their sound on the soft winds borne,
> As of old on each quiet sabbath morn, –

---

* *Cumberland Pacquet*, 12 February 1839. This was the poem that helped me describe William's wedding.

How 'of old' can a memory be, for a young man just into his twenties? The rhythms of the next lines seem exhausted.

> I hear their toll – their solemn toll,
> As it telleth of some departed soul, –
> And then – oh! then – a spell is thrown
> O'er my throbbing heart, and I feel alone;
> For that knell hath long since marshall'd those,
> Most lov'd on earth, to their last repose;
> Yet it soothes me still – for oh! 'tis sweet
> The long-lost friends of our heart to greet,
> Though but in dreams: – and such is the spell
> That breathes in that deep funereal bell.

I decided this was our William, writing – very simply – of his emotions upon hearing, for the first time in seven years, the bells of Cleator* or perhaps another church.

They are the words of a very lonely, death-haunted man.

All William's words had been preoccupying me for so long that I'd started to be taken over by them. I noticed that his combative and convoluted prose style was entering into everything I was writing. And when I wrote about him, I did it in a sort of mock nineteenth century way.

For example, in the first draft of the section above, I wrote:

---

* I knew they could not be the bells of Hensingham Old Church, because it did not have bells in the tower. It was too poor. At most it had a single bell to call parishioners to service. Gordon Gray, a local expert, asserts that 'our local peals of bells have all been installed since the date of the poem'. *The Carlisle Diocesan Guild Bell Ringers' Newsletter*, p. 17. Hensingham Old Church, becoming derelict, was demolished in 1949.

Either this is an act of extreme literary sophistication – the co-option of an absent father's emotional world by a present-in-the-scene-depicted son, the total ventriloquism and then publication under initials that almost all the *Pacquet*'s readers would take as indicating William Snr. Either that, of which William Jnr. hardly seems capable, or this is our William writing – very simply – without Hardyesque irony – of his emotions upon hearing, for the first time in seven years, the bells of Hensingham church; bells within whose dinning reach he had grown up.

This was bad. This was showing off.

But I blamed William.

Having got so into him that I'd watched him write his poem 'The Lakes', it was as if things had now gone a stage further. He was taking control of my pen. The rhythms I fell into were his. When I tried to produce simple, direct sentences, he started to add asides and sub-clauses.

Something similarly uncanny happens, occasionally, when I'm writing very fast in a notebook – my handwriting starts to look exactly like my father's. When I notice this, I try to stop it immediately. I make the letters less loopy, more spiky. But if I look back up the page, it's as if he's written that part. I really used to get creeped out by this, now I don't mind as much.

When I was growing up, my father's handwriting used to be particularly distinctive because he always wrote with a particular kind of blue felt-tip pen. He would sign cheques and leave notes for my mother. It was something I knew very well. And this was how I discovered that Father Christmas didn't exist. Or rather, that my father was Father Christmas – because, one year, I realized that Father Christmas, although his handwriting was a little disguised, had left a gift tag for me written in blue felt-tip pen.

My father only wrote as Father Christmas once a year. If I didn't take care, I would be writing full time as William. And, unless I got a grip on myself, I would produce something as dense and – to most people – as unreadable as *Henry & Mary*.

'The Sky is Clear' was published a few days after 'The Bells'. When I looked at it closely, I found it could only be describing Canada, not Cumbria.

The landscape seems uninhabited, except for the poet – no populous town of Whitehaven, no farms. Instead, there are green fields and, at the same time, parched earth, and most tellingly of all the words, 'Through the giant forest the loud wind howls'.

As far as I know, Cumberland in 1839 boasted no giant forest, whereas Canada was still mostly that very thing.

Here, I saw very clearly William confronting his isolation. As Wordsworth did in dozens of poems,* William forces himself to draw moral comfort from the sights of Nature.

> Know that the summer's cloud or shower
> Comes but to freshen the fruit and flower –
> That joy would lose its dearest zest,
> If the gloom of grief ne'er touched thy breast...

There wasn't much else but Nature that could give him comfort.

But the poem that gave William's emotions on returning to Cumbria most directly was 'Stanzas Written Near Black Combe'. It starts with

---

* E.g., 'My heart leaps up' and 'Calm is all nature as a resting wheel'.

a quotation from a travel book I was unable to track down. I thought, perhaps, that William had made the quote up — because it's so fitting. The book was called *Journal of a Tour to the Lakes and Mountains of Cumberland*. The part William extracted or invented is about the towering chunk of rock known as Black Combe fell.

> This mountain, in itself one of the finest in Cumberland, gains additional interest from being the last of his native hills which the outward-bound Cumberland mariner beholds, and consequently the first that meets his view on his return homewards.

I can't describe William's desolation any better than this.

> How beautiful this scene! sea, land, and sky
> Are calm alike and motionless, save when
> Some light and fleecy cloud skims o'er the high
> Cerelean arch, o'ershadowing it, and then
> Diffusing breaks, and all looks gay again, –
> Borrowing a passive splendour from those beams
> Imperial, which, alike o'er lawn and fen,
> Scatter the radiance of their silver streams,
> Till earth awhile like some sweet spot of poesy seems.

> How softly on the meditative mind
> Comes the deep influence of external things!
> When some sweet thought, within the heart enshrined
> For years, at one remembered object springs.
> E'en now the syren memory o'er me flings
> Her magic robe, as at thy feet I lie,
> Majestic mountain! And the thoughts she brings
> Are those which rose when, first a wanderer, I
> Beheld thy rugged form fade in the eastern sky.

The fears – the hopes – the chaste regret which steals
On all whose home-land lessens to the view
In tears and gloom, – when first the wanderer feels
His heart sink, and hopes vanish in the dew
Of distance dim. Can ever prospect new
Gladden his heart as this hath done? What though
The Iris of his youth has melted now,
Life is not all a desert path – there grow
Some flowers ever on the wildest spots below.

Hail rugged mount! that, frowning o'er the main,
Art still to those who wander o'er the sea
That laves thy feet, a mine whose every vein
Is of deep thoughts and feelings – now to me
A fountain of pure song! How few there be,
Wanderers from Cumbria's soil, who have not proved
How they adored her, as they wept to see
Thy lessening form! The lovely or the loved,
Aged or young – none, none may gaze on thee unmoved.

Yet not alike the feelings all that pour
At sight of thee. You little barque whose prow
Is pointing now to Fleswick's glassy shore,
Bears on her deck, I wean, a goody row
Of manly forms, and hearts whose pulses flow
Denotes their ecstasy: for they have felt
What 'tis from home, and love, and friends to go,
We know not where; – and now with hopes they melt
To press those household gods to which they oft have knelt.

Muse we no more; – for see! the evening sun
Hath tinged the mountain with a golden haze –
The distant cottages are waxing dun –
The deer now leave the covert side to graze
In silence undisturbed – the cotter's gaze
Is homeward bent – the heron leaves the stream
Where Esk meandering its tribute lays
At ocean's mighty feet, – and all things seem
To borrow from the time the halo of a dream.

And I, whose soul hath melted into song
In gazing on this prospect, now must turn
To home and cold reality. Too long
Perhaps the time now spent in thoughts that burn.
Yet why so? He whose heart hath been an urn
Long time for buried joys, may deem it well
If out delay the hour when he must mourn.
I love and thank thee, then, majestic Fell!
And feel a sweet regret in bidding thee *Farewell.*

18th August 1840

William's longing is pure. Away from the sight of his native hills, he was an incomplete man; life elsewhere was less meaningful, less alive. In Canada, he felt an addenda to himself.

But we can be sure that he returned – Canada is where William lived out the sad remainder of his life, and where he died and was buried.

There's no account of his return journey. It was probably much the same as his first sea voyage to Montréal – with the big difference that William must have known he would never see Cumberland again.

Cold reality, indeed.

It can't be said other than directly: William never mentions his children. He seems, on all written evidence, to have longed for Cumbria more than for his daughters and sons. A conventional poet, in many ways, he didn't publish the conventional poem this would seem to call for – or, if he did, I haven't found it. The closest he came was in the line:

What, 'tis from home, and love, and friends to go, ...

But it is some words quoted in *Wrestling and Wrestlers*, and the sentiments that preface them, which seem to catch William best:[*]

Suffering, however, from 'home sickness' — a craving often fatal to natives of mountainous regions — his mental as well as bodily powers began failing before attaining his sixtieth year.

"I gaze on the snow clad plain, see the cataract's foam,
And sigh for the hills and dales of my far distant home.

"Dearly lov'd scenes of my youth, for ever adieu,
Like mist on the mountains ye fade from my view,
Save at night in my dreams."

These words are from a poem apparently called 'The Emigrant'. I wasn't, in all my librarying and Googling, able to trace it, but it seems to me to have William's tone, and the geography is correct for St Anne's Parish.

The area surrounding Montréal *is* fairly flat – although the city, of course, centres on Mount Royal. This wasn't anything like William's

---

[*]   *Wrestling and Wrestlers: Biographical Sketches of Celebrated Athletes of the Northern Ring*, Wordsworth Press, 1893, pp. 69–70.

native hills. It was a very distant cousin, three-peaked, climbable for a view of a slightly bumpy horizon. North of Montréal, William would have felt both agoraphobic and claustrophobic. He would have felt terribly homesick.*

I wanted to assume that it wasn't just neglect – that William's feelings for his children were too strong to find expression in verse. This is not even to mention what he might or might not have wanted to say to his wife, Betty.

I have heard there were letters home; they did survive into the twentieth century, but were in such a tattered state they were destroyed.

---

* The Wikipedia entry on 'Homesickness' is fascinatingly exact: 'The term was coined in 1688 by Johannes Hofer (1669–1752) in his Basel dissertation. Hofer introduced *nostalgia* or *mal du pays* "homesickness" for the condition also known as *mal du Suisse* "Swiss illness" or *Schweizerheimweh* "Swiss homesickness," because of its frequent occurrence in Swiss mercenaries who in the plains of lowlands of France or Italy were pining for their native mountain landscapes. Symptoms were also thought to include fainting, high fever, indigestion, stomach pain, and death. Military physicians hypothesized that the malady was due to damage to the victims' brain cells and ear drums by the constant clanging of cowbells in the pastures of Switzerland', https://en.wikipedia.org/wiki/Nostalgia, retrieved, 2 November 2016, 10:52.

21

PASS ON TO THE END

The Memoirist wrote that '... the author of *Wrestliana* sleeps "the sleep that knows no breaking", far from the tombs of his fathers and the homes of his friends and his family', and quoted these sad lines by Felicia Dorothea Hemans as William's epitaph:[*]

> He was the loved of all, yet none
> O'er his low bed may weep.

As William emerges from the landscape of Cumbria, so he disappears into the landscape of Canada.

When I visited Ile Jesus, staying in a chain motel beside an eight-lane highway, eating in a nearby supermall, I found it hard to see beneath the dusty concrete sprawl.

---

[*] 'The Graves of a Household', *Miscellaneous Poems*, Felicia Dorothea Hemans, quoted from *Women Poets of the Nineteenth Century*, edited by Alfred H. Miles, George Routledge & Sons, 1907; www.bartleby.com/293/39.html, retrieved 6 January 2016, 11:36. This poem describes the resting places of four children who once 'fill'd one home with glee'. Although very fitting for William's epitaph, the Memoirist transposes his resting place with another. For the first of the children it is said: 'One, 'midst the forests of the West, / By a dark stream is laid – / The Indian knows his place of rest, / Far in the cedar-shade'. Yet the grave William's is compared to is oceanic. 'The sea, the blue lone sea, hath one – / He lies where pearls lie deep; / *He* was the loved of all, yet none / O'er his low bed may weep'. William is seen to be not just incorporated into some corner of a foreign field but unreachably submerged; Lycidas, not Adonais.

Dark details of wood and frozen mud against white and yet more white, canals with vast rafts of logs floating seawards, farms pluming woodsmoke above plains of stripland – this is where William fades.

All final accounts of him, and his last poems, have William full of nostalgia for the hills of home.

Why then did he stay? My only explanation is, because he could not return. Either it wasn't safe for him, or however modest a Canadian schoolmaster's income, it was still more than he would have earned in Whitehaven. What could he have done? By this time, the mines and factories of Industrial Revolution were employing most of the workers that weren't farming. A gentleman couldn't do that. William was no longer strong enough for manual labour.

I sensed that one of the things Canada afforded William was privacy: he didn't want those who had seen him as Champion of the Green to witness his physical decline. In other words, he properly retired – from the ring, from society, from view.

Silence, then the 'Letters', thousands of words between the 1st and the 11th of June 1840, then again silence.

William had always produced his words and his works intermittently, rapidly, manically.

On this evidence, it would be easy to say William was 'clinically depressed', or that he suffered from 'bipolar disorder'. I preferred to try to see him through the words of his own time.

The chance the 'Letters' gave him, of once again speaking to the people he cared about most, those who lived where he had grown up and perhaps had seen him wrestle – this chance 'galvanized' William. We still talk of being 'galvanized into action' without always realizing the origin: the application of electrical currents to stimulate dead muscles. This was a great scientific discovery of William's time. Remember the twitching frog in the biology lab at school? An electrical current – the idea that he could still flow, had currency – brought

William back from the dead. His great energy surged through him one final time.

Then, as far as I could find out, it failed.

Is it possible for a man to die of homesickness? I have already quoted *Wrestling and Wrestlers* that it is a 'craving often fatal to natives of mountainous regions'.

There are several accounts of William's decline.

> For some time before his death, they who knew him best had observed a gradual failure of his intellectual powers. He did not appear to suffer from any particular disease, but died quietly and tranquilly of something like a general break-up of the system. Sixty-two, it may be said, is scarcely the age of natural decay; but in his case the constitution had been heavily tried in the fullness of his strength, and his long exile from all that were near and dear to him must necessarily have hastened the consummation.[*]

We can be a little more specific about the onset: 'his mental as well as bodily powers began failing before attaining his sixtieth year'. This gives a date of around 1844 or 1845.

He seems to have been looked after. The Memoirist said,

> ... the last few years of his life were spent in the house of a Cumberland family of the name of Forster, at a place called La Chine, about nine miles distant from Montreal, ...

Mrs Cubby, William's granddaughter, disagreed.

---

[*] 'Memoir of the Author', *Henry & Mary*, 2nd ed., pp. x–xi.

When William Litt died, ... he was living with some people hailing from the Ewe and Lamb, Padstow. They were relations of his. I believe their name was Ewart.[*]

Whilst in Montréal, I spent a lot of time in libraries, trying to trace the Ewarts or Hewitts, the Forsters or Fosters. I couldn't find them. Church records had plenty of Fosters, a few Ewarts, no Forsters or Hewetts – but none of them were in the right place at the right time.

I came to think it likely that William was last heard of, by the Memoirist, in Lachine – near the canal, where he'd gone soon after arriving. This was down to the South west of Montréal city. Later, he moved up to Saint-Eustache, then down to Laval, but for some reason the Memoirist didn't hear about this.

Mrs Cubby, reporting the names of the family he lived with, gets the date of his death wrong by three years. If nothing else, it suggests that William's last private letter was sent around that time.

I wanted to find the best medical explanation I could for William's cause of death.

The best person I could ask was my cousin John. The eldest son of my father's elder brother,[†] he's an eminent doctor in Australia. He has taught physicians at the University of Flinders, and been an A&E specialist for decades.

When I sent John all the evidence I had, of William's final years, he replied with a long, detailed email – including some possible diagnoses.

---

[*] *Cleator Moor Notes, News, and Views* [By "Denton".] 'Henry and Mary Again', *Cumberland Pacquet*, 21 March 1929.
[†] He was also called John – the Litt tradition of naming first and second sons John and William has stuck.

He said William did not die young. In fact, 'dying at age 62 years would be better than the general population in the 1840s'.*

William's mental decline was probably dementia, and this might be linked to diabetes, high cholesterol or high blood pressure. 'These do tend to run in the current Litt generations, although not in their 60s'.

As I read this, I was thinking of my father, as I knew John was. His decline sounds just like William's – 'a general break-up of the system' – and that makes me think that's what's likely to happen to me, too.

After living a long while in 99 Dunstable Street, my parents downsized. They sold all the Georgian furniture, tea caddies and teapots. They moved to a small house a few houses along from where my mother's mother once lived. Meanwhile, they had my father's old antiques workshop converted – according to my mother's strict vision – into a comfortable home with big sofas and a large kitchen.

When she died, we sprinkled some of my mother's ashes on the flowerbeds that surround the house on three sides.

My father lives inside whatever is left of my mother.

He watches antiques shows, and a lot of other shows, on the TV. He has diabetes, high cholesterol and high blood pressure. He doesn't get as much exercise as he should. He eats Waitrose ready meals.

My father wanted me to write about William, and followed my research with great interest, but was always distanced from it. I think he formed an idea of William that he wanted to keep.

When I asked him once to sum up William in one word, he said, 'Tough'.

My father wanted a hero, not a man falling apart.

However much I and my sisters visit or phone, I think my father feels as isolated as William did in Canada.

---

* Private communication, 5 October 2015.

If William had diabetes, said my cousin John, he would have suffered muscle wasting. He would also 'have been noticeably thirsty and drinking a lot of fluid and weeing a lot'.

Against the starkness of John's diagnosis, I put Bill and Margaret's suggestion. They have read and thought about William more than anyone, much more than I have.

'William Litt,' they write, 'did not die of any particular illness. He died of a broken heart, full of regret for his loved ones and his forced banishment'.

> 'William Lett, Schoolmaster of the Parish of St Rose County of Terrebonne & District of Montreal died on the 5th day of November in the year One thousand Eight hundred and Fifty and was buried by me in the seventh day of the same year.' Witnesses present, C. Smallwood M.D., W. Ol. Stephens, T.A. Young, Missionary.[*]

T.A. Young wrote this in the record he kept of births, deaths and marriages in his parish.

With Vicki's help, I was able to turn the initials into names – Charles Smallwood M.D., William Oliver Stephens, Thomas Ainslie Young – and then turn the names into people.

Dr Charles Smallwood was born in Birmingham, England, and moved to Saint-Martin in the early 1830s. Of all the people who lived in that area, he was the one I most hoped had been William's good friend – he was the one I would have chosen to have at the bedside on the 5th of November 1850 when William died, aged sixty-four.

---

[*] Ancestry-Quebec Vital Registers-Records & Church Register [Droin Collection] 1621–1967; Burial-Laval, Anglican Saint Vincent de Paul, Reg.

Charles Smallwood was a great scientific pioneer. He was the first man to observe the structure of snowflakes.

In one his 'Letters', already quoted, William gave very detailed yearly high and low temperatures for the area where he lived, he also mentioned 'the thermometer';* I was delighted when I found the obvious source for this precise scientific information – Charles Smallwood's weather observatory in Saint-Martin.

William couldn't have missed it. Everyone on the island must have known it as a landmark – the mast for collecting atmospheric readings stood eighty feet high.

Charles Smallwood's 'Meteorological Register 1849 to 1855' is kept in the archives of McGill University, in Montréal. It is a big, beautiful, water-damaged ledger, using sewn-together pages printed for double entry bookkeeping. I felt extremely privileged to be allowed to handle it.

We have nothing else of William's last day but facts and omissions. Smallwood made very regular entries at 7, 9, 12, 3, 6 and 9 o'clock every day. On November 5th, he missed two. Perhaps he was at William's bedside.

There is no entry for 7 am on William's final day. At 9 am there was 'Rain,' by three it was 'Clear,' by 6 pm, 'Mostly clear' and at 9 pm 'Overcast'. The wind was east–north–east. The temperature around 46,3 Fahrenheit. Winter had not started. The first snow shower came on November 22nd.

The day of William's funeral, the 7th, was colder – only rising to 41 F. The wind had shifted to the north-west. It started 'Clear frosty' and stayed clear into the evening.

---

* Letter No. 7.

To attend the funeral, William Oliver Stephens would only have had to walk thirty paces – out the front door of his handsome wooden house, with one gable, and across the muddy Saint Eustache road.

William Oliver Stephens was a gentleman farmer, growing mainly potatoes. The land the church was built on had been his gift, and in grateful thanks the congregation called it Saint-Stephen's.

Charles Smallwood would have played the organ, which he himself had built.

Since the beginning of 1850, the Reverend Thomas Ainslie Young – only 24-years-old – had buried in the small graveyard in front of Saint-Stephen's two women, Mary Content, Daughter of Edward Hannah Schoolmaster of the Parish of St Martin and of his wife Margaret, and Mary Henderson, wife of William Wright Senior; and Edward Snell, son of John Snell, brewer. There were not that many deaths.

Saint-Stephen's church was a neat substantial stone building, 43-ft long by 33-ft wide, and contained about 125 sittings. The congregation averaged around fifty.[*]

Inside the church there was a large centre aisle and two smaller ones. The whole service was performed within the chancel.

Thomas Ainslie Young would have given the usual readings from the Book of Common Prayer – 'We brought nothing into this world, and it is certain we can carry nothing out' – earth to earth – although William, if he had been alive, would have insisted that Laval earth was very different, and very inferior, to that of Cleator Moor.

Vicki Onufriu's mother was Greek, and she has that intense, olive skinned look – coupled with a punky bob shaved up the sides and

---

[*] 'The Church', 2 September 1842.

back. Later she told me, 'I'm always on the side that lost – the Greeks, the Patriotes, the Irish – no wonder I'm called "Victoria"'.

We met, as arranged. We swapped snippets we'd learned about William over an espresso in the metro station café. Then we took a bus to Saint-Martin.

I didn't know what I was hoping for. Vicki had already told me there was 'nothing to see'. The original church of Saint-Stephen's had been knocked down years before. I'd assumed it must have been made of wood; she told me I was wrong, it had been a modest but sturdy building of stone. I had thought you couldn't just build houses on top of graves, however old; Vicki said, no, two houses had gone up in the 1950s. The one nearest the road was right on top of where the grave would have been.

Why go to a place that's guaranteed to disappoint you? I suppose because there may be one detail, one thing learned, that you wouldn't otherwise have known.

We got off the bus beside a grey field. The sidewalks were the sort that no one is expected to walk on – chunks of poured concrete dusty with winter's pale mud. We crossed to where Vicki's map said Saint-Stephen's had been.

I had thought I would cry.

I didn't.

There was no grave. There was nowhere to stand and look down. Instead, there were two ugly condos surrounded by trucks, boats. A black car was for sale, six hundred dollars.

It was an intersection, and soft drinks bottles were there, and lots of cigarette butts.

'I don't know what to do,' I said to Vicki. I hadn't brought flowers. I wasn't sure about saying a prayer out loud. If there had been an empty field, it would have been easier.

Running off into the distance, up 110e Avenue, were spruce condos, less than three years old – each generation of them smaller and closer together.

'I feel sorry for you,' said Vicki.

We briefly talked about knocking on the door of the condo. Vicki looked at the speedboats. 'I don't think they're very interested in history.'

I thought of the Hartleys, their quiet passion. I wished they'd been there with me.

There was nothing to focus on. William could be over here, or over there. The church might have meant very little to him.

I didn't cry.

My father would have cried. I could have phoned him up, and told him where I was, and he'd have cried down the phone – and that would have made me cry.

My father is better at crying than I am.

Looking back, I really regret not phoning him. It would have been the right thing to do.

Vicki saw I was sad. She told me she understood how I felt. Her historical subjects weren't her family but she spent so long researching them that she got to know them like relatives. Sometimes, she said, she got emotional seeing a name that was no longer on a list, a list that name had appeared on year after year. We might have hugged but didn't.

'I feel sorry for you,' she said, again.

We took a photograph.

Not a very good photograph.

We crossed at the intersection and went to visit the brothers Goyer.

The Goyers have lived in the fine house built by William Oliver Stephens for three generations. It has a tin roof and a new porch but the elegant light grey stone in correct proportions was there in William's time. The land around it is now grass or cultivated. Developers wanting to build more condos had made offer after offer, all refused. The brothers, only two left out of three, now in their nineties, had always said no. They still farmed, and sold their vegetables to those who wanted the *best* vegetables – the Spanish, the Greeks.

Inside the house, up a few concrete steps, things don't move. Once they find a place, they stay there for decades. The walls were blue, the broad doorframes and skirting boards yellow, the next room green. We sat at the kitchen table.

The brothers were strong men who had grown old. One of them gave long explanations, the other followed with terse footnotes. They had the photographs out ready – of their root cellar, or *caveau à legumes*, looking like an Anglo-Saxon burial mound beside and behind the house, trees growing out of a hillock big enough to swallow a bus shelter. It wasn't open yet, they said; they would open it in a week. I didn't quite understand why they thought it was so important. Vicki explained. Parts of the root cellar – a stone stoop, a piece of an arch – probably came from Saint-Stephen's church. They were things William might have seen and touched. Broken up and half buried, they were the closest I was ever going to get to seeing his grave.

I was still feeling bad about not having cried. Perhaps there was some detail here. I asked if the Goyer brothers remembered, as children, playing on the ground opposite, where the church had been.

'We always played this side of the road. Our uncle, with his eight children, lived and farmed opposite.'

The Goyer's elder brother had died, his house had been left empty, broken into, squatted then demolished.

They didn't want to say more about this. The older brother told me he liked the Queen. He asked me if we had supermarkets in England.

What was the ground where the church had been – what was it like, before the two condos were built there?

The elder brother spoke for a while. I couldn't always understand his accent, but he made a pushing gesture with his hands – I thought he was miming mowing a lawn.

Vicki translated: the old church land was farmed. The elder brother hadn't been mowing but ploughing – following behind an imaginary horse. This would have been in the 1930s. The condos were built twenty years later.

'My uncle,' he said, veg-musing, 'grew tomatoes, beans, potatoes, carrots…' He paused, trying to think of the word in English. At last it came, 'Cucumber.'

As he ploughed, his Uncle turned up bones.

22

BLOODLINE

I came back from Canada meaning to finish this book quickly. All the research was done. I just needed to put it together.

Six months later, I am still working.

Much of that time I have been struggling to take my writing back from William. Somehow, he'd muscled into almost every sentence I'd written about him.

He was a bit of a bully.

The whole book was starting to become more his than mine, and I really did have to wrestle it back from him.

I don't want to relive the fight for you, paragraph by paragraph. But overall I realized* that I'd become pompous, that I wasn't saying what I meant but showing what I was capable of. I was being Williamesque. At times it felt as if William was being me. Together, we were writing a bad book. This was humbling. He probably felt it, too.

I needed to put some distance between us.

From first word to last, I went through de-Williaming myself.

It was time to sum him up.

The worst that can be said about William (and as I've mentioned earlier) is said by the writers of *Wrestling and Wrestlers*.

---

* With more than a little help from my editors, Sam and Elly.

The truth… is that from the time he left the paternal roof, his course through a checkered life to the bitter end, was marked by a series of disastrous failures.[*]

This is absolute, devastating, and wrong.

William's own view of himself had already been smuggled into *Henry & Mary* – it is the explanation of Henry's downfall.

The greatest misfortune of his life had been the want of some honourable and determined aim, which, by pointing out a road to happiness and independence, would, at the same time, have furnished ample employment to a genius so fertile by devising and pursuing the necessary means for attaining them…[†]

Writing about himself, in a letter sent not many years before he died, William said:

I look upon it that the most important thing for youth is always to have some object in view, some aim and end, the attainment of which shall find occupation for both mind and body and to which everything else should be made subservient. I am satisfied my own failures and sorrows have all sprung from a want of this kind in early life.[‡]

The Memoirist, always kindly, saves his saddest words for his farewell:

But we cannot close this hasty sketch of the life and character of William Litt, without an expression of our feeling, that he was certainly capable

---

[*] *Wrestling and Wrestlers: Biographical Sketches of Celebrated Athletes of the Northern Ring*, Wordsworth Press, 1893, p. 69.

[†] *Henry & Mary*, 1st ed., p. 280; 2nd ed., p. 160.

[‡] Quoted by the Memoirist in *Henry & Mary*, 2nd ed, p. vi.

of much more than he ever accomplished, and that it is impossible to speak, even with the utmost partiality, of what he *was* without at the same time some sentiment of regret for what he *might have been*.

Perspectives change; both of the occupations in which William was a success, sport and art, were not seen as fitting for a gentleman.

He was thought of as a great loser in life.

In many ways, he was. He lost his country, his family, his health.

I still like William, even having lived with him for so long. I think he was an admirable man. But his desire to be liked by everyone, at every moment, undermined him. He needed to care less about his reputation. It is a waste of energy to try to win every battle. Sometimes it's necessary to lose.

Mainly, William's contemporaries thought him a failure because he didn't make money. There was, so far as we know, almost no legacy for his children. Betty continued to live close to poverty, if not quite destitute. Hers was the hardest life. However much he was able to send home of his schoolmaster's wages, William left her with the children; she raised them. We have no way of knowing what she might or might not have been like.

What of the children? What of the male line between William and my father?

William's eldest child, my great-great grandfather William Jnr, was the most successful of them. His brother John became a carpenter. He died in Liverpool in 1854. Joseph, a mariner, 'died in Calcutta, as the result of an accident aboard ship'.* Of William Jnr's sisters, Nanny lived the

---

* *Cleator Moor, Notes, News and Views.* [by "Denton"]. 'Henry and Mary Again', *Cumberland Pacquet*, 21 March 1929.

longest – until 1900. She was the mother of Mrs Cubby, who gave the fondest account of William's life. Elizabeth, a dressmaker, lived until 1867. The youngest child, Hannah, had died in 1847, aged 15 – William may have heard news of this.

He also lived to learn that William Jnr, who had previously won distinction as a student in the Royal Veterinary College, London, had been awarded a certificate of thanks by them. This entitled him to the rank of Honorary Fellow of the London Veterinary Association. The work he was recognized for was a thesis on the hock-joint of the horse.

William Jnr was a success in his profession and, it seems, elsewhere. In response to an enquirer, his eldest son wrote:

Figure 24. William Jnr, who was said to look very like his father. I am still hoping that a painting of William will turn up.

He was a very highly educated man, a brilliant speaker, a very fair poet and a voluminous writer – principally for the press – in his spare moments. Hampered by a large family he was compelled to adhere to the drudgery of a comparatively unremunerative profession, bring afraid to sacrifice the small substance for what might have proved an unsubstantial shadow... I believe the finest speech he ever delivered was in proposing "The Memory of Clive [of India]" at the inauguration of the Clive Statue in the Market Square in Shrewsbury.*

After William Jnr died, in 1864, a meeting of the Royal College of Veterinary Surgeons at the Plough and Harrow Hotel in Edgbaston offered conventional Victorian-era condolences to his widow, Edith, and then broke into real feeling when it said, 'His death will be greatly lamented, not only by yourself, family, and friends, but by the profession at large, for whose advancement he laboured incessantly, especially with his pen'.

Another writer, it seems.

William Jnr's first son was called William, and was also a vet, but I am descended from William Jnr's fourth son, John, not a vet but a doctor, also in Shropshire. John died young, aged 38, after marrying Emma Phethean and having just one son, John Percy.

I possess one object that belonged to John, my great-grandfather, a strange sort of family heirloom, it hangs high in our front hallway and is five and a half paces in length – it is an oar, of the kind used in the Oxford–Cambridge Boat Race. About a quarter as heavy as it looks, the long shaft ends in a blade wooden, gilded, painted with a crest showing three lions, the initials P.B.C, and listing the names of the places where (I initially presumed) it raced.†

---

* Private letter.
† Shrewsbury, Bridgeworth, Chester, Stourport, Burton-on-Trent, Tewkesbury, Worcester, Bedford, Hereford, Bath, Manchester.

Figure 25. John Litt.

My father had told me about John – that he was a professional oarsman, and that he died of heart fever, or because his heart exploded
(due to effort).

It turned out, on some research, that John Litt was a gentleman–amateur oarsman – a very successful one. The P.B.C. on the oar stands for
Pengwern Boat Club. They still race out of Shrewsbury. The painted
names of the places he *raced* were, I discovered, the names of the places
his coxed four *won*. The crew comprised J. Cock, St J.C. Crampton
and W.P. Mitchell. In August 1877, they were in the final of the West
of England Challenge Vase.*

> The race, which was a most interesting one, was splendidly rowed, the
> crews being almost level for about half the distance. The Shrewsbury
> men spurted, and gained when near the enclosure, a slight lead, and
> though the Avon appeared to increase their speed, they could not

---

* *Bath Chronicle and Weekly Gazette*, 9 August 1877.

name up for what they had lost, and the race was eventually won by Shrewsbury by a short half length. Time, 3m. 11secs.

For this the prize was 100 guineas.

Rower John's only son, John Percy, was born on July 2nd 1887. He, too, attended Shrewsbury School. He, too, became a doctor – a G.P. I have his war record. Between 1915 and 1919, he was promoted from Captain to Major. As part of the Royal Army Medical Corps, he served in the Expeditionary Forces to Gallipoli and Salonica. He was decorated a Chevalier of the Greek Order of the Redeemer (5th Class).

During his military career, he was mainly in charge of sanitation. One commanding officer noted, 'He has had many difficulties to overcome and has proved that he possesses administrative ability of a high order'.

Figure 26. My father's father, John Percy.

He was a very strong swimmer, my father says. The story goes that, stationed in Constantinople, he wanted to swim the Hellespont – as Byron had done – but wasn't granted permission. There is no doubt that he would have made it across.

I've found out that each male generation between William and my father wrote, wrote something – even my father wrote some newspaper columns on antiques, and left a play behind from his Dublin years.

'It's in your blood,' my father said, after I announced I wanted to be a writer. I used to doubt it – I can't any more.

And what about me? Am I a success or a failure, in comparison to William? To my father?

Figure 27. Me.

23

TOUCHLINE

In Cumberland and Westmorland wrestling, there is no touchline or, rather, there is more than a touchline. The divide between the ring and the rest of the world is more emphatic.

When it takes place outdoors, there is a rope, looped between thin iron posts with hoops at the top. This can be circular or square. The crowd is kept back; the wrestlers, entering, have to decide whether to hike themselves over or dip under. Sometimes, within the rope, there is also a circle of strewn sawdust – the bag remaining off to one side, to repair the ground on muddy days.

Indoors, the edge of the mat is all.

A couple who are friends of mine didn't want to know the sex of their child before it was born. The romance of only discovering 'It's a boy!' or 'It's a girl!' was something they wanted left for the delivery room. So they specifically asked at the three-month scan *not* to be told. But then the bright skeleton appeared on the screen and, routinely, the nurse began to go through their usual spiel – 'That's the spine. That's the heart. That's the scrotum.'

And with that single word, 'scrotum', the couple's future world turned from a sludgy mixture of sparkly pink and dull camouflage into a definite boyish palate of green, brown, grey and black.

Ballet lessons, shared lipsticks, getting deafened at boyband concerts – all suddenly went pop.

Instead, there was football.*

Hours and hours of football.

When I found out that Henry would be a boy, I anticipated him learning to ride a bike and me and him kicking a football back and forth.

And that is the thing I now most often *do* do – with him and George – play football.

Dad vs. Lads.

A kickabout in the park is one thing. But if boys get serious, and most of them do, there's the team, the training, the match.

Six, eight or ten years after they are born, you are likely to find yourself separated from your son by a long straight white line painted on grass or astroturf or some other surface. They will be playing, and you will be reduced to watching them win, lose, draw, cheat, get sent off or get injured. They will be a competitor and you will be nothing more than a spectator – at best and worst, their biggest fan.

If you want, you can go and get a cup of tea and a bacon sandwich, or sit in the steamed-up car. Because for all the direct effect you will have, once the whistle is blown, you might as well be at work on the other side of the world. Or in prison. Equally, you might be dead, cremated, buried.

It's just possible they may listen to your shouted advice ('Pass the bloody ball!'), and this may change the game for the better – it's unlikely. ('Dad, shut *up*!')

The touchline isn't a symbol of something. This isn't 'like' fatherhood, 'like' it's going to be for the rest of their lives. Being behind a line of some sort *is* being a father. The touchline just makes it explicit.

---

* Terms and conditions apply. Other childhoods are also available.

What the touchline means is the opposite of what it says – it's the don't-touch line, it's the all-you-can-do-is-shout line. Your control and influence is reduced to barked instructions, screamed celebrations, significant facial expressions, coded hand signals (if you're sadly desperate).

If you want to retain your dignity, pray silently and without moving your lips. Otherwise say *Come on!*, say *Referee!*, say *No!!*, say *Yes!!!*

As my sons were being born I felt helpless, and that feeling has never gone away – in fact, it has intensified.

The most useful thing I ever did for my sons was feed them, from a bottle or a spoon. I suppose cleaning their bottoms, washing their little bodies, drying their folds – that was necessary, too.

I also, twice, saved George from drowning in a holiday swimming pool.

The feeding and cleaning, however, could have been done by any stranger – male or female – brought in off the street.

It didn't have to be me.

What's left, apart from these essentials, is bringing them up, teaching them how to be human beings. And men.

Good men.

And then, after or before the match on the real pitch, comes something worse – comes your son getting dropped from the team. If the coach is a coward, and has texted or emailed you, you have to explain this to your son, just as you have to explain that granny has died or that grandpa will never again know who they are when they go to give him a hug.

'You've been dropped.' It's like taking a hammer to their glassy confidence. You/they start out with a recognizable F.A. Cup-shaped chalice and finish with, if you're lucky, not shards and smithereens but an angular piece of abstract art. Let them glue it back together, with psychoanalytic help, in the years to come.

'You're out.' The coach, who was your friend, becomes a force for evil in the world. The team-mates, who you supported and who supported your child, become toxic. You define the extent of your magnanimity in direct relation to their results: if you celebrate when they lose, you become a less moral person.

'Well, good luck to them', is perfectly ambivalent – it can mean just what it says, or the exact opposite. You are unlikely to know, even as you say it, what you mean by it.

My job as a father is to stand on the touchline. I have thought about this a lot. What do my sons learn of life, through sport? What does it mean? For them? For me?

I am superstitious, I have recognized this about myself; I take the touchline very seriously. I feel similarly about cutting across the corner of a football pitch, when the action is up at the other end (so the pitch is *live*, the rules apply), as I do – within a churchyard – about stepping on a grave.

I feel the full significance of the touchline when I see other fathers casually crossing it, to get a better look at the game. I shudder in horror. It's not that they don't *know*, it's that they are presuming – even as non-players – to have a place there, too. But they have no place.

What sport means to me changes all the time. My values change in relation to it. As a boy, I loved the impatience of John McEnroe, as an adult, I revere the patience – the other side of the net – of Bjorn Borg.*

The longer I go on, the more football seems to be the problem.

---

* I also admire the foolishness of Borg, attempting to make a comeback still playing with a wooden racquet.

I regret that we live too far away from Cumberland for Henry and George to take part in wrestling. From all I've learned of it, it's a better sport than football. It teaches better things. Although I'm sure the boys and girls who take it up also want Barcelona away strips, they are playing an anti-football. C&WW shows an alternative.

It could have been, if William Litt had been a different man, that I ended writing about another non-writing occupation – ceramics or pigeon fancying or competition vegetable growing or Morris dancing or cheese-mongering or bookbinding, and in that, and in the people involved in that, I might have found something essential.

I am very glad William led me to wrestling. I think it's where I needed to go, to learn what I needed to learn.

However much I neglect it, I still have a body. I realize now that this body was capable of more than I gave it the chance of doing.

Lots of life is like a fight, but even more like a wrestling match.

But however much its forms might change, there is something essential – on an animal level – about fighting. Boxing, paradoxically, despite its brutality is a very sophisticated form of combat. Most playground fights turn into wrestling matches – either Cornish or Icelandic, with clothes or belts being grabbed.

Wrestling is – as far as we know – a universal human activity. It was also, most likely, one of the very earliest leisure activities. Children, who weren't yet old enough to hunt, would playfight, as do chimpanzees. I wouldn't make this claim for Morris Dancing, cheesemongering, bookbinding. And I wouldn't, of course, make it for writing – or even for storytelling. However, perhaps in the form of retelling the fight, re-enacting the hunt, it came closely after fighting – the action replay: that, I think, is also essentially human (not animal).

Then what does this tell us? Surely this is what we should be hoping to create – a human society that permits small conflicts, unserious, in which there is a clear outcome.

We desperately need a model of conflict that results in a winner but does not result in the destruction of their opponent. Perhaps wrestling could be this – if one opponent was not there, the other opponent would fall face first into the mud.*

What do we do with all our young men? How can we allow them to fight without destroying themselves and also, perhaps, us?

'You're scared of everything,' says George, when my prohibitions vex him. 'When I'm twenty metres from a cliff you say, "Don't fall off the cliff, George" – and I'm like twenty metres away. You're *paranoia*.' I try to explain that I am trying to keep him safe, and that's my job, and he says, 'But I'm like twenty metres away. Dad, you're scared of *everything*.' And perhaps I am.

Perhaps, after all, I am an apology for a man; in which case this could be my apology for mankind.

When my sons cross the touchline, I am scared for them. I have some idea what faces them.

I, too, deal in a line, but a very different one, black not white: a long, extremely broken line that is miles and years long, and passes through this sentence, as the tip of the pen loops and squiggles and zigzags, jumps to i-dot, j-dot, t-cross, doubles back to cross out stupidities and wrongnesses of all sorts. I clove to this line and the line has come to cleave to me.

What we have of William's that is most worthwhile is the product of a similar inky line. But he could not have written with such authority had he not entered the ring many times, and successfully. His physical involvement is where his authority came from.

I had no such involvement – my world was word-bound, and had been for decades.

It is less so now.

---

* 'He that wrestles with us strengthens our nerves, and sharpens our skill. Our antagonist is our helper.' Edmund Burke, *Reflections on the French Revolution*, Dent, 1910, p. 163.

PART THREE

SHAKING HANDS

24

CHAMPION

26 October 1811

Having laid aside his hat and coat, William Litt walks proudly into the ring. His eyes move upwards, judging what he sees. This is the beginning of the science. There is grass and there are people and then there are high hills and then there is the sky, and he is familiar with all of them.

He is familiar with the grass, because, since he began at the nobler art, he has often been thrown down upon it. The ground has bruised him but never seriously broken him. That is why he is still here. But today, as he would say, he does not intend to renew his acquaintance with his Mother Earth.

He is familiar with the people, and the people are divided up as absolutely as the other things he sees. There is grass, then people, high hills, and then sky. The people are labourers, yeomen, gentlemen and the nobility. And he knows all of them – he has sported with the labourers, drunk with the yeomen, read poetry to the gentlemen and received the patronage of the nobility.

He is familiar with the high hills – Weddicar, Whillymoor, Blake Fell, Hen Comb, Grike. When he has to travel, and he has enough time, he prefers to walk. This is Cumberland, what he will later call in a poem his 'Mountain Home'. And when – years from now – he is in exile, and dying, it is the hills for which he will yearn. It is this yearning for the hills that will kill him.

And he is familiar with the sky. He has grown up on the most westerly point of Northern England, where there are sails to be looked out for and sunsets to be admired. Where the clouds are examined for signs of tempest by dozens of sailors, awaiting the tide that will take them to Manhattan or Quebec. Where the rain or lack of rain is discussed by gentlemen farmers, like his father, who worry over the wheat and potatoes. Where poets have come, in order to be closer to the sky and the hills but not necessarily to the people.

This is Arlecdon Moor, about four miles east of Whitehaven. It is common ground, wasteland – but not for too many years longer now. His father, who holds the position of 'Commissioner for the Inclosure of Waste Lands', will have something to say about that; and he will have something to say in return, in print. He will regret that the green tops of vegetables now wave over the place where the mighty have fallen.

But for today, Arlecdon Moor is his domain. This is where the best wrestling in the best style takes place, and where, as part of the festivities of the Arlecdon Fair, he has wrestled for around half a decade.

Undefeated.

Never once thrown.

And this has made him, in the North, very famous. Wrestling is the most popular sport, from Whitehaven to Keswick, from Carlisle to Liverpool. William Litt's name is familiar as a household word. Football, he will later write, is an exercise that has dwindled down to nothing, compared to the estimation in which it was formerly held. It is wrestling which grips the crowds.

Supposing two individuals, one a celebrated Wrestler, and the other a distinguished football-player, are present at any place of amusement where there is a large collection of people; the Wrestler will be noticed and gazed at by almost every person present; while the other will be regarded with comparative indifference.

And what do they see, the crowd encircling William as he walks towards the other man?

His hair is dark. His skin is pale. He is about six feet tall. Years later, a friend will remember him possessing a rare combination of physical strength, with the most perfect symmetry of form. His countenance and manner, the friend will write, with regret, were manifestly thoughtful and pleasing. Another witness will remember him most distinctly as a tall, straight, handsome, respectable, mild-looking, well-dressed man.

He is dressed conventionally, as far as wrestling goes, apart from one detail – of which some observers disapprove. He has on a loose white linen shirt, stout leather breeches buttoned at the waist and gartered just below the knee, but instead of the usual white stockings and leather slippers, he is wearing top-boots. This distinguishes William, is quite eccentric – perhaps even a little showy, a little arrogant.

Top-boots, as sported by jockeys, are the closest thing England has had to national dress. They became popular a hundred years before today, but not for Wrestlers. Top-boots usually end just below the knee, and often have a higher, softer leather cuff turned down to form the distinctive pale leather 'top'. They are tightly fitted, to show off a fine leg, and leather hoops are needed to pull them on.

Perhaps the boots are part of William's image – a Gentleman Jim of the wrestling ring, a man who wears a white flannel suit down a coalmine. Their leather soles can't be all that practical for getting a grip upon the grass, unless he's had them specially cobbled. They are very different from the rough wooden shapes that Harry Graham hews from alder trees, in the groves up near the borders.

Today is the 26th of October 1811 – a Saturday. The labourers, fancy free, have come for some fun. The swains. The plebeians. This bout has been talked of for weeks. It is to be a battle of acknowledged champions. At stake is 60 guineas. The greatest sum ever yet wrestled for in Cumberland or Westmorland. Enough money to buy a farm.

The man awaiting William upon the green is Harry Graham of Brigham, a small village eight miles to the north of here. No apology for a man, he is around 22 years of age, by occupation a clogger – and is, in his own opinion, a competent match for any Wrestler whatsoever. He is more than that – when William comes to write his own account of this most famous of bouts, he will say, 'No Wrestler ever entered a ring in higher condition, or with greater confidence than Harry Graham.'

Except, perhaps, William Litt – upon his home turf, before his home crowd, in previous years.

But William does not wish to fight this day. Only a few weeks ago he was suffering from 'extreme illness', and asked for a respite – time to recover, before the bout. This request was refused. He still feels a great listlessness, just as he did when losing to Joseph Bird at Carlisle Races, but if he doesn't go ahead with this match William will forfeit six guineas.

There is no need for a so-called 'writer' – within the ring – to take the wrestlers' names; every man, woman and child here knows who William is, and has an opinion on whether he'll win or not. Most have put money on him, a very few against him.

Nor is there need for a crier, to call William out of the crowd of Wrestlers, standing or lying, such as that which assembles to contest for the belt at Carlisle Races. Here, today, there are only two.

This challenge match has come about because of some loose words of Harry Graham's associates, and a wager that followed therefrom. The day after the Carlisle Races, William had umpired a bout between Harry Graham and the great Tom Nicholson – in which Harry Graham was fortuitously victorious. Circumstances, William believes, had been very much in Harry Graham's favour. Both wrestlers had spent the preceding evening in a manner that was neither sober nor prudential. Tom Nicholson having just won the belt at the Carlisle Races, and with so many friends wishing to celebrate with him, found himself – the next morning – quite the *less fit* of the combatants.

After William had declared Harry Graham victorious, three throws to one, William overheard Graham's friends give out that he was 'a match for any man in the kingdom'. William stoutly refused to acquiesce to this assertion; Tom Nicholson remained the better wrestler – and, when it came to it, William was prepared to put the case to issue.

And now the moment for proving or disproving has arrived.

The umpire gives the word, 'Tek hod', and the men do.

Although to an outsider the men would look terribly awkward, William is so accustomed to this position that he finds nothing embarrassing or unmanly about it. Quite the contrary, of all occupations this is the one most becoming the healthy male. To enter a contest, one on one, with another.

William has believed this since, twenty years ago, as a boy, he first witnessed Wrestlers like Jemmy Fawcett and William Ponsonby and Adam Dodd, and wished to emulate them. To become a hero like them.

At this moment, William is very conscious of his breathing. To win the bout he will need his wind, so he breathes freely. Mostly, however, his attention is fully upon where he and his opponent touch – the breast and chest. Here is where a wrestler learns the most important things. Does the opponent hold tight or slack? Is he trying to begin by leaning to the left? A straight stander or not? William already has detailed intelligence of Harry Graham, but still Graham may change his approach. A wrestler needs to be all live sensation. 'It is the *feel* and not the *sight*,' William will one day write, 'which generally regulates the movements of a good Wrestler, especially at the commencement of a contest'.

William and Harry Graham set for the bout. Right leg forward, left leg back – as if each were trying to walk straight through the other; which, in a way, they are. Their wills are opposed in a very simple way. One must thwart the other.

The texture of Graham's rough hempen shirt is against William's left wrist and the top of William's right hand, which are already starting to feel hot, chafed.

The umpire is content that both men have an equal hold. It has not taken hours, as sometimes it does; occasionally, bouts are even delayed until the following day. This is good, this speed in coming to grips. Harry Graham is here to wrestle, not merely sport.

'On guard,' says the umpire.

This bout is the best of eleven falls. A fall could be won by William breaking Harry Graham's hold, parting his hands, but this isn't likely, and isn't glorious. What William must do – somehow – is lift Graham off the ground then throw him down upon it. Either that or kick at his legs and unbalance him, till he goes down – goes unmistakably down. But not so hard, of course, as to injure him.

William wants this contest to be fair but decisive, so all the good judges, the knowledgeable onlookers, will agree he was the best man. In particular, he wishes to convince the Egremontians. It must be no dogfall of a bout.

'Justice, and fair play between man and man, should be the invariable motto of every Englishman.'

William's right ear is against Harry Graham's left ear. This is the closest William ever comes to another man, because it is as close as any man may legitimately come. Now is when William is able to tell, by smell, whether – as some wrestlers do – his opponent has partaken of the 'waters of life'. This may make William's task easier, though to some it lends a wildness and energy they would otherwise lack.

William feels his feet easy and firm upon the ground.

And 'Wrestle!' calls the umpire.

Harry Graham instantly makes vigorous play. He is known for his activity.

The world, for William, is suddenly nothing but muscle and grass. What was far away disappears, and what was close by now seems almost inside him. He finds it hard to tell what is his weight and what his opponent's – both must be used.

The beginning is important. To come back from falls down is difficult, for Harry Graham knows that William has to attack, and this gives him an advantage. Graham can wait, respond. The beginning needs to go well.

And it does not go well.

William is looking up at Harry Graham, and behind him at the pale sky – because William has been thrown, thrown again, and again.

But the loss of three falls, instead of depressing, only rouses William's energies; the listlessness which pervaded his whole frame at the start of the contest now gives place to that animated feeling arising from exercise, and the situation in which he is now placed.

The situation being that his friends are looking on, Robert Gibson among them. William cannot allow himself to be defeated, not with honour at stake.

When William's eyes accidentally meet those of his particular friends, they are surprised to discern in them that peculiar expression which clearly indicates he feels himself perfectly at home.

Yes, he is another Antaeus – invincible on his home turf. Hercules figured out Antaeus' weakness. By holding Antaeus aloft, breaking the link between man and land, Hercules won.

But Harry is no Hercules; although by some pounds the heavier man, the advantages of length and strength are much against him.

A change has taken place in William. The situation is essentially altered. He well knows that Harry Graham, against a wrestler such as himself, has not the slightest chance whatsoever.

This is the moment of mystery that all sportsmen know – the man who is losing suddenly becomes aware, with complete surety, that he will triumph. He *sees*. Each grass blade. Each eyelash. His hands are more than hands. A god has descended, and the human form it has taken is William's.

Perhaps Harry Graham senses this, for when the time comes to take hold again he pins William's right arm down on William's ribs, and grasps William as tightly as he can to his breast. This draws boos from the crowd. Harry ignores this, however – maintaining a grip that will give him an unfair advantage.

Perfectly aware of Harry Graham's intentions, William regulates his own actions accordingly. He takes a gentle hold of Harry's back, and stands as far away from him as he will allow, feet apart. Then, shifting forwards, William offers his body to his opponent's grasp in a way that makes it impossible for him to refuse, without seeming weak.

Harry gives a grunt of satisfaction. He tries to pull William as close to him as he can. He is ready to push against William with all his strength. William resists for the moment, until the referee shouts 'Wrestle!' But then William gives way, stops throwing the weight of his body forwards and, at the same instant, he strikes his opponent's heel with an inside clip. Harry Graham is off-balance, outwitted, not meeting the resistance he expected.

The instant his heel is struck, Harry Graham falls violently backwards – and in the act of falling, throws his hands loose; allowing William, therefore, to go lightly over, instead of falling heavily upon him.

To describe the electrical effect this scientific performance has upon the immense multitude is impossible.

William walks instantly to that part of the ring from which he had advanced, while the discomfited Harry Graham, after rising and looking for a moment after William, his newly-revived antagonist, with no very enviable sensations (he knows he is beaten), follows William's example, being well aware that the best method of escaping the critical scrutiny of the crowd is to smile, and seem indifferent to the outcome.

William wins the next fall, and the next, and the next! And instead of the expected victory, Harry Graham is somewhat obligated to fortune for the one fall out of the other eight!

Eight falls to four.

The shouts of victory for the Champion of the Green.

He has won.

The other man has lost.

They shake hands.

ACKNOWLEDGEMENTS

Dad; Leigh, Henry & George; Aunt Shirley; Georgina & Charlotte; Uncle Tony; Australian Cousins John, Sandy, James, Sue, Jane.

Bill & Margaret Hartley, for thirty years of research into the Litts & Hartleys; & their daughter Jane, for perspective.

Roger & Sue Robson, & all their family, Simon, Andrea, George & Eddie, Ian, Catherine, Anna & Gemma, for putting me up and setting me right.

Rebecca Shawcross, Shoe Resources Officer, Northampton Museums & Art Gallery, for Top-Boots.

Olga Patricia Holin, for The Fight Between Carter and Oliver catalogue image.

Josh Clayton, Jarndyce Antiquarian Books, for *Henry & Mary* information.

Aoife Monks, for typefaces.

Dr James Kneale, for pubs.

André Robichaud, for Montréal.

Vicki Onufriu, for Saint-Martin.

Dr Richard Virr, Archivist, Diocese of Montreal, James Sweeny, Archivist, Diocese of Quebec, and Lucy McCann at the Bodleian Library, for Reverend T.A. Young.

Pippa Griffin, for ponies.

Gordon Gray, for village bells (leading to my first appearance in *The Carlisle Diocesan Guild Bell Ringers' Newsletter*, Issue 30).

Faith Lawrence, Ian McMillan, for Verbing.

Ms Victoria Slonosky, McGill University, Quebec, for research into William's possible friendship with Charles Smallwood.

Cathryn Summerhayes, for agenting.

Mic Cheetham & Andrew Kidd, for previous agenting.

Jenn Ashworth, for dissecting.

Rachel Seiffert, for librarying.

Alex Warwick and David Cunningham, for housing.

Matthew Nichols and Guy Jaouen, for *Wrestliana 2*.

Cocteau Twins and Nick Drake, for life-support.

I received a grant from The Society of Authors' Authors' Foundation, which was bloody fantastic.

I would also like to acknowledge the support of Birkbeck College, and all my colleagues there.

PHOTOGRAPH AND OTHER CREDITS

The photographs on pages 63, 106 and 109 are by unknown press photographers.

I took most of the photographs of the 2015 wrestling. But those on pages 189 (Figure 16) and 192 (Figure 19) are by Jill Robson.

Photographs of me winning like a boss in the chapter 'Actually Wrestling' were taken by Linda Scott, Chairman (sic) of the CWWA Wrestling Body.

The photograph on page 287 is by the great John Minihan, taken in Cork, 2015.

The painting on page 198 appeared in the show 'Sporting Art in Britain' organized by Christie's, 6–22 January 2003. The title is 'The Fight Between Carter and Oliver at Gretna Green, October 4th, 1816'. It is in a Private Collection.

GALLEY BEGGAR PRESS

We hope that you've enjoyed *Wrestliana*. If you'd like to find out more about Toby, along with some of his fellow authors, head to www.galleybeggar.co.uk.

There, you'll also find information about our subscription scheme, 'Galley Buddies', which is there to ensure we can continue to put out ambitious and unusual books like *Wrestliana*.

Subscribers to Galley Beggar Press:

- · Receive limited editions (printed in a run of 500) of our four next titles.
- · Have their name included in a special acknowledgements section at the back of our books.
- · Are sent regular invitations to our launches, talks, and annual summer and GBP Short Story Prize parties.
- · Enjoy a 20% discount code for the purchase of any of our backlist (as well as for general use throughout our online shop).

WHY BE A GALLEY BUDDY?

At Galley Beggar Press we don't want to compromise on the excellence of the writing we put out, or the physical quality of our books. We've also enjoyed numerous successes and prize nominations since we set up, in 2012. Almost all of our authors have gone on to be longlisted, shortlisted, or the winners of over twenty of the world's most prestigious awards.

But publishing for the sake of art and for love is a risky commercial strategy. In order to keep putting out the very best books that we can, and to continue to support new and talented writers, we ourselves need some help. The money we receive from our Galley Buddy subscription scheme is an essential part of keeping us going.

By becoming a Galley Buddy, you help us to launch and foster a new generation of writers.

To join today, head to:
https://www.galleybeggar.co.uk/subscribe

FRIENDS OF GALLEY BEGGAR PRESS

Galley Beggar Press would like to thank the following individuals, without the generous support of whom our books would not be possible:

Jo Ayoubi · Linda Bailey · Edward Baines · Rachel Barnes · Paul Bassett Davies · Jaimie Batchan · Tim Benson · Mark Blackburn · Jessica Bonder · Naomi Booth · Hilary Botten · Greg Bowman · Ben Brooks · Stuart Carter · Leigh Chambers · Enrico Cioni · Alan Crilly · Toby Day · Paul Dettman · Janet Dowling · Allyson Fisher · Simon Fraser · Gerry Feehily · Paul Fulcher · Phil Gibby · Ashley Goldberg · Carl Gosling · Simon Goudie · Neil Griffiths · Robbie Guillory · Drew Gummerson · America Hart · David Hebblethwaite · Penelope Hewett Brown · Hugh Hudson · Bex Hughes · Agri Ismail · Alice Jolly · Diana Jordison · Riona Judge McCormack · Brian Kirk · Jacqueline Knott · Phillip Lane · Jackie Law · Joyce Lille-Robinson · Jerome Love · Benjamin Lyons-Grose · Philip Makatrewicz · Anil Malhotra · Robert Mason · Adrian Masters · Jon McGregor · Leona Medlin · C.S. Mee · Marilyn Messenger · Tina Meyer · Ian Mond · Linda Nathan · Catherine Nicholson · Seb Ohsan-Berthelsen · John O'Donnell · Liz O'Sullivan · Eliza O'Toole · Chris Parker · Victoria Parsons · Roland Pascoe · Nicola Paterson · Jonathan Pool · Alex Preston · Richard Price · Polly Randall · Barbara Renel · Pete Renton · Ian Rimell · Jack Gwilym Roberts · Libby Ruffle · Seb Ohsan-Berthelsen · Richard Sheehan · Ben Smith · Chris Smith · Hazel Smith · John Steciuk · Nicholas Stone · Juliet Sutcliffe · Helen Swain · Ewan Tant · Sam Thorp · Eloise Touni · Margaret Tongue · Anthony Trevelyan · Edward Valiente · Stephen Walker · Steve Walsh · Bianca Winter · Ian Young · Rupert Ziziros · Sara Zo · Carsten Zwaaneveld